Chicago's BIG TEAMS

BIG

Chicago's TEAMS

Great Moments of the
Cubs, Bears, White Sox, Blackhawks and Bulls

Lew Freedman

FIREFLY BOOKS

A FIREFLY BOOK

Published by Firefly Books Ltd. 2015

FIRST PRINTING

Publisher Cataloging-in-Publication Data (U.S.)

Freedman, Lew, 1951– .

    Chicago's big teams : great moments of the Cubs, Bears, White Sox, Blackhawks and Bulls / Lew Freedman.

[240] pages : color photographs ; cm.

Includes index.

Summary: "A look into the histories and heroes of these Chicago franchises: Cubs, Bears, White Sox, Blackhawks and Bulls. The book also honors Soldier Field, Wrigley Field, US Cellular Field, United Center, Comiskey Park and Chicago Stadium." – from Publisher.

ISBN-13: 978-1-77085-582-3

1. Professional sports—Illinois—Chicago—History. 2. Sports franchises—Illinois—Chicago—History. 3. Stadiums—Illinois—Chicago—History. I. Title.

796.09773 dc23   GV584.5C4F7443 2015

Library and Archives Canada Cataloguing in Publication
Freedman, Lew, 1951–, author
    Chicago's big teams : great moments of the Cubs, Bears, White Sox, Blackhawks and Bulls / Lew Freedman.

Includes index.
ISBN 978-1-77085-582-3 (bound)

    1. Professional sports—Illinois—Chicago—History. 2. Sports franchises—Illinois—Chicago—History. 3. Stadiums—Illinois—Chicago—History. I. Title.

GV584.5.C4F74 2015   796.09773'11   C2015-902801-9

Published in the United States by
Firefly Books (U.S.) Inc.
P.O. Box 1338, Ellicott Station
Buffalo, New York 14205

Published in Canada by
Firefly Books Ltd.
50 Staples Avenue, Unit 1
Richmond Hill, Ontario L4B 0A7

Cover and interior design: Gareth Lind/LINDdesign

Infographics and illustrations provided by:
Tony Rodono at CityPrintsMapArt.com

Printed in China

CUBS

BEARS

WHITE SOX

BLACKHAWKS

BULLS

INTRODUCTION

When poet Carl Sandburg wrote that Chicago was a "city of big shoulders" he was not referring to the professional athletes who came to represent the Windy City on playing fields. Rather, he was speaking of work ethic, a roll-up-the-sleeves way of life and a robust nature.

ROOT *for the* HOME TEAM
But You Can Pick Only One Baseball Club

Sandburg's Chicago celebrated the blue-collar man who invested sweat in his endeavors, and while style might be applauded, somehow, it was the athlete who put out similar efforts to those who cheered him on who became most revered.

Maybe that has something to do with the Chicago sports fan being particularly attracted to teams that play physically, hit hard, and above all, compete with grit.

Chicago is a 21st-century city that not only is represented by all four major team sports—football, basketball, hockey and baseball—but also is still blessed with two Major League Baseball franchises, one in each league, both with longevity.

Chicago baseball has been around as close to forever as is officially possible. Yet rarely will be found even the most devoted local to the sport who splits allegiance between the Chicago Cubs and the Chicago White Sox. The main thing such fans share is the Red Line, the commuter train that connects North Side Wrigley Field and South Side U.S. Cellular Field (still better known as Comiskey Park). There are family feuds over the Sox and Cubs, but only transplants to ChiTown say they are simply baseball fans and root for both.

There are no such divisions in support for the Bears, perhaps the chief unifier among franchises in town. Nor the Bulls in basketball or the Blackhawks in hockey, which have made it easy to ride bandwagons in recent years.

Chicago sports fans truly do have a buffet to choose from in sating their appetites, although the dish most commonly eaten is the thick-crust, deep-dish pizza sold at Uno's or Giodarno's. Suitably, as a city that once flexed its muscles in the stockyards, other highly coveted eats are beef sandwiches and hotdogs. Chicago is king of the wiener, with the widest selection of the highest-quality dogs in the country. Portillo's, Gold Coast Dogs and Lucky Dog all produce hotdogs better

than those served at the ballpark, and they are never, ever to be consumed with ketchup.

Chicago sports fans also have a long memory. They know all the important dates. They know the last time the Cubs won the World Series (though so does almost everyone else). They know the year the White Sox won the World Series under Ozzie, and they know (sadly) the year the White Sox threw the World Series. They know the year the Bears last won the Super Bowl. They still smile about the Jordan era, although they're getting a bit impatient for a successor. And they cherish how the Blackhawks rebuilt and won Stanley Cups after an eternity without one.

There are icons never to be forgotten, part of that long memory, whose names are uttered with reverence. Michael Jordan is one of them, and yes, deep down they know they will probably not see his likes again. Walter Payton, too, whose nickname "Sweetness" belies his real rugged nature

on the field. George Halas started it all with the Bears and he devoted his life to that team. Mike Ditka, of course, remembered as "Iron Mike" the player and, who would have ever guessed it until it happened, as "Da Coach" all those years later. Bobby Hull is one of the city's gods, and it is good to have him back in the fold with the Hawks. Baseball memories are the longest, with nobody alive who saw crackerjack throwers Big Ed Walsh and Mordecai "Three Finger" Brown actually throw. But they are still part of the lore.

Chicago sports fans know they are lucky to have such a smorgasbord of wonders in their rooting DNA. And with the exception of having to choose Sox or Cubs, they long for another championship banner to be raised at the United Center or Soldier Field, or another pennant flag to fly at the right ballpark. Sandburg's city of big shoulders can certainly carry a few more professional crowns.

Chicago
CUBS

FOREVER
Mr.
CUB

National League
CHAMPS
AGAIN
...and
AGAIN

GREATNESS
JUST OUT *of* REACH

CURSES!
FOILED AGAIN

The LOVE

ABLE LOSERS

Just because no one alive saw it happen doesn't mean the Chicago Cubs never won a World Series. They have just been in a slump for more than 100 years. Anyone can have a bad century, as the joke around Chicago goes.

Cubs fans are devoted but fatalistic—waiting, waiting, waiting for the someday miracle that will allow them to witness another World Series championship. They have been waiting since 1908, which actually marked the end of what could be termed a Cubs mini-dynasty, after the club won the National League pennant in 1906, 1907 and 1908 and captured two World Series in a row. There was another pennant in 1910 and more celebration in 1918 before the 11 seemingly long years until 1929, when the Cubs again started to win NL pennants with regularity. But after their pennant win in 1945, when they were supposedly cursed, they have never won another. That's a long time.

There has never been a more apropos line to describe the emotions of Cubs supporters than the famous phrase "Hope springs eternal in the human breast." Originally penned by English poet Alexander Pope in an essay intended to facilitate understanding of God's seemingly random acts, his prose now befits a fandom that is certain an act of God is their only hope. Come every April, those fans do let their cynicism fade for a short while, at least as long as it takes for the team to fade from contention.

But a franchise that was founded in 1876, concurrent with the creation of the National League, has been around long enough to have numerous special moments and to field many special players, team victory aside for the last 70 years.

Action from Game 5 of the 1907 World Series between the Chicago Cubs and Detroit Tigers at Detroit's Bennett Park. The Cubs won 2–0 to clinch their first World Series championship.

Overleaf: Logan Watkins reacts after committing a throwing error in 2014.

At various times, before they settled on baby bears as their nickname affiliate, the Cubs were called the White Stockings, Colts and Orphans. They have been the Cubs since 1903. That is the official team name, though in conversation the Cubs have also been called "the North Siders" because of their location on that side of Chicago, "the Cubbies" as a gesture of affection, and "the Lovable Losers" as a realistic assessment of their usual situation of late.

Wrigley Field is the iconic ball park associated with the Cubs, and although it is more than 100 years old—and one of the most revered structures in Major League Baseball—the Cubs and their forebears under those long-faded nicknames played for pay at several locales around the community until 1916. The field actually opened as Weeghman Park in 1914 under the supervision of Charles Weeghman. He owned the Chicago Whales, a team that played during the short life of the Federal League, which competed with the American League and National League.

After the team and league became defunct, Weeghman sold the ballpark to P.K. Wrigley, the chewing gum magnate whose family operated the Cubs. It went through life between 1920 and 1926 as Cubs Park before adopting the Wrigley name, which it has borne since.

One of the greatest of all Cubs players was on their first roster, when they were the White Stockings. That was Adrian "Cap" Anson, a Hall of Famer and longtime player-manager. Anson was a brilliant player but an avowed racist who insisted on closing the sport to African-Americans. That is the stain on his reputation from the vantage point of a more enlightened America. He actually appeared in games over a 27-year period before the turn of the 20th century, collecting 3,435 hits, batting .334 and becoming one of the few men to drive in more than 2,000 runs with 2,075 RBIs. Anson won four batting titles and eight RBI titles. There are no statistics available about how many friends or enemies he made.

Baseball's Deadball Era, ending in 1920, was a good time for the scrappy Cubs. They won pennants and produced stars, not the least being the famed Tinkers to Evers to Chance double-play infield combination immortalized in poetry. Joe Tinker, Frank Chance and Johnny Evers all ultimately were enshrined in the Baseball Hall of Fame, partially for their glove work and partially because their names rhymed conveniently with other words.

Many years passed before the Cubs were rejuvenated. Although they never could quite capture that elusive World Series title again, the North Siders fell into a peculiar pattern, winning pennants every three years starting in 1929 and ending in 1938. No one guessed that when the Cubs threw in an additional pennant in 1945 it

would be the last to wave at their famed ballpark until, well, forever so far.

There was no shortage of great Cubs players during this period, or even later, when occasionally it seemed certain the squad would return to glory. Outfielder Hack Wilson's hacks in 1930 produced one of the greatest slugging feats of all time. His 56 home runs remained a National League record until 1998 when it was twice broken by Mark McGwire (70) and Sammy Sosa (66), who set a new Cubs record, too. Wilson's mind-boggling 191 runs batted in that season, however, remains a Major League standard 85 years after he set the mark.

The Cubs may have fallen short in the final standings year after year, but they often fielded appealing players. No player to wear a Cubs uniform has ever been more popular than Hall of Famer Ernie Banks, who broke into the lineup as a 22-year-old shortstop in 1953.

Remembered for always being sunny in public, always optimistic in words, Banks' best-known comment about the sport he loved was "Let's play two." That was his expressed desire to play every day, and twice on some days.

The Cubs have endured close-call losses in the 1960s and in the 2000s, gaining the reputation of heartbreakers for their fans. They have coped with a goat's curse and a fan's interference with a ball in play at the wrong time.

There was always a feeling that anything could happen at Wrigley, especially if the wind was blowing out. That was hitter's weather, and the ball might fly across the street to threaten those watching on apartment building rooftops. How else to explain a 1979 game that ended 23–22, Philadelphia Phillies on top? Wags joked that Chicago missed an extra point.

The Cubs developed a national fan following when WGN television became a so-called superstation and televised Cubs games all over the country. In those days there were no lights at Wrigley Field, and with all contests played during the day, followers enthusiastically enjoyed baseball on air even when it butted up against the most popular daytime soap operas.

The whole country could sing along with broadcaster Harry Caray when he threw open the booth's windows during the seventh-inning stretch and belted out "Take Me Out to the Ball Game." It became such a tradition that it has continued with guest singers since Caray died in 1998. Soaking up sun in the stands looked like so much fun that fans made long driving pilgrimages to participate, and even a play was written about the experience, called *Bleacher Bums*. The Cubs definitely permeated the culture.

Everyone knows the Cubs' day is coming. They just hope it arrives soon. On the splendid day when the Chicago Cubs do win the World Series, the city will lose its sanity and on a day following soon after, a parade of a million or more silly believers will celebrate with the biggest party in Chicago's history.

YEAR FOUNDED: 1876

Founded as Chicago White Stockings; changed to Cubs in 1903

WORLD SERIES CHAMPIONS

1907   1908

NATIONAL LEAGUE PENNANTS WON

1876	1880	1881	1882	1885
1886	1906	1907	1908	
1910	1918	1929	1932	1935
	1938	1945		

RETIRED NUMBERS

10	**14**	**23**
Ron Santos	Ernie Banks	Ryne Sandberg
26	**31**	**31**
Billy Williams	Greg Maddux	Ferguson Jenkins

HALL OF FAMERS

Cap Anson

Ernie Banks

Mordecai Brown

Frank Chance

Kiki Cuyler

Johnny Evers

Gabby Hartnett

Billy Herman

Ferguson Jenkins

King Kelly

Ryne Sandberg

Ron Santo

Bruce Sutter

Joe Tinker

Billy Williams

Hack Wilson

THEME SONG
"Go Cubs Go"

BATTING AVG.
.336

Riggs Stephenson
Bill Madlock

HOME RUNS
545

Sammy Sosa

RUNS BATTED IN
1880

Cap Anson

GAMES WON
201

Charlie Root

EARNED RUN AVG.
1.78

Albert Spalding

STRIKEOUTS
2038

Ferguson Jenkins

Chicago CUBS

CHAPTER 1

The Foundations of Success

The last time the Chicago Cubs won the World Series, it was 1908. They topped the Detroit Tigers in five games, with Orval Overall earning the 2–0 victory in Game 5.

That year the Cubs won 99 games in the regular season, and although they had to fend off the New York Giants and Pittsburgh Pirates in the closing days of the pennant race, they claimed their third straight National League flag.

Overall, a right-hander, played just seven years in the majors but won 108 games and was twice a 20-game winner. His career ERA was 2.23. Despite being the pitcher on the mound when the Cubs won the World Series—his second win of the final—it is his mound compatriot, Mordecai "Three-Finger" Brown, who is more fondly remembered.

A Hall of Famer with a lifetime record of 239-130 and a brilliant ERA of 2.06, Brown won the other two games for the Cubs that fall when they clinched their second straight World Series crown. A monument was erected in Brown's memory in his hometown of Nyesville, Indiana.

Brown acquired his nickname because as a seven-year-old he was in a farm accident in which his right forefinger was cut off in a feed

Chicago Cubs' World Series pitching stars Orval Overall, left, and Mordecai "Three Finger" Brown.

chopper. While the hand was still healing, Brown took a fall and badly broke his middle finger, leaving it turned at an angle. A by-product was Brown's ability to hurl a wicked curveball—some say the best ever seen.

Brown was the cornerstone of the pitching staff when the Cubs were great. Six times he won at least 20 games in a season. When he wrote a book about pitching, his stature was described in the book as "the World's Greatest Baseball Pitcher."

"That old paw served me pretty well in its time," Brown said. "It gave me a firmer grip on the ball. All I knew is that I had all the fingers I needed."

Brown's Cubs won National League pennants in 1906, 1907, 1908 and 1910. The club added another pennant in 1918, two years after Brown retired, and altogether, the five NL titles represent the greatest sustained span of team success. There were no long waits for World Series appearances. The 1906 team, by record alone, was one of the greatest of all time. Chicago finished 116-36. That was 20 games ahead of the second-place Giants. The .763 winning percentage remains the best in baseball history, and only the 2001 Seattle Mariners, who finished 116-46, ever won as many games.

Yet in one of the sport's greatest upsets, the Cubs did not win the World Series that year. Somehow, the crosstown rival Chicago White Sox shut them down. Nicknamed "the Hitless Wonders" because of their lousy hitting, the Sox upset the Cubs for the Series in six games despite hitting a measly .198.

The Cubs made up for their dismal showing in 1906 by winning the franchise's first World Series in 1907 after winning 107 games in the regular season. They met the Tigers for the first of two straight Chicago-Detroit showdowns and

OVERALL, CHICAGO NAT'L

swept them, 4-0, with four different pitchers getting wins. The first game actually ended 3–3 in 12 innings before being stopped on account of closing-in darkness. So the teams started all over again, and then the Cubs won four straight. There have been three tie games in World Series history, all of them played by 1922, long before lights were routine in ballparks and in games that ran long enough to crowd sunset.

Chicago's celebrated infield trio immortalized by Franklin P. Adams' poem, "Baseball's Sad Lexicon," are seen here in 1910. From left to right: shortstop Joe Tinker, second baseman Johnny Evers and first baseman Frank Chance.

★ ★ ★ ★

During the Deadball Era, power hitting was of no real consequence. Getting on base, advancing the runner, playing for one run at a time manufactured from walks, the hit-and-run and stolen bases, that was the way to get ahead. Couple that so-called scientific game with fine pitching, and a team could do all right. Being solid in the field was a great aid to a team's pitchers and demoralizing to foes. This was the era of Wee Willie Keeler's famous comment about hitting success. "Hit 'em where they ain't," he said. Offense was all about dropping singles in between outfielders, not hitting the ball over their heads and over the fences.

The Cubs of that time were blessed with a fielding group that has lived on in the sport's lore. The foundation of their reputations was based on an ability to turn a double play with the best of them.

Frank Chance—also manager between 1905 and 1912 and called "the Peerless Leader" because he had everyone's respect—lined up at first base. He was on the receiving end of throws from shortstop Joe Tinker and second baseman Johnny Evers when they completed double plays.

Although all three players were quite competent and oftentimes excellent, it is conceded that the trio would not have ended up honored in the Baseball Hall of Fame if not for the creative mind of Franklin P. Adams, who normally bent over to scoop up dropped pencils, not ground balls.

In 1910, Adams was a columnist in the employ of the *New York Evening Mail,* not a Chicago newspaper, when he wrote a little ditty called "Baseball's Sad Lexicon." It was all about the Tinkers-to-Evers-to-Chance double-play combination that erased so many base runners, snuffing so many rallies. The poem far outlasted the fielders' shared experience between 1902 and 1912.

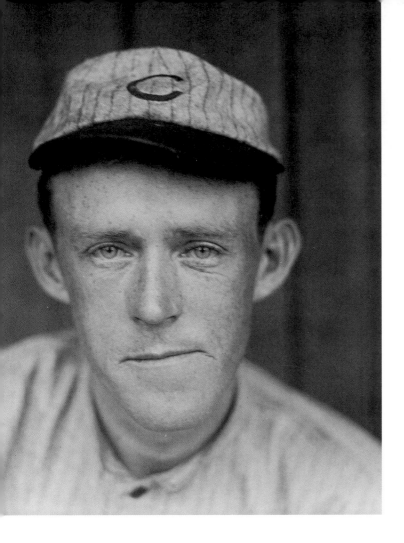

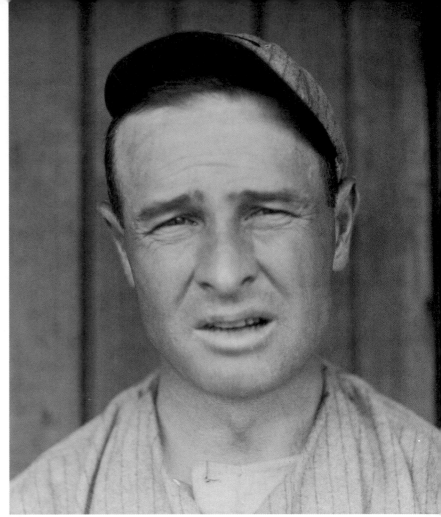

The name of Adams' column was "Always in Good Humor." The original poem appeared on July 12, and that is what is generally remembered, although others added some of their own verses later. In part, this is what Adams wrote:

These are the saddest of possible words:
"Tinkers to Evers to Chance."
Trio of bear cubs and fleeter than birds,
Tinkers and Evers and Chance.

Adams was actually on his way to the Polo Grounds to watch a Giants game when he wrote the poem, never imagining it would be remembered so long. The puffery greatly enhanced the images of the trio involved.

Second baseman Evers' image, more than the others', needed a little burnishing. He was not going to be voted the friendliest guy on the diamond and was nicknamed "Crab" because of

his grumpiness. He even feuded with Tinker. For years the duo did not speak a word to one another except for quick team business when a ball was struck or a runner was coming. Years later Evers said the two did not talk right through two World Series and longer—because he was mad. He blamed Tinker for an unnecessarily hard throw that broke his right index finger, which did not heal straight.

Although diplomacy was not his strong suit, in some ways Evers owned a leader-like personality. He needed to be pugnacious because although his height was generously listed at 5-foot-9, he weighed just 125 pounds. He was built more like a long-distance runner than a baseball player.

Evers played 18 seasons in the big leagues, batted .270, won the 1914 Most Valuable Player award and then managed both the Cubs and the White Sox. When Evers passed away in 1947, renowned baseball scribe Fred Lieb explained

REULBACH'S GREAT
DOUBLE

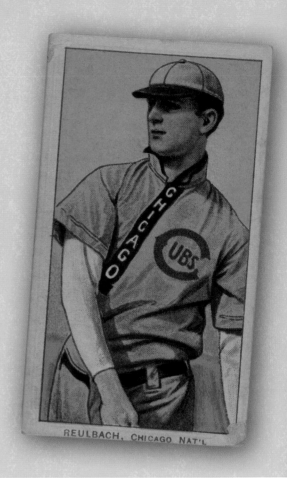
REULBACH, CHICAGO NAT'L

Ed Reulbach will forever be associated with the Chicago Cubs' 1908 season. However, because that is the last year the team won a World Series, his accomplishments are often forgotten.

The right-hander won a career-high 24 games for the Cubs that season, and on September 26 in Brooklyn, he performed a feat no other Major League pitcher has ever matched.

In that day's doubleheader, Reulbach won two games over the Brooklyn Dodgers (then using the nickname Superbas) and both games were shutouts. Reulbach won the opener, 5-0, and the nightcap, 3-0.

American League pitchers have 10 times pitched two complete-game victories in one day, and National League pitchers have done it 35 times. The last time it was accomplished was 1926. However, no pitcher has ever hurled two shutouts.

him this way in *The Sporting News*: "The truculent little gladiator, who packed more aggressiveness in his frame than any other player of his size."

Joe Tinker played 15 years in the majors, most of them with the Cubs, and accumulated a .262 batting average and a .938 fielding average at short. He led the National League in fielding four times, in chances three times, in putouts twice and in assists twice. He also stole 336 bases with a single-season high of 41. Later, he managed some minor league teams.

Tinker was a principal in one of the most controversial plays in baseball history. Forever known as "Merkle's Boner," the game and play in question dramatically altered the outcome of the 1908 season.

The Cubs and Giants entered the September 23 contest tied for first place in the NL. With the season quickly drawing to a close, each and every point was crucial. Fred Merkle, a 19-year-old

Giants rookie who made his first career start that game, failed to run to second base when teammate Al Bridwell struck a walk-off single, scoring a runner. Instead, Merkle ran to the clubhouse as Giants fans flooded the field. Tinker and Evers were near second base. Somehow Evers retrieved the ball and stepped on the bag.

"Both Evers and I saw what he had done," Tinker said. "Evers started yelling to Artie Hofman in center field for the ball and I started for Bob Emalie, the base umpire, to make sure he saw what Merkle had done."

The game, initially registered as a 2-1 victory for the Giants, was overturned overnight and replayed the next day. The Cubs won, essentially clinching their pennant, as the Giants could not gain ground over the final few contests of the season.

In double plays, whether Tinker fielded it, Evers threw it or they both touched it, the ball always ended up in Frank Chance's glove at first as they tried to nab the second runner. Chance was six feet tall and weighed 190 pounds, a fairly big lad for the times. He started his 17-year Major League career in 1898, and he could both run and hit. Chance's lifetime average was .296. He drove in as many as 81 runs in a season and twice led the National League in stolen bases. One season his on-base percentage was .450 and he batted as high as .327.

Chance was admired by the other players and served as player-manager between 1905 and 1912, presiding over the four pennant winners and the two World Series titles.

When Chance was in the majors, players did not have numbers on their jerseys. He once said that his Cubs teams had more superstitious players on the roster than any other, including him. Chance liked the number 13, and when he traveled by train he always asked for berth 13. His explanation was that "a number so frequently dodged by the average traveler has been a lucky charm to me."

Chance was the manager of the White Sox when he got sick and died from a lingering illness in 1924 at age 48. With conceivably many more years of managing ahead, he finished with a sterling overall record of 946-648.

Testimony to Chance's all-around character came from a somewhat unlikely source. Giants manager John McGraw, who gave no quarter and expected no friendship on the diamond, thought highly of Chance.

"Chance was a great baseball man because he could fight desperately on the field and then forget his enmities afterward," McGraw said.

★ ★ ★ ★

The one pennant Chance and the Cubs missed between 1906 and 1910 may have been due to the absence of a single player—catcher Johnny Kling. Kling was a glue guy. He hit .272 lifetime but was more important to team fielding and chemistry. That season Kling complained that he was underpaid and held out for more money. When owner Charles Comiskey did not ante up, Kling turned to his alternative source of income. It so happened that Kling not only had his own pool hall in Kansas City but was also a terrific pool player. He frequently won big tournaments in baseball's off-season.

In 1909 Kling made his living with his cue stick, winning a world pool championship instead of vying for baseball's top prize. Despite winning 104 games, the Cubs finished 6½ games behind the Pittsburgh Pirates for the 1909 pennant. With Kling behind home plate, many like to think the Cubs' fortunes could have been better.

Kling was back in 1910, and the Cubs won the pennant for the fourth time in five years. After that, there was an eight-year gap for big celebrations by the Cubs faithful, and while 1917 was not one of the finest Cubs seasons, it did contain one of the finest games of all time at Weeghman Park.

★ ★ ★ ★

May 2, 1917. Hippo Vaughn was on the mound for the Cubs and Fred Toney for the Cincinnati Reds. Back and forth the hurlers dueled, completing nine innings without either man allowing a hit. It is still the only time in Major League history two pitchers have thrown concurrent nine-inning no-hitters. Vaughn finally gave up two hits in the 10th inning and the Reds won 1–0. Toney preserved his no-hitter.

When the Cubs claimed another pennant in 1918, all the major players from the early pennant champs were gone. The only truly famous player on that NL championship roster was Hall of Fame pitcher Grover Cleveland Alexander. "Old Pete," who'd won at least 27 games five times in his career with Philadelphia, pitched only a few games (2-1) after being acquired from the Phillies. Alexander would reach such an exalted figure just once more in his career, and it was with the Cubs in 1920.

From Tinkers to Evers to Chance, to Three-Finger Brown and Johnny Kling, the Cubs of the early 1900s featured some of the greatest players and proudest moments in franchise history. For Cubs fans, more than most, these moments are never to be forgotten and always to be cherished.

Chicago CUBS

CHAPTER 2

The Friendly Confines

Wrigley Field is probably the most beloved building in Chicago. Now more than a century old—its 100th birthday was celebrated at the beginning of the 2014 baseball season—it is a throwback to an earlier, more innocent age of the sport.

Cubs fans gather outside the Wrigley Field box office on October 9, 1945, in hope of securing tickets to Game 7 of the 1945 World Series, which was played the next day.

Quaintness is one of the main words used to describe the home of the Chicago Cubs. Often called cozy as well, with the ability to hold more than 40,000 fans, it is hardly Little League–sized.

Located smack in the middle of a congested neighborhood that grew up around it, Wrigley Field is short on parking but long on nostalgia. As the longest-standing structure in Major League Baseball besides Fenway Park, Wrigley evokes a bygone era when the ball was dead but the team was lively.

From the bright green grass and green walls, to the unique ivy on outfield fences, Wrigley touches a chord with fans everywhere with a romanticized image that entices them to visit—watching a game

played at Wrigley is on every serious baseball fan's bucket list.

The venerable and venerated structure at 1060 West Addison Street on Chicago's North Side was designed by architect Zachary Taylor Davis and his brother Charles. Zachary made himself known by designing Comiskey Park on the city's South Side, which opened in 1910. This was the period when Major League team owners were investing in new ballparks made out of steel and concrete, and with much larger capacities than

had previously been seen. This new generation of ballparks replaced smaller, older wooden structures that had a tendency to burn down.

Charles Weeghman, who paid $250,000—half the minimum salary in 2014 of the last player on a 25-man roster—to build the stadium, did so because he desperately wanted in to big-league baseball. A wealthy Chicago businessman who made his money through a chain of lunch counters, Weeghman owned the Chicago Whales. His club played in the newly formed and ill-fated Federal League, which

A field-level view of Wrigley Field during a game between the Chicago Cubs and Pittsburgh Pirates in 2011. Neighboring rooftop bleachers can be seen beyond the iconic ivy-covered outfield walls.

was supposed to compete with the established National League and American League. The Federal lasted two seasons (1914–15), with Weeghman's Whales winning the title in the final season.

The Cubs moved in the next season, 1916, and four years later, Weeghman sold the park to the Wrigley family, the chewing gum magnates that owned the Cubs. Initially, they called the stadium Cubs Park, but it morphed into Wrigley Field in 1926 and has displayed that name ever since.

When Weeghman opened the park it could hold about 14,000 people, sufficient for the times. Since, it has been altered so many times—in major ways and small—that it seems the listed capacity has changed almost as often as the Cubs' batting order. As of the last major renovation in 2006 the park can hold 41,118 fans for a game. With plans to renovate and expand through 2018, Wrigley is only going to get more modernized.

Despite putting more bums in seats, Wrigley has long been considered a cozy little place, far removed from the 1970s era of multipurpose, cookie-cutter stadiums of little personality that could seat 65,000 fans. Those parks were never going to be intimate settings for baseball. But Wrigley has always managed to maintain an old-time aura and a smaller feel.

Part of that is undoubtedly due to the most famous change that has been made at Wrigley. Owner P.K. Wrigley had requested some beautification to his ballpark. In 1937, during the stadium's first renovation, ivy was planted to cover the brick outfield walls. The look was not original but was adopted from a similar scene at Perry Stadium, a minor league park in Indianapolis. The ivy installation was supervised by team executive Bill Veeck. This is the same Bill Veeck who gained greater fame as a colorful owner of the crosstown rival White Sox. His father, Bill Veeck Sr., was

president of the Cubs for many years, and the younger Bill grew up working for the team. Shifting between behind-the-scenes positions, Bill Jr., a future Hall of Famer, learned the baseball business with the Cubs. To this day, the ivy in the outfield is one of the park's most revered features.

It was chatty infielder Ernie Banks who bestowed another of Wrigley's much-loved unique traits when he began referring to the home field as "the Friendly Confines." His homage to the only ballpark he called home had a feel-good ring to it and has become part of the cultural vernacular of Wrigley Field.

With its green walls, ivy decoration and long-established history, Wrigley shows well on television, and when the WGN Superstation began broadcasting Cubs games nationwide in the late 1970s it created a wide-ranging "Cubs Nation." Many of the citizens lived elsewhere and featured on their bucket lists the desire to see a game in person at Wrigley before they died.

When they arrived, only to discover that it was virtually impossible to park their cars with the out-of-state plates in the neighborhood around Wrigley without shelling out $30 or so, those visitors might also have been surprised to learn that the ballpark's interior was not to be confused with a tiny little bandbox, and its layout was not particularly quirky. The dimensions are 355 feet down the left-field line, 368 feet to left center and right center, 400 feet to dead center, and 353 feet down the right-field line. No cheap home runs to be had with those measurements.

Wrigley was built for the times in a residential neighborhood, with no thought given to the future massive influx of automobiles. It is a ballpark easily accessible on the city's Red Line elevated train, and anyone who chooses any other form of transportation, besides coming on foot if they are willing to hoof it a reasonable distance, is considered to be mad. Pre- and postgame traffic jams accompany every Cubs home game.

One of the fan-pleasing aspects of Wrigley, especially over the decades, when seating was inexpensive and the games were all played during the day, was watching from the bleachers. Make that the sun-drenched bleachers. It was as reliable a place to gain a tan as the beaches of nearby Lake Michigan. Near the end of his life, after he had divested ownership of the White Sox for the second time, Bill Veeck Jr. used to mingle with the masses in Wrigley's bleachers. There were many regulars who followed the Cubs from nowhere else, never thinking to buy a box seat. They became friends through the common interest of rooting the Cubs to victory and agonizing in defeat. The same faces came all the time, and they may not all have known each other's names, but they knew their allegiances.

The Wrigley bleachers have been mythologized in newspaper stories, in books and even in theater through a play called *Bleacher Bums.*

Lonnie Wheeler, the author of the book *Bleachers: A Summer in Wrigley Field,* wrote that the bleachers were much, much more than a gathering place to watch baseball. "They were a neighborhood, a bar, a depot, a beach, an office, a church, a home." It was pretty much a subdivision that had a Neighborhood Watch, too, because the residents looked out for one another and wondered about others' health if they were absent.

TV found the sights in the bleachers irresistible. Camera shots featured shirtless, muscular college guys and young women in halter tops. For a while there was a fellow named Jerry Pritikin out there. After flirting with the name "Bleacher Creature," he switched his appellation to "Bleacher Preacher" and rotated his T-shirts. One example was: "We Believe!"

★ ★ ★ ★

Wrigley has been around for so long that many suggested it was haunted, infiltrated by ghosts of Cubs past or other phenomena. There was a period of time when the bullpen phone rang when the park was empty. Whether that was just a wrong number or the reprise of a past Cubs manager still seeking help on the mound was unknown. Play-by-play man Harry Caray once prevailed upon management to hire paranormal researchers to check out the park. Bill Murray, who is a Cubs superfan, may have been a ghost buster on screen, but he was not among those experts. The paranormal guys actually reported finding significant activity—whatever that meant—in the bleacher area. Nobody was surprised.

Nothing captured the imagination of Cubs fans like Harry Caray's seventh-inning-stretch maestro routine from the radio booth above the stands, leading "Take Me Out to the Ball Game." He actually brought it with him from the White Sox when (who else?) Bill Veeck pressured him to try it, though Caray was reticent about showing off his singing voice in public. It ended up being a trademark. A statue of Caray, microphone in hand as he sings, greets fans outside the ballpark.

The view from behind home plate stretches beyond the ivy and the ballpark's walls. It is a reminder that the fan is very much in a city environment. Apartment buildings across the street loom over the right-field wall, and in one of the most unusual arrangements in any big-league city they have become an extension of the arena. What was once a more casual experience—those who rented across the street wandered up to the roof to watch a game in progress for free—slowly turned into a big-money business. As the demand for Cubs tickets grew, so did the rooftop phenomena. Residents brought friends over to watch. Parties were organized around the game. Landlords became entrepreneurs, installing seats on the roofs and selling space, even concessions. It all assumed a squatter's rights kind of

atmosphere, and when the team owners wished to expand the ball park, install billboard-type advertising and essentially block some of the views, apartment owners protested vociferously.

The crazy situation only intensified over time. What had once been a pleasant perk had evolved into big business. Eventually, Cubs ownership and the rooftop owners negotiated, and the landlords now pay a percentage of their profits to the team in exchange for unimpeded access. Periodically, the war flares up, each side distrustful of the other. Cubs ownership is incredulous that the product they spend a fortune on fielding should be fair game for others thinking they have a divine right to watch.

★ ★ ★ ★

When it comes to controversy surrounding Wrigley, though, nothing could compete with the notion of installing lights for night play, joining the rest of the MLB stadiums. From the opening of the park in 1914 through early August of 1988, every single Cubs home game was played during the day.

By that time years had elapsed since all other Major League teams had become invested in night baseball. For those clubs the move was already afoot to play the vast majority of games at night, and now day games, except on Sundays or holidays, are a comparative rarity. The Cubs and Wrigley were the last holdout. The Wrigleys flirted with installing lights in 1942, but after acquiring the stanchions ended up turning the metal over to the war effort during World War II.

In 1988, the team needed civic approval, but once acquired things were set for an August 8 game versus the Philadelphia Phillies. Festivities were held, the game began…and it was rained out in the fourth inning. After all the hoopla, the situation left the Cubs open to being the butt of jokes. "The first time I tried it with the lights on it was pretty much of a washout, too," said comedian David Letterman.

The in-the-books first official night game took

HARRY CARAY

🏾 There is a statue honoring Harry Caray outside of Wrigley Field. A restaurant with his name on it endures in Chicago. So does the tradition of his singing "Take Me Out to the Ball Game" during the seventh-inning stretch at Wrigley—except now the task is handled by special guests as opposed to the gravel-voiced play-by-play man. "Holy Cow!" as Caray would put it.

Caray, with his almost comical oversized glasses, was witty, acerbic, bombastic and always entertaining.

Well known in the business from his lifetime of announcing—first with the St. Louis Cardinals, then with the Oakland Athletics and later with the Chicago White Sox—Caray became a legend after he joined the Cubs, partially through super-station WGN, which brought his style to the masses nationwide.

His Cubs tenure began in 1981, but it was toward the end of his long career, when he was white-haired and in fading health. He suffered a stroke in 1987 and died in 1998.

place the next night when the Cubs beat the New York Mets.

Even today, the Cubs play a set number of restricted night games per season so as to less disrupt the neighborhood, and the city council must approve any change. Thirty-five were scheduled for 2014.

Before the lights changed the situation, a Cubs player kept home-game hours as if he were an office worker. Coming in a few hours before the first pitch, playing in the afternoon and then finishing up in a reasonable three-hour-time period meant he could almost work nine to five.

Combined with the beautiful setting, Wrigley was an enviable place to play.

Alvin Dark, who spent the 1958 and 1959 seasons with the Cubs but was a full-career National Leaguer and someone who also managed in the NL, loved Wrigley.

"Every player should be accorded the privilege of at least one season with the Chicago Cubs," he said. "That's baseball as it should be played—in God's sunshine—and that's really living."

Whether it was Ernie Banks, another Cubs player, new fans or longtime fans, undoubtedly they all agreed with Dark's sunny assessment.

Chicago CUBS

CHAPTER 3

National League Champs Again ...and Again

With the 1920s quickly coming to a close, Chicago Cubs fans were fretting. What had happened to their great and glorious championship team? It had been so long without a pennant the faithful were becoming doubters. Would the North Siders ever again reign supreme over the Giants, Reds and Cardinals?

Chicago's "Murderers' Row" of 1929. From left to right: Kiki Cuyler, right field; Rogers Hornsby, second base; Hack Wilson, center field; Charlie Grimm, first base; and Riggs Stephenson, left field.

Spoiled by the Cubs' five pennants and two World Series titles between 1906 and 1918, the supporters were getting impatient. They wanted to see the red, white and blue bunting mounted on Wrigley's walls announcing the World Series was in town.

Of course, those fans could not see into the future when an 11-year gap between pennants would be the equivalent of a snap of the fingers. And, in the shadow of the Great Depression, the Cubs rode a 98-54 record to the 1929 pennant. Fans were jubilant and cheered the exploits of some of the best players ever to wear the local uniform. Their Cubs

were again the toast of the National League.

The team drew nearly 1.5 million fans that season, best in the league and a club attendance mark that stood until 1969. Those 1929 Cubs were certainly worth a look: a great show that outdistanced the Pittsburgh Pirates by 10½ games in the standings.

The Cubbies featured a trio of great starting pitchers in Pat Malone (22 wins), Charlie Root (19) and Guy Bush (18), who never had to worry about run support. The Cubs' hitting was phenomenal. The great Rogers Hornsby manned second base, hit .380, bashed 39 home runs and drove in 149 runs. And that didn't even lead the team. Stocky outfielder Hack Wilson clubbed 39 homers, too, but knocked in 159 runs while batting .345. Underrated Riggs Stephenson batted .362, and Kiki Cuyler—bound for the Hall of Fame like Hornsby and Wilson—batted .360.

Hack Wilson, the Major League single-season RBI record holder, set the mark with 191 RBIs in 1930. He had led the league in 1929 as well, with 159 — good for 22nd on the all-time list.

In the World Series, the Cubs were up against the American League juggernaut Philadelphia Athletics, winners of 104 games and the team that kicked off the second Connie Mack dynasty. As owner-manager of the A's, Mack had fielded superb teams in the 1910 era, but he sold off his best players when Federal League bloodhounds came sniffing around offering bigger contracts than he could afford. An entire generation later Mack's bunch was loaded, outscoring foes 901-615, despite being viewed as a pitching-first team.

Athletics ace George Earnshaw won 24 games and Lefty Grove 20, but in one of the boldest maneuvers a manager ever attempted, Mack chose little-used Howard Ehmke as his Series opening-game starter. Even Mack's Hall of Fame catcher Mickey Cochrane tried to talk him out of it. But Ehmke flummoxed the Cubs in the first game, and they ultimately fell, 4-1, in the best-of-seven series.

Cubs manager Joe McCarthy, a brilliant field leader and future Hall of Famer who was underappreciated by ownership, led the 1929 team. Rather than be rewarded for taking his team to their first pennant in more than a decade, McCarthy was fired for not winning the World Series. It was a rash and incorrect move, and McCarthy later masterminded the New York Yankees to eight American League pennants and seven World Series crowns.

The Cubs were not exactly chopped liver in 1930. The lively ball was a decade old, but it became the jackrabbit ball that season, a definite year of the hitter. Even the laggards in the standings had a deep reserve of .300 batsmen.

This was Hack Wilson's year. He was one of five starters in the Cubs lineup who hit at least .335. But Wilson's .356 average was the least of his power numbers. The barrel-chested but short (5-foot-6) outfielder with dainty feet and thickly muscled arms—called by some, "the Little Round Man"—belted a National League record 56 home runs that year. His RBI total was so astonishing that it has almost never been approached. At the time his mark was recorded at 190, but historical research later upgraded the number to 191 RBIs. The next closest total is Lou Gehrig's 185 the very next season, and in the decades since, no one has ever come closer to topping Wilson.

And Wilson never pretended that he had a keen discernment of the strike zone. The stocky outfielder merely had a remarkable intuitive ability to decide what to hit.

"Any ball I can reach I'm going to swing at," Wilson said.

On the back of Wilson's work at the plate, the Cubs tried gamely to repeat as National League champs, but 90 wins wasn't enough to keep up with the St. Louis Cardinals.

A likable man, Wilson's career—and life—was undone by a too-strong devotion to alcohol. But there was really no one else ever like him, and his 1930 season won't soon be forgotten.

★ ★ ★ ★

New York Yankees star Babe Ruth clubs his famous "called shot" during the 1932 World Series.

The Cubs' 1929 pennant was the beginning of a strange cycle. They next won the NL title three years later in 1932, then three years after that in 1935, and yet again three years later in 1938.

Second baseman Hornsby started 1932 as manager but was replaced by Charlie Grimm partway through the season. Hornsby's temperament was his downfall. The high standard of play he demanded of himself over the course of his career made him push his players to strive for the same standards; when they couldn't, or wouldn't, Hornsby could be overbearing and unlikable. Grimm, on the other hand, had a more even-keeled approach, and the Cubs took off with the managerial swap. As a player-manager that year, Grimm hit .301, and under his charge the Cubs went 37-18 down the stretch to finish with 90 victories, four games ahead of the Pirates.

"The players make you," Grimm said of his methods. "It's up to the manager to mold the players and keep them together."

For decades after his playing career, Grimm was on call whenever the Cubs needed him to fill in as a coach, manager or broadcaster. "Jolly Cholly" was always popular with the Cubs' front office.

Unfortunately, Grimm's fairy tale ran out in the Series when the Cubs met the Yankees, winners of 107 games and featuring stars Babe Ruth and Lou Gehrig in the lineup.

New York swept the 1932 final, but the defining moment of the Series, and one of the most epochal occurrences in Wrigley Field history, took place in the fifth inning of the third game: Ruth's "called shot."

After Cubs players and Wrigley fans hooted him, insulted him and called him names, Ruth stepped to the plate with elevated blood pressure and intensity. But he didn't let the heckling interfere with his concentration. Accounts indicate that Ruth took a couple of strikes from Charlie Root and then waved his arm or bat to indicate where he was going to deposit Root's next pitch. There are disputes over the facts of the encounter, but no dispute over the home run that sailed out of the park. Just what Ruth signaled has been debated for nearly 85 years, but he never confirmed nor denied the details. The astonishing blow under severe harassment merely added to the Ruth mystique. He was tickled he had pulled off the trick and called himself a "lucky SOB."

★ ★ ★ ★

The Cubs didn't get lucky again until 1935. Grimm, who played the banjo and sang in his spare time, sometimes entertaining his players, was in charge, managing Chicago to a 100-54 record. It was a grand performance for a well-balanced team that was not laden with superstars but had solid players at every position.

Gabby Hartnett was a leader at catcher. Outfielder Augie Galan, in the early stages of a 16-year-career that would see him chosen for three All-Star Teams, turned in his best all-around season with a .314 average, a league-leading 133 runs and 22 stolen bases. Future Hall of Fame second baseman Billy Herman batted .341, but more surprising was outfielder Frank Demaree, who hit .325 in 107 games.

Demaree is not a familiar name to most baseball fans, but he was a first-rate player. He batted .350 for the Cubs the next year and in 12 big-league seasons averaged .299 and made two All-Star Teams. He bounced between several teams but was a member of five pennant winners, four in the National League and one in the American League. Despite being a guy teams could count on at the plate, Demaree never led a league in a major statistical category except for grounding into double plays in 1937.

Somewhat overshadowing Demaree's unforeseen season was a rookie at first base who made the startling jump directly from high school at age 18 to starting for his hometown Major League club. One minute Phil Cavarretta was shopping for a suit to wear to his Lane Tech graduation and the next he was batting .275 with 82 RBIs for the Cubs. It's hard to say who was more surprised at

his success, Cavarretta, the Cubs or the Wrigley fans. No one had ever come out of nowhere like that for the Cubs.

Cavarretta was not so long removed from his youthful days of sneaking into Wrigley Field to watch games. He said as a novice first baseman he had no idea how to play hitters. Herman, at second, who was a 10-time All-Star, gave him the insight he needed in the field that first year, and Grimm provided special tutoring.

"The '35 team was probably the best team I played on," Cavarretta said of his 22-year career.

The Cubs won 21 games in a row in late September 1935 to clinch the pennant and get their shot at the American League champion Detroit Tigers. The Tigers—led by Hall of Famers Hank Greenberg, who had 170 RBIs that season; Mickey Cochrane, who batted .319; Charlie Gehringer, who hit .330; and Goose Goslin, who contributed 109 RBIs—held off the Cubs in the Series, 4-2.

★ ★ ★ ★

But the North Siders would get still another shot at a World Series title in 1938. It was a battle to win the pennant that season, but in those days the Cubs were seen as a clutch team—not one that folded when the chips were down (the World Series aside). They had experienced a long run featuring many star players who riveted the cheering Wrigley fans' focus.

Indeed, it took timely hitting for the Cubs to edge the Pittsburgh Pirates. The season came down to a three-game set at Wrigley Field. The Cubs took the first game and trailed the Pirates by a half game in the standings on September 28 when Game 2's result collided with fate. It was 5–5 entering the ninth inning, and umpires warned both teams that the fading daylight meant that would be the last inning. If regulation play ended in a tie, then everything would start fresh the next day, not resume from that point.

Nearing the end of his career at 37, Gabby Hartnett had taken over as player-manager midway through the season. He appeared in just 87 games, but this was one of them. Hartnett came to the plate with two outs in the bottom of the ninth. Pitcher Mace Brown worked the count to 0-2. But then Hartnett slammed a deep fly ball to center field. Those in the infield and fans sitting behind the plate lost track of the ball in the gathering darkness.

The ball landed in the bleachers for a home run, moving the Cubs into first place. As the wild celebration played out, a sportswriter termed the blast "the Homer in the Gloamin'," *gloaming* being another word for twilight. The clever description stuck, and the blow remains one of the most famous home runs in Cubs history. Fans leaped from the stands and chased Hartnett around the bases. Chicago prevailed the next day 10–1 and clinched the title days later.

At that time the new Baseball Hall of Fame was just opening its doors in Cooperstown—the first class of players wouldn't be inducted for another year—and administrators were busily collecting memorabilia for display. A Hartnett hat and catcher's mask were the first artifacts acquired.

Riding the momentum created by Hartnett's marveled-at homer and the emergence of Stan Hack, the Cubs thought they could break their World Series jinx.

For the previous few years the Cubs had played Hack as an up-and-comer at third base, but by 1938 he was a full-fledged star. Hack batted .320 that season and was on his way to five All-Star selections.

But, just like the Cubs' 1932 bid, the American League champion New York Yankees rolled in a four-game sweep.

The way things had played out for the eager, seasoned and successful Cubs over the last decade, there was no reason for the faithful to believe they wouldn't be back very soon for another shot at a World Series title.

However, there were changes to come, not only

Gabby Hartnett warms up prior to a game in 1932. Hartnett was named the National League MVP in 1935.

in the baseball world but in the real world as well. By the time the Cubs won another pennant in 1945, much of the team had turned over, and the world had turned over as the result of a brutal and widespread World War II.

Almost as if he had been preserved in a time machine, Charlie Grimm was manager again in '45, guiding the Cubs to a 98-56 record. Stan Hack was still around, hitting .323 with his usual reliable élan. And Cavarretta was now the veteran leader. He had been 4-F during the war because of hearing problems and played all the way through.

The 1945 season, which had begun before peace broke out and finished after the war reached its weary conclusion, was Cavarretta's finest. He batted .355 and won the National League MVP award.

A newcomer in the outfield, Andy Pafko, who

Rogers Hornsby batted .358 lifetime on his way to the Hall of Fame. Most of his best stickwork was achieved with the St. Louis Cardinals during his 23-year career, but he stopped by with the Cubs from 1929 to 1932.

The second baseman won the 1929 National League Most Valuable Player award and helped carry the Cubs to a pennant while slugging 39 homers with 149 runs batted in and a .380 batting average.

Hornsby became player-manager the next season, and he held that job for about two years as his playing career wound down. However, Hornsby was a better player than leader, and his tough-love approach alienated his men with strict rules and high expectations. He was ousted 99 games into the 1932 season.

ROGERS HORNSBY

would enjoy a very solid big-league career, batted .298 with 110 RBIs that year. Pafko loved Wrigley, Chicago and that 1945 team for the rest of his 92 years and was popular with the fans.

The Cubs won the first game, third game and sixth game of the Series against the Detroit Tigers, with Hank Borowy winning twice and Claude Passeau once. But they dropped the decisive contest in stunning fashion, being outscored by six runs in the seventh game.

More notable, in hindsight since it has taken on such power in legend, was an incident that happened at Wrigley Field before the start of the Series' fourth game, a 4–1 loss for the Cubs. This is when the Curse of the Billy Goat is said to have taken hold.

There is no question this is a wacky occurrence. Billy Sianis, the Greek owner of the popular Billy Goat Tavern, came to the game leading his pet goat. Why anyone would do this has been forever lost in translation or mythology. Notwithstanding that Sianis was an upstanding citizen, he was turned away at the gate as fans complained about the smell of the goat.

He became enraged as he departed and leveled a curse on the Cubs. The exact phrasing has been lost to time. Sometimes it is repeated with a thick accent mimicking Sianis' speech. Other times a follow-up telegram to P.K. Wrigley is cited. The bottom line was that because Sianis' goat was repelled, the curse he leveled on the team meant it would never play in the World Series again.

It sounded ludicrous, but as the years passed without another Cubs pennant, the story of the curse gained currency. Many Cubs players and managers have passed through the clubhouse over the years ridiculing the curse, saying they didn't believe in it, they weren't present for it and it would not affect their play and prospects.

However, leaving no possible remedy unexamined, at various times different curse-busting methods were tried. Periodically, Sam Sianis, the nephew of the long-departed Billy, shepherded a goat into Wrigley with the aim of breaking the curse. He did so on opening day in 1984 and 1989 and both years the Cubs won their National League divisions. But they didn't stick around in the playoffs long enough to advance to the World Series. The younger Sianis said the alleged antidote to the curse is rooted in the Cubs organization's showing a special fondness for goats. Apparently, the team hasn't been sincere enough.

At least three times since 2007 goats were anonymously butchered and their remains hung on the Harry Caray statue outside of Wrigley Field, or delivered to the team's offices. The gory efforts were interpreted as curse-breaking attempts, though no written messages were left. A by-product of the curse that grew in acceptance over the years is that the team participating in the World Series with the most ex-Cubs on its roster will lose.

To some this is all equivalent to voodoo and explainable in other ways than blaming the 100-plus years of World Series futility on a goat. Those discounting the Billy Goat Curse believe it is simply a case of Cubs management making

Phil Cavarretta is seen here in 1945, the year he won the National League batting title and MVP.

repeated mistakes in judgment on managers and players and of those managers and players screwing up on the field.

The fact remains that the Cubs have not won a pennant since 1945 when the curse was first uttered, and they don't seem to be getting any closer. After that most recent pennant, the Cubs morphed into lovable losers, but the Cubs faithful hope the team can shed that label—and finally bust the curse.

Chicago CUBS

CHAPTER 4

Forever Mr. Cub

To have met Ernie Banks was to know him and to have met Ernie Banks was to like him. To say the man was friendly wouldn't do the legend justice. Banks, who also went by the affable "Mr. Cub," may have been the most popular athlete in Chicago history. Hardly ever was a discouraging word heard from Banks, or a negative one about him.

Ernie Banks poses with bats at spring training in the early 1950s.

To have talked sports or life with Banks was akin to a ride on a roller coaster. His chats took exhilarating twists and turns on the way to the intended destination. Someone, say, may have wanted to discuss the occasion of the Hall of Famer's 500th career home run, but Banks—as he was wont to do—might have detoured. He may have spoken of his love for bowties, or he may have made a personal inquiry about the other's love life, just to make sure they were doing okay. Then,

Ernie Banks unwinds one of his long and elegant swings on August 31, 1955, in Brooklyn, New York, in a game against the Dodgers. He finished third in the National League that year with 44 home runs and first in extra base hits, with 82.

eventually, he'd discuss the big shot.

Banks' signature comment, which applies to baseball, but when you think about it, could also be applied to life, is his legendary statement "Let's play two." The way Banks remembered the day he first uttered the words, it was 100 degrees on the thermometer, the sun was out, the grass was green and the atmosphere seemed primed for baseball. The words have been invoked ever since as description for the perpetually optimistic, positive demeanor Banks possessed.

When playing your entire career for the Chicago Cubs during fallow times, like Banks did, staying positive was a challenge. Banks persevered, first at shortstop, then at first base, for 19 seasons in a Cubs uniform, from the early 1950s to the early 1970s, when they won nothing and frequently finished in last place. He gave his all, did his best, and that was very good indeed. Over 2,528 games, his labors produced 512 home runs, 1,636 runs batted in, 14 All-Star appearances and two Most Valuable Player awards, but no pennants.

The Ernie Banks story began in 1931 in Dallas, Texas, where he was born the second oldest of 12 children. There were no organized baseball teams for him to play on as a youth, and the slender Banks, who grew to be 6-foot-1 and 180 pounds as a Major Leaguer, started out as a softball player.

By age 19 in 1950 Banks was playing for the Kansas City Monarchs, one of the last grand institutions of the fading Negro Leagues. Former star James "Cool Papa" Bell noticed Banks early on, and Jackie Robinson invited him to barnstorm. In Kansas City he came under the tutelage of manager Buck O'Neil. O'Neil, a savvy baseball man, known for his patience with young players, was a hugely influential presence in Banks' life. A few years later, after the Monarchs had folded and Banks had served two years in the Army, O'Neil was scouting for the Cubs and steered Banks to the team that represented his future. Ultimately, O'Neil became the first African-American coach in the majors for the Cubs, too.

It should be noted that O'Neil was also admired

500TH

🏐 "Mr. Cub" launched his 500th career home run on May 12, 1970, at Wrigley Field. The blast made him just the ninth player in baseball history to reach the milestone.

His home run was part of an 11-inning 5–4 Chicago victory, and it came off of Atlanta Braves hurler Pat Jarvis. Banks knocked the homer in the second inning on a fastball thrown on a 1-1 count. The bases-empty smack also gave him 1,600 career runs batted in.

"I felt the ball had a good chance," Banks said of it clearing the wall in left-center.

Fans gave the Cubs legend a four-minute standing ovation after the shot.

Banks retired after the 1971 season at 40, with 512 home runs.

HOME RUN

as a man who always had a positive attitude about the game, even when discriminatory hardships might have turned him bitter. His approach definitely rubbed off on Banks.

In 1953 Banks made his big-league debut, batting .314 in 10 games. He and teammate Gene Baker, another African-American, were brought to the majors together, but Banks played first, making him the first black player to appear in a game for the Cubs.

From there Banks became a starter and a star. Besides being one of the best hitting shortstops in the game, he was durable, rarely missing games. Banks' batting was characterized by great wrist action. He was wiry and stronger than he looked, and in his second full season in the majors Banks bashed 44 home runs.

As the nation grappled with its own dark history of race relations and struggled with the burgeoning Civil Rights Movement, Banks was a low-key figure. He said he did not experience much discrimination, but that he and Baker lived with segregation. As National Book Award winner Richard Wright wrote in his novel *Invisible Man*, it was quite possible during that period in America to be black and ignored.

That described Banks' early days with the Cubs. "For a while it was like I was there, but I wasn't there," Banks said.

Eventually, the world caught up to Banks' openness, friendliness and talent. Before the 1950s were over Banks had won two National League home-run crowns and two RBI titles. In 1958, and 1959, he performed the near impossible—playing so well for losing teams that he twice was named league MVP.

In 1960 a sportswriter broke a story suggesting that the Milwaukee Braves had offered six players, plus cash, to the Cubs for Banks. If true, the rumor was intriguing since several of the Braves, including outfielder Bill Bruton, pitcher Joey Jay and shortstop Johnny Logan, were first-rate players. But Banks wasn't going anywhere. Owner P.K. Wrigley said he would never trade him.

During the seasons when Banks was at his absolute best the Cubs finished so far back in the standings they would have needed a GPS to find first place. Banks evidenced a kind of stoicism as the Cubs continued to lose during his career, but he never seemed to let the losing ruin his mood for long. It became a ritual at spring training for Banks to predict good things for the Cubs in the season ahead, often in rhyme. In 1962 he said, "The Cubs are due in '62." In 1969 he said, "The Cubs are gonna shine in '69." They were nice thoughts, but no crystal-ball forecast panned out—in those years or any others.

Banks was a chatterbox on the field. Teammates like Ron Santo, Don Kessinger and Glenn Beckert said he kept up a constant stream of talk during the action. That was funny to them, but they all admired the way Banks interacted with the public.

Much later, long after Banks retired, the team went on a good run in 1984. The Cubs finished first in the NL East with 96 wins and advanced to the National League Championship Series. A keen observer of Chicago's progress in the playoffs, Banks said, "My ship has come in. Good things come to those who wait ... and wait ... and wait."

Actually, Banks realized his perennial optimism had been joked about, and sometimes he even joked about it. Once, as he coped with a forecast that spoke of haziness with a threat of rain, Banks said, "Lovely night to play three."

Banks was always appreciated in Chicago, on and off the field. By 1964 he'd cracked more than 350 career home runs. August 15 of that season was proclaimed "Ernie Banks Day" in Chicago by Mayor Richard J. Daley. The festivities included an on-field Wrigley ceremony where Banks was showered with gifts. They included a Dodge station wagon, a diamond ring, a transistor radio and savings bonds for his three children.

The player's acceptance speech was gracious and worthy of the best of politicians.

"I want to thank God for making me an American and giving me the ability to be a Major League player," Banks said. "I will be forever grateful."

As a player, even when he lost a step in the field and switched to covering first base, Banks kept on ticking and was forever upbeat. Sportswriters asked him more about how he could keep up his attitude than his toe-hold on a starting position.

"I always believe," Banks said of making those pennant predictions. "Some people think I don't. Some people think I should be in a lunatic asylum. But I say it every year and I believe it every year. It doesn't cost you anything to be happy. Am I ever grouchy? Well, I'm not going to say I jump out of bed every morning and start putting on my Cubs uniform while humming a tune. Sometimes I give myself a pep talk, and as I look into the mirror in the bathroom I tell myself I'm the luckiest guy alive."

There are worse ways to go through life.

When Banks retired after the 1971 season he was 40. His No. 14 jersey was retired. One of his notable statistics was his proclivity for hitting grand-slam homers. In 1955 alone he hit five, and he added seven more over his career. It was obvious Banks was going to be a Hall of Famer and merely had to wait the predetermined amount of time before selection. When he was inducted in Cooperstown, New York, in 1977, some amongst the thousands of fans cheering for him held up a banner reading, "America Loves Ernie Banks."

President Barack Obama awards Baseball Hall of Famer Ernie Banks with the Presidential Medal of Freedom, November 20, 2013.

With a twinkle in his eye, Banks glanced skyward and said, "There's sunshine, fresh air, and the team is behind us. Let's play two."

Acknowledging he did not have the proper temperament to become a Major League manager, Banks sometimes expressed loftier goals for his postretirement life. He thought about becoming president of the Cubs and leading the front office. At other times he said he would like to do something meaningful for mankind and win the Nobel Peace Prize. (Perhaps finding a way to bring the Cubs a World Series title was the ticket to a Nobel Prize?)

Whenever he could he always thanked Cubs fans and said the experience of playing every day at Wrigley Field couldn't be topped.

"It's unfortunate I didn't get to a World Series," he said. "My World Series was winning the respect of the fans, the media and my family. That and building friendships. That's what counts, things that will last."

If not for Banks, the nickname Mr. Cub might well have been applied to another of Chicago's greats, but it truly belongs to Banks, and he always took pride in being called Mr. Cub. It meant more to him, in more ways, than most fans knew.

"That's kind of what my life has always been about," Banks said of being Mr. Cub. "I wanted to finish my career with one team, in one city, one mayor, one park, one owner. I did that. My career was very unique and I am proud of it."

The statue honoring Banks at Wrigley Field was unveiled at the beginning of the 2008 baseball season. The inscription, "Let's Play Two," could not have been more right, and never has a permanent connection between player and team been more appropriately solidified.

"Even when I am no longer around, this will be here," Banks said, "When I'm not here, I will be *here.*"

Chicago CUBS

Greatness Just Out of Reach

Ron Santo's Major League debut was a beauty, one of the only good things to come out of the Cubs' 1960 season—make that the early 1960s.

Called up from the Cubs' affiliate in Houston, the rookie third baseman was a nervous wreck prior to a doubleheader against the Pirates in Pittsburgh. Soothed by Cubs star Ernie Banks, Santo collected himself and notched two hits and scored three runs in his first game. He added another hit and two RBIs in the second match. After that he knew he would be fine.

It was a nice surprise for Cubs fans. Santo, a coveted high school star in the Seattle area who was scouted by many teams but chose to sign with the Cubs because of what he saw of Wrigley on television, finished fourth in Rookie of the Year voting. It was a welcome result for a franchise that had little to boast about outside of Banks' heroics in the previous seasons. Santo went on to slug 342 career home runs, drive in 1,331 and win five Gold Gloves. He was a nine-time All-Star.

But sometimes it seemed as if the Cubs were cursed in more ways

Ron Santo poses at spring training in the 1960s; Santo was a six-time All-Star over the decade.

CHICAGO'S BIG TEAMS

than one. Second baseman Ken Hubbs, a home-grown talent, debuted on the heels of Santo in 1961 for a 10-game stint and was named the 1962 NL Rookie of the Year. He also won a Gold Glove, and it looked like a future filled with promise. Yet in February of 1964, a few months after completion of his third season, the popular Hubbs was killed in a plane crash at 22 years old—he was at the controls. Religious and affable, Hubbs made friends with fans and didn't drink or smoke. Given his short time on earth and shorter time with the Cubs, he left a strong impact.

When it came to smiles and making friends, Hubbs was a younger Ernie Banks. Those who knew him never forgot him. There were 1,300

mourners at his funeral in the small California town where he grew up, and the headstone on his grave reads simply, "Our Ken."

Hubbs was supposed to be part of the Cubs' 1960s future. Instead, his death left a gaping what-if hole.

★ ★ ★ ★

In the wake of the Hubbs tragedy, the Cubs' core became Santo and Banks along with catcher Randy Hundley, second baseman Glenn Beckert and shortstop Don Kessinger. They played the infield together right through to the end of the decade. In fact, all five players were named to

Chicago Cubs rookie second baseman Ken Hubbs is surrounded by young fans after he tied the National League record of 57 consecutive games without an error, in Chicago, August 14, 1962.

coaches, with each of them taking turns as the boss. So, in 1961 and 1962 the Cubs had several managers in a job share that was widely ridiculed and never worked well.

The problems were numerous. Originally, there were eight coaches. Over the next few years as people came and went, 24 different men became members of "the College of Coaches." There was overlapping authority, contradictory advice given, players who didn't know what was wanted, and pitchers confused by different voices. On the field the Cubs were as lousy as ever. The club's 59-103 season record in 1962 represented the 16th straight nonwinning season.

Although the "experiment" lasted on the books until 1965, by 1963 Bob Kennedy, who led the team to a more respectable 82-80 record, was the acknowledged "head coach" and the carousel had stopped spinning.

But management still bumbled. Always fingered as the biggest personnel mistake in team history is the 1964 trade of outfielder Lou Brock for pitcher Ernie Broglio. At the time Brock was a young player still finding himself. Broglio had been a 20-game winner for the Cardinals. As soon as Broglio came to the Cubs, arm soreness interfered with his effectiveness. Brock blossomed into a Hall of Famer, collecting more than 3,000 hits and stealing 938 bases.

When Durocher was hired for the 1966 season, the move shook things up with an earthquake's power. Brash and colorful, used to winning, Durocher had not inhabited a dugout for 11 years. He had won a pennant with the Dodgers and two with the Giants, as well as a World Series with the Giants. He had mentored Jackie Robinson and Willie Mays. That followed a long playing career with the Yankees, Reds, Cardinals and Dodgers characterized by a fiery style. Durocher

the All-Star Team in 1969. These mid-1960s North Siders helped swap the Cubs' losing ways for winning streaks, even if they could never go all the way.

Controversial Hall of Fame manager Leo Durocher, who had managed both the Dodgers and the Giants, was brought in to help this group of stars find their form. His hiring in 1966 spelled the end of one of the more bizarre management structures in the majors.

The brainchild of owner P.K. Wrigley was to rotate the manager's job among a group of was a three-time All-Star shortstop who played on two World Series champions.

Although usually taken out of context, Durocher was famous for uttering the phrase "Nice guys finish last." At the very least it reflected his sentiments. Later, he added his own interpretation to the remark: "I never said that you can't be a nice guy and win. I said that if I was playing third base and my mother rounded third with the winning run, I'd trip her up."

In 1965, the year before Durocher began his crusade for a Cubs pennant, the team finished 72-90, good for eighth place in the 10-team league. When he was introduced to the press he declared, "This is not an eighth-place club." He was right. Under Durocher, the next season the team finished 59-103 and placed an embarrassing 10th.

Improvement, and even excitement, followed. It took just one year. In 1967 the Cubs won 87 games and attendance jumped by 342,000. In 1968 the Cubs attracted more than a million fans for the first time since 1952. They weren't pennant contenders, but they were winners for a second year in a row. Then things really got interesting.

Cubs manager Leo Durocher argues with umpire Shag Crawford on May 23, 1966, in the second game of a doubleheader against the Atlanta Braves. Durocher was tossed out of the first game for staging a similar argument.

The 1969 season seemed to belong to the Cubs from the outset. The players were gelling. Wrigley was rocking. More than 1.6 million fans came out.

Besides their superb infield, the Cubs possessed more nuclear armaments. Outfielder Billy Williams, who had been Rookie of the Year in 1961, blossomed into an All-Star.

The 6-foot-1, 170-pound lefty batter, often called "Sweet Swinging Billy Williams" because of his beautiful touch with the bat, became a Hall of Famer on the strength of 426 home runs, 1,476 runs batted in and a lifetime average of .290. He also played in 1,117 consecutive games—for a time

that was the National League record. Cardinals great Stan Musial previously held the record, and Williams bested Musial's tally of 896 games played in a doubleheader against the Cardinals in 1968. What's more, it was on "Billy Williams Day" at Wrigley Field. Not shy of the big stage, Williams' second game featured four hits, three runs and three runs batted in. He took home a car, a watch, a fishing boat and a pool table, among other gifts.

Much like Banks, Williams was so revered by the Cubs that in 2010 a statue of him was erected outside of Wrigley Field.

Right-hander Bill Hands, who went 20-14 with a 2.48 ERA, recorded a career year in 1969. Ken Holtzman no-hit the Braves in August on the way to his 17-14 season (and recorded another no-hitter for the Cubs in 1971). But the main intimidator

RON SANTO

The shame of it is that when Ron Santo was finally inducted into the Baseball Hall of Fame in 2012, he wasn't alive to enjoy it. The third baseman had succumbed to the multitude of illnesses that ganged up on him as an offshoot of his nearly lifelong battle with diabetes.

Never has there been a more enthusiastic Cubs booster (except perhaps old teammate Ernie Banks).

After retirement from a 15-year career (14 with the Cubs), the beloved Santo spent another two decades as a team broadcaster.

The nine-time All-Star and five-time Gold Glove winner batted .277, with 342 home runs and 1,331 RBIs. He kept his health status secret for most of his career, but later in life he raised millions of dollars for diabetes research.

was Ferguson Jenkins, who went 21-15 and struck out 273 batters.

Jenkins was definitely optimistic entering the 1969 season. He believed Durocher had infused a downtrodden organization with an infectious positive outlook. Nearly a quarter of a century after the Cubs won their last pennant, the players felt this was their year.

"Even before the 1969 season began, we expected it to be a big year for the Cubs," Jenkins said. "Leo Durocher's plan was in place. His winning attitude had taken root in the organization."

Santo added that he felt the Cubs were a much more solid team than they had been the previous two years. "Every time I went out there I thought we could win," he said. "Every game."

Baseball was marking its 100th anniversary in the United States—acknowledging the Cincinnati Red Stockings as the first professional team. It was also the first year the word *playoffs* was added to baseball's lexicon, as the new American League and National League Championship Series were created.

The Cubs won the season opener on April 8, 7–6 in 11 innings to start the season in first place. They remained there throughout April, past May, into June, through July, beyond August and well into September. The lead was as much as nine games several times, the latest being August 16. Cubs fever swept Chicago like the flip side of a flu epidemic.

In June, when Cubs outfielder Jim Hickman ended a game with a three-run homer against the Montreal Expos, as Santo ran off the field in celebration he leaped in the air and clicked his heels together like a dancer.

Fans swooned. There was immediate and broad-based reaction to the spontaneous gesture. After that it was expected of Santo to click his heels together after every win. It became a trademark and a symbol of the joy Cubs Nation was feeling.

"I ran down the left-field line, listening to the cheers from the fans," Santo said of the inaugural click, "and for no particular reason I jumped into the air—and clicked my heels. It

"Sweet Swinging" Billy Williams poses at spring training in 1964, his second of six All-Star seasons.

was a reaction. It was out of jubilation. I had never done that before—ever. Little did I realize it would be associated with me for the rest of my life."

Still, after the peak lead was established the Cubs began to fade, a little at a time at first, and then came an eight-game losing streak at the beginning of September, culminating with a showdown against the Mets.

For 143 straight games the Cubs were No. 1, in first place and loving it. Delirious crowds filled Wrigley. And then it was over. The Mets sprinted past. The Cubs traveled to Shea Stadium in New York for a two-game set September 8 and 9, leading the division by 1½ games. It was 2–2 in the first game when a single to Hickman sent a Mets baserunner towards home from second. Hickman's throw was on the mark and the Cubs believed the tag was made. But the call went against Chicago, the run stood and the Cubs lost 3–2. That dropped the lead to a half game.

The next day Tom Seaver beat the Cubs 7–1 for his 21st victory. During the game, while Santo

A black cat crosses the path of Ron Santo as he waits his turn at bat in a crucial game against the New York Mets in 1969. The Cubs went on to lose the game and, ultimately, the pennant. The Mets went on to win the World Series.

stood in the on-deck circle, a black cat darted out and ran past him. Santo was superstitious and couldn't believe his eyes. It is probably the only time in Major League history a black cat made a run-by at a ball park.

"I was studying Billy Williams at the plate when all of a sudden a black cat jumped out of the third base stands!" Santo said. "He ran in front of me, stopped to stare, and headed toward our dugout, where he glared at Leo who was stooped on the front step of the dugout. I don't like to walk under ladders. I throw salt over my shoulder and don't light three cigarettes on one match. I especially don't like black cats in my path."

Especially if they are New York Mets cats.

The next day the Cubs lost to the Phillies and fell out of first place for the first time all year. They continued to stumble down the stretch, and the Mets pulled away. When the season ended the Cubs were eight full games behind New York.

Many years later Hands revisited the season. "When you start to lose like we did, it's hard not to keep on losing," he said. "It's a mental thing."

There was much talk that the Cubs' starting pitchers were overworked by Durocher in late summer and that he should have gone to his bench more. The Mets were credited with great pitching. Some people thought about the Billy Goat Curse.

"We broke down as a team—that simple," Beckert said.

★ ★ ★ ★

It would be accurate to say that the Leo Durocher tenure as Cubs manager peaked on August 16 when the team was nine games ahead in the standings, the whole world was seashells and flowers, and one of the most fun summers in Chicago history was playing out.

Still, Durocher had tempted fate a few times. Mostly because of ego, he foolishly sought to diminish Ernie Banks, repeatedly bringing in younger players to challenge Banks' foothold on first base. In the end Banks was always restored to the position.

All would have been forgiven by a desperate fan base, and hungry players, too, if the Cubs finished first in 1969 and went all the way. There would probably be a statue of Durocher in bronze outside Wrigley now, too.

Just how Durocher stirred up people against him was explored in print almost immediately after that season's World Series—the one the Cubs should have been in. It was suggested that Durocher was feared and disliked, even if he won.

There was no denying that Durocher had uplifted the franchise from last place to almost first place and had filled the ballpark to overflowing. But the number of wins declined year by year after 1969, and Durocher was ousted after 90 games of the 1972 season.

That meant he missed seeing one of the greatest games in Cubs history. On September 2, Milt Pappas turned in the gem of his 17-year, 209-victory career. Pappas twirled a no-hitter, beating the Padres, 8–0. As great an achievement as that is, Pappas has felt for the last 40-plus years that he was robbed of a perfect game.

In the eighth inning, after teammates began conspicuously giving him the silent treatment, Pappas noted aloud that he was pitching a no-hitter. He thought it would relax him, but it didn't. In the top of the ninth Pappas surrendered a blooper to John Jeter. He thought it was going to drop in.

"And Billy Williams came out of left field on his white charger," Pappas said.

Williams made the grab and a ground-ball out followed. After retiring the first 26 batters and with two strikes on Larry Stahl, Pappas threw two close pitches that plate umpire Bruce Froemming called balls. The result was a perfect game turned into

Milt Pappas in spring training in 1971, the year he would throw his famous no-hitter.

a no-hitter. Years later Pappas noted that when Stahl walked to first, "I was livid" at Froemming. Ron Santo soothed Pappas on the mound, reminding him he still had a no-hitter at stake. The last out came on a pop-up to second base.

The next time the Cubs fared as well as they had in 1969, it was 1984. By then the team was no longer owned by the Wrigley clan. Heirs of P.K. Wrigley, faced with tax difficulties, sold the Cubs to the Tribune Company.

After so many lean years, some fans were starting to get edgy about that Billy Goat Curse thing. Maybe it was real, after all. Maybe the Cubs never would make it back to the World Series. You just couldn't say that around Ernie Banks, though. Banks had retired his bat but not his optimism. In 1984, when the Cubs won the NL East, the franchise named Banks an honorary team member. They didn't win it all that year, or the year after that, but Banks kept believing. Even after his death in 2015, the optimism he engendered lives on with the club.

Chicago CUBS

CHAPTER 6

Curses! Foiled Again

Dallas Green was on top of the world after his 1980 Philadelphia Phillies captured the World Series. Looking for a new challenge, he became general manager of the Chicago Cubs in 1982, determined to be the guy that reshaped the franchise and made it a winner.

Green looked like the smartest guy in the room when he fleeced the Phils of players who made an instant impact in Chicago. Veterans like Bob Dernier and Gary Matthews were helpful. Second baseman Ryne Sandberg became a Hall of Famer. Philadelphia may have let Green walk out the door, but they forgot to change the locks.

But for the first two years of Green's time at the helm, the Cubs were dismal, finishing 73-89 in 1982 and 71-91 in 1983. Lee Elia was the Cubs' bench boss for both those seasons, and he didn't even make it all the way through 1983. In April, after a home defeat to the Dodgers, feeling the pressure of criticism and fan booing, Elia lost it in a postgame press conference. He went ballistic in a long rant heavily sprinkled with

Ryne Sandberg slides and steals home against the San Diego Padres in 1984; Sandberg was voted the National League MVP at the conclusion of the year.

curse words. It was a soliloquy that left sports-writers open-mouthed. Elia was defending his players, but he attacked the fans. The rant lives on in baseball lore as one of the all-time blow-ups by a manager. And although he may not have been fired as a direct result of the rant, it certainly hastened his departure.

By 1984 the Cubs had the look of a contender for the first time in 15 years. Some of their play-ers were a little long in the tooth, but they could still snarl. Larry Bowa, another ex-Phillie, was at shortstop. Ron Cey and Davey Lopes came from the Dodgers. Dennis Eckersley was on his way to the Hall of Fame as a combined starter-closer. Lee Smith was overpowering in the bullpen.

Touched by fairy dust, Rick Sutcliffe went 16-1 with a 2.69 earned run average after being traded by the Cleveland Indians. It was easy enough for the Indians to part with Sutcliffe after he went

4-5 with a 5.15 ERA in Cleveland. His page-turn of a season won him the National League Cy Young Award.

The Cubs could hit, too. Catcher Jody Davis, Leon Durham, Keith Moreland (yet another ex-Phillie), Cey and Matthews were practically their own lumber company. Probably no one had more fun coming to the ballpark than new manager Jim Frey, who presided over a 96-65 masterpiece of a season. For the first time Wrigley Field attendance topped two million. The turn-stiles clicked for 2,107,655 fans.

The season was the coming-out party for Sandberg. He batted .314 with 19 home runs and 84 runs batted in. He stroked 19 triples and stole 32 bases. He won his second of nine Gold Glove awards, made the All-Star Team for the first of 10 selections and was named National League Most Valuable Player. Those glitzy performances led to

Cubs hurlers Rick Sutcliffe, left, and Greg Maddux. Sutcliffe led the staff in 1984 with a remarkable 16-1 record; Maddux led the staff with a career-high 20 wins in 1992.

Sandberg's induction into the Hall of Fame.

On June 23 of that season Sandberg had the best single game of his career. The Cubs bested the St. Louis Cardinals 12–11 in 11 innings, with Sandberg bashing out five hits (including two home runs), driving in seven runs and scoring twice. For the rest of his life people have been talking with him about "the Ryne Sandberg Game."

"It seems like everybody was at that game," he said. "I guess they were, one way or another, in person, watching on TV, or listening on the radio."

The Cubs finished the season as the champs of the NL Eastern Division, which earned them the opportunity to play the San Diego Padres, the Western Division champs, for the right to advance to the World Series. This was the first time since 1945 the Cubs reached the postseason. At the time the NLCS was the best three out of five.

Chicago opened with Sutcliffe, who continued to be mesmerizing in a 13–0 victory. The Cubs went up 2–0 as southpaw Steve Trout won the only playoff game of his career, 4–2. Fans were dancing in the aisles at Wrigley. The Cubs were one game away from the Series as long as they could steal a win in California.

They could not. The Padres won 7–1, 7–5, 6–3, beating Sutcliffe in the finale, a group of results not so different from a Roger Federer tennis score. The player who took the most grief was first base-man Durham, who let a ground ball go through his legs. The error led to a tie game at 3–3 in the decisive contest before San Diego pulled away. In the end, 1984 was as rotten as George Orwell had predicted it would be. Teased again.

✱ ✱ ✱ ✱

From that apex the Cubs promptly went into a long slide. Even as Cubs Nation grew across the United States because of team exposure on broadcast station WGN, the club slipped back into the doldrums immediately with losing records, starting in 1985. In 1993, after three straight losing seasons, the Cubs hopped above .500 with an 84-78 record and set a new Wrigley attendance record with 2,653,763 spectators.

Defying logic, baseball history and the common sporting belief that fans flock to see winners and stay home when their team flounders, the Cubs began an unprecedented and unexpected run of good fortune at the box office. Although the team did not finish first at all, regularly notched losing records and only occasionally produced good seasons, attendance kept climbing. The attendance mark was broken again in 1999, crossing over 2.8 million. Then, for eight seasons in a row, starting in 2004, the Cubs drew more than 3 million fans per season. The record of 3,300,200 was established in 2008—the most recent season fans could get their hopes up.

It seemed that Cubs fans didn't care if they were slapped in the face, stood up or told they could only be friends from now on; they couldn't let go of their mistress. People from afar—and that included White Sox fans across town—could not fathom the depth of the allegiance in the face of constant losing, often in a heartbreaking manner, such as that experienced in 1969 and 1984.

"The longest running daytime soap opera in history," said Chicago broadcaster Arne Harris of the Cubs, "and the only one without a doctor in it."

Steve Stone, a Chicago broadcaster who had a successful pitching career that included a Cy Young Award, likes to answer "How long are you planning on living?" when a fan asks if the Cubs will break the curse in their lifetime.

★ ★ ★ ★

Following the 1984 meltdown, and before the Cubs revived again, one of the bright spots fans could get excited about was the promotion to the majors of one of the greatest pitchers of all time. With the passage of time and the accomplishments he registered with the Atlanta Braves, many non-Cubs baseball fans may not even remember that Greg Maddux's formative years were spent in Chicago.

Maddux was more a methodical genius than a flamethrower on the mound—he outfoxed batters with his control rather than blowing fastballs past them. At 6 feet tall and 170 pounds, Maddux was small for a modern-era star pitcher. But his 23-year Major League career produced 355 victories with 3,371 strikeouts and a 3.16 earned run average. He was chosen for eight All-Star Teams and won 18 Gold Gloves and four Cy Young Awards.

Maddux was 20 when he broke in with the Cubs in 1986 and pitched through the 1992 season in Chicago. That year he finished 20-11 and won his first Cy Young. However, his contract had expired and the Cubs chose not to compete on the open market for Maddux's long-term services. It was a serious misjudgment, and the best pitcher of his generation got away, only to lead the Braves to triumph after triumph.

"I really think that with the money they were going to have to pay me to stay, they would rather have had three pitchers," Maddux said. "They'd rather have three for the price of one."

Of course in Maddux's case he really was worth three other pitchers. He proved it in Atlanta. Still, many years later, Maddux has retained fond memories of Chicago. When he was inducted into the Baseball Hall of Fame, he went in without having a team insignia on the cap displayed on his plaque; it was too tough to choose between Chicago and Atlanta.

Before Maddux left he was a key participant in the Cubs' 1989 success—a second shot at the NLCS title. Some might call the 93-69 season a fluke since it represented a jump of 16 wins from 1988, and in 1990 the Cubs sunk again. But, in between, good fun was had by a team sparked offensively by Sandberg and first baseman Mark Grace (.314), Andre Dawson (21 homers), surprising Dwight Smith (.324) and Shawon Dunston

(19 steals, .278). The hurlers, led by Maddux (19 wins), Mike Bielecki (18), Sutcliffe (16) and reliever Mitch "Wild Thing" Williams (36 saves), did their part, too. But the 1989 NLCS was another disappointment, as San Francisco easily marched to a 4-1 series win.

Dawson was another ex-Cub voted into the Hall of Fame. Although "the Hawk" did a higher percentage of damage while playing for the Montreal Expos, he was a significant addition to the Cubs. Dawson, who was starting to feel the strain of playing on weakening knees, became a free agent and chose the Cubs primarily because they played all their home games on real grass as opposed to artificial grass, a situation he believed would greatly benefit his health.

A one-time Rookie of the Year in Montreal, Dawson was a bargain hire. He signed for $700,000, a large pay cut. No one expected how terrifically he would play for the Cubs. In 1987, when Dawson was 32, he won the NL's Most Valuable Player award in his first Chicago campaign when he slammed a league-leading 49 homers and knocked in a league-best 137 runs.

In all, Dawson was chosen for eight All-Star Teams, won eight Gold Gloves in the outfield and was enshrined in the Hall of Fame in 2010.

"My six years with the Cubs pretty much got my career rejuvenated," Dawson said. "As far as I'm concerned there is no better place to play. But to come to Chicago, the warmth of the Friendly Confines and the knowledge of the fans ... the thing that they do best is allow you to enjoy yourself and have fun."

That may be because Cubs fans have always been able to make their own fun, since so often the team does not provide it on the field.

★ ★ ★ ★

The Cubs recorded just two winning seasons in the next eight after their flirt with the NLCS in 1989 and before another apparent blip on the radar with a 90-73 mark in 1998.

That season featured the great chase as the St. Louis Cardinals' Mark McGwire and the Cubs' Sammy Sosa laid siege to Roger Maris' 1961 single-season record of 61 homers. McGwire won the chase that riveted the nation most of the summer, setting a new record with 70 four-baggers. Sosa finished with 66 and a league-leading 158 RBIs. He also won the MVP award.

Another large part of the Cubs' success was rookie starting pitcher Kerry Wood, who went 13-6; pitched a one-hit, 20-strikeout gem in only his fifth start; and collected the NL Rookie of the Year award.

Despite their record and obvious strengths, though, the Cubs wilted in the playoffs and were swept aptly by the Braves in the National League Division Series.

Sosa would play with the Cubs until 2004 and go on to win two home-run titles and another RBI title. The seven-time All-Star finished his career with 609 homers, eighth on the all-time list. He was beloved by Cubs supporters most of the time he played, but at the tail end of his career and in retirement, the slugger came under suspicion for performance-enhancing drug use, something McGwire admitted to doing. That tarnished Sosa's reputation, and so far during his short stay on the Hall of Fame ballot, his support has been lukewarm.

★ ★ ★ ★

Fed up with long-term mediocrity that saw the Cubs finish no higher than third from 1999 to 2002, management made a big-name hire when it brought in Dusty Baker as manager in 2003. Baker had taken the San Francisco Giants to the World Series in 2002. He led the Cubs to an 88-74 mark, first place in their division and a 21 game improvement from their dismal 67-95 line the season before.

Baker's Cubs had a young pitching staff that featured Wood (14-11), Mark Prior (18-6) and Carlos

Andre Dawson hits a 15th-inning walk-off single against the St. Louis Cardinals in 1990. That season was one of Dawson's eight All-Star campaigns.

RYNE SANDBERG

Bestowed with the unusual first name of Ryne because his parents were baseball fans and liked pitcher Ryne Duren, Ryne Sandberg channeled his baseball-fueled name into a Hall of Fame career as a second baseman for the Cubs after the Philadelphia Phillies foolishly included him in a trade.

The 1984 season was Sandberg's do-it-all year and the most memorable of his career. He won the National League Most Valuable Player award and among other things batted .314 and hit 19 triples.

Overall, Sandberg was a 10-time All-Star and won nine Gold Glove awards. After retiring in 1997 at 37, Sandberg decided to stay in baseball, and he worked his way up through the minors to become a Major League manager. He began as interim manager for the Philadelphia Phillies in 2013 and led the club in 2014.

Zambrano (13-11). Sosa was still swinging well, too, as he smacked 40 home runs and drove in 109.

The Cubs rode the feel-good vibes into the playoffs. They battled past the Atlanta Braves, 3-2, in the Division Series and brought a 3-2 National League Championship Series lead home to Wrigley Field against the Florida Marlins. World Series fever was a communicable disease in Chicago as the sixth game began. The team was poised to break through and reach the Series for the first time in 58 years.

The Cubs led the Marlins 3–0 entering the top of the eighth inning with Prior in charge on the mound. Rarely has such joy infected so many as the anticipation of the Cubs' advancing to the Series grew more intense with each pitch.

And then it all unraveled in the most unlikely of ways. Just when it seemed the Cubs would work their way out of the inning, Florida second baseman Luis Castillo lofted a high fly down the left-field line that was drifting foul. Chicago's Moises Alou sought to get a bead on it. As the ball fell from the sky, a Cubs fan sitting near the fence reached out to grab it. The ball bounced off his hands, and Castillo stayed alive at the plate.

The fan, Steve Bartman, had to be escorted out of his seat for protection against irate home fans. From there, Prior lost command, the Cubs made

Steve Bartman interferes with Cubs left fielder Moises Alou as the pair reach for a foul ball off the bat of the Florida Marlins' Luis Castillo in the sixth game of the NLCS. Five outs away from eliminating the Marlins and capturing their first NL pennant since 1945, the Cubs faltered after the play and ultimately lost the NLCS. The Marlins went on to win the World Series.

an error, and the Marlins pushed across eight runs to win the game, 8–3.

At first Alou said he would not have caught the ball anyway, though he later waffled on the matter, sometimes indicating he might have had a chance. No matter. The Cubs had another chance, a seventh game at home. Chicago led that one, too, 5–3, going into the fifth. That chance also evaporated, the Cubs falling 9–6. Florida went on to win the World Series, and the devastating end to the season made the Cubs believe they were haunted—if not by the Billy Goat Curse then by some other evil spirit.

Bartman was castigated, vilified and initially harassed. He placed himself under virtual house arrest, refused to grant interviews and wisely made himself difficult to recognize. For some he remains an object of scorn, but his innocent lunge for the ball did not prevent Prior from terminating a rally.

The ball itself later appeared in the possession of Harry Caray's Restaurant upon the expenditure of $100,000 to whoever came up with it in the postmuff scramble. Later, restaurant operators blew up the ball in a highly publicized ceremony. That could be construed as another way to spike the Billy Goat Curse once and for all.

★ ★ ★ ★

In 2008, under Lou Piniella's managerial guidance, the Cubs won 97 games and advanced to the play-offs once more. They lost three straight games to the Los Angeles Dodgers. And since, it feels like a steadily sinking ship.

A new ownership group, the Ricketts family, bought the team in 2009. They have big plans to renovate Wrigley. They hired bright, young front office leaders. They are rebuilding the Major League roster top to bottom. Yet very little has gone right on the field so far. The latest addition to the cause is manager Joe Maddon. He's next in line to try to lift the curse. He'll need all the luck he can get.

Chicago BEARS

MONS
of the

TERS
MIDWAY

For most, George Halas is remembered as jut-jawed and craggy-faced, as if his head were one of the busts on Mount Rushmore. If ever the National Football League chiseled its own sculptures of Founding Fathers, Halas would definitely be one of them.

He was present at the creation of the league, was a tireless advocate for pro football, outlasted all of his competitors and built the Chicago Bears into a fearsome wild bunch of tacklers and blockers who in many ways set the tone for the league.

It was Halas who emerged as the league's strong man. He was actively involved at the NFL's organizational meeting in a Hupmobile showroom in Canton, Ohio—so crowded with rich, optimistic football-franchise-owning hopefuls that many could not find a place to sit except for the running boards of the vehicles.

Bears head coach and all-time figurehead George Halas, as seen in 1961.

Overleaf: Brian Urlacher surveys the Carolina Panthers' offense and readies the Bears' defense at Soldier Field on Sunday, October 28, 2012.

In those days, albeit briefly, the Bears were the Decatur Staleys, a team formed through the largesse of an Illinois starch manufacturing company that turned Halas loose to make a football team the company would be proud of on the gridiron. When Staley management decided to stick with starch as the firm's primary reason for existing, Halas took over the team, renamed it the Bears because he was a Chicago Cubs baseball fan, and chose the same orange and blue team colors sported by his alma mater, the University of Illinois.

The tie to the Cubs was more than simply emotional. For a half century—1920 to 1970—the Bears also called Wrigley Field home. They abandoned Wrigley for the more spacious Soldier Field only when the NFL set a 50,000-seat minimum for stadium capacity as it merged with the American Football League.

The Chicago Bears' history is a glorious one, spotlighted with great victories and star players, though the early success stemmed from the fertile mind and personnel judgment of Halas, who as player, coach, and owner influenced the fortunes of the franchise for 63 years until he passed away at 88 in 1983.

The son of Chicago Czech-Bohemian immigrants, Halas was a top-notch all-around athlete who not only was an end in football but also briefly played Major League Baseball with the New York Yankees. Halas coached great players and coaxed great seasons out of the team from its inception.

Chicago under Halas won its first NFL title in 1921 and won them regularly thereafter in the 1930s and 1940s (the team's most accomplished decade). They won again in 1963, when Halas' acumen earned him the league's Coach of the Year Award. That '63 championship was one of the club's most satisfying achievements, holding off the Green Bay Packers at the height of their brilliance and also vengefully taming their longtime rival in New York, the Giants.

Chicago and Green Bay enjoy the longest-standing rivalry in the NFL and one of the most intense rivalries in all of sport. Dating back to 1921, as of the end of the 2014 NFL season, the Bears and Packers had played 191 times, with Chicago ahead 93 wins to the Packers' 92, and the clubs have tied six times. Although every newly hired Bears coach understands that the ultimate goal is to win championships, he also realizes that the second most important task before him is to beat Green Bay.

The Bears helped the NFL succeed when there was still doubt, by turning loose the dashing Red Grange as he made his transition from college household name to the pros. Their hulking, bruising batterers adopted the catchy nickname "Monsters of the Midway," and in 1940, their 73–0 massacre of the Washington Redskins represented perfection on the field and remains the most startling and lopsided score ever recorded in a National Football League game, championship or otherwise.

Few, if any, teams owned a decade the way Chicago dominated the 1940s, with four world titles and one other championship-game appearance despite the fracturing of the roster by World War II. As the passing game became more significant in the offense than ever before, opening up the field and introducing a more exciting style of play to the sport, the Bears were in the forefront with Hall of Fame quarterback Sid Luckman leading the way.

Appropriately for a team priding itself on the number of black and blue marks its defense left on opposing ball carriers, the 1950 Bears sported Bill George, who improvised during a game and wound up inventing the position of middle linebacker, forever changing the complexion of NFL defenses. George became the first in a line of superb Chicago middle linebackers who cut a swath through foes' offenses as they carved paths to the Pro Football Hall of Fame in Canton. George begat Dick Butkus, who begat Mike Singletary, who begat Brian Urlacher.

Halas, in collusion with the perfectly-built-for-the-role Mike Ditka, his No. 1 draft choice out of the University of Pittsburgh in 1961, reinvented the tight end role. Ditka, who stood 6-foot-3 and weighed 230 pounds and was nicknamed "Iron Mike," came out of Pennsylvania coal country and was considered as tough as saddle leather. Ditka helped make the 1963 Bears champions.

That high point aside, the 1960s were grim for the Bears, a period when the club was probably at its worst. Yet the Bears managed to entertain with some stunningly brilliant players and touch the nation's heart with tragically sad stories.

In 1964, at training camp in Indiana, the Bears' preparation for a title defense was demoralized by the death of two players, halfback Willie Galimore and end John Farrington, in an automobile accident. In 1970, fullback Brian Piccolo died from cancer at 26. The mixed backfield couple of the white Piccolo and the African-American Gale

Sayers was a rarity. The roommates cared deeply for one another as friends, and their relationship and Piccolo's death were explored in the tear-provoking movie *Brian's Song*.

Sayers, an All-American out of Kansas, was potentially the most lethal all-around runner ever, winning rushing titles and leading the league in kickoff returns. He scored six touchdowns in one game. But his career was cut short when devastating knee injuries resulted in his retirement at age 29.

Seemingly indestructible as a player, Ditka and Halas had a falling out, but they reconciled when the Old Man was dying. Halas anointed Ditka as the new coach of the Bears in 1982 with the mission of rebuilding the franchise, which had fallen on hard times.

Ditka fulfilled his assignment, and his 1985 Bears were probably the most colorful team in the history of the game, devouring opponents with a frightfully overpowering defense (tip of the helmet to defensive coordinator Buddy Ryan) and a wild cast of characters who loved to play as hard as they hit. The never-bashful quarterback Jim McMahon was a ringleader of the fun bunch, but all were anchored by the work ethic and fabulous production of running back Walter Payton.

That group had the audacity to record a rap song called "The Super Bowl Shuffle" even before the team won the Super Bowl, which it did. More surprisingly, the humorous, well-put-together single was well received by the music world, selling more than half a million copies. The Bears became so culturally hip that the TV comedy show *Saturday Night Live* featured the skit "Bill Swerski's Superfans," famous for its running gag line "Da Bears."

In the 2000s, the Bears are still owned by descendents of George Halas. The club at long last reached another Super Bowl in the 2006 playoffs but fell to Peyton Manning's powerful Indianapolis Colts. The Halas family is still working hard to make the Bears kings of the league George helped establish. After all, that is what Halas most coveted—one more championship.

YEAR FOUNDED: 1920

Founded as Decatur Staleys; changed to Chicago Bears in 1922

SUPER BOWL CHAMPIONS

1921 1932 1933 1940 1941 1943 1946 1963 1985

RETIRED NUMBERS

3	5	7	28	34
Bronko Nagurski	George McAfee	George Halas	Willie Galimore	Walter Payton

40	41	42	51	56
Gale Sayers	Brian Piccolo	Sid Luckman	Dick Butkus	Bill Hewitt

61	66	77	89
Bill George	Clyde Turner	Red Grange	Mike Ditka

PASSING

137
TOUCHDOWN PASSES

Sid Luckman

RUSHING

16726
YARDS

Walter Payton

RECEIVING

492
PASSES CAUGHT

Walter Payton

SCORING

1116
POINTS

Kevin Butler

HALL OF FAMERS

Doug Atkins

George Blanda

Dick Butkus

George Connor

Richard Dent

Mike Ditka

Paddy Driscol

Jim Finks

Danny Fortmann

Bill George

Red Grange

George Halas

Dan Hampton

Ed Healey

Bill Hewitt

Stan Jones

Sid Luckman

Link Lyman

George McAfee

George Musso

Bronko Nagurski

Walter Payton

Gale Sayers

Mike Singletary

Joe Stydahar

George Trafton

Clyde Turner

Chicago BEARS

CHAPTER 7

The Galloping Twenties

Red Grange may have owned the best sports nickname of all time. "The Galloping Ghost" was a seemingly wispy, speedy, untouchable figure outrunning behemoth tacklers left behind in the mud.

But he also may have been the most important pro football player of all time. Once revered as a godlike figure of the gridiron at the University of Illinois, he made the glitziest of all transitions to the pros.

America was exhaling and seeking to let loose after World War I despite the puritanical imposition of Prohibition that was supposed to eliminate liquor but instead drove imbibing underground. The National Football League, previously a slapdash group of teams made up of players who had real jobs during the week, was the new sport in town, and the task of teams such as the Chicago Bears was to show the public that this was the best brand of ball ever displayed.

It was the age of the American sporting hero: Babe Ruth's arcing home runs that disappeared into the gloaming seemed to uplift the national pastime even higher in estimation. Jack Dempsey was the

Red Grange, fresh off playing amateur ball with the University of Illinois, is seen as a pro with the Chicago Bears during their barnstorming tour of 1925.

most popular heavyweight champion boxing had ever seen. "Big" Bill Tilden ruled the world of tennis. Golf's Bobby Jones popularized the phrase grand slam even more than the Babe did.

To sports fans, the only professional team sport that truly mattered was baseball, although hockey, too, was trying to find its footing in this era of the fast-stepping Charleston. For football, there was notable allegiance to the alma mater, however, and old alums still linked by good-old-days memories to their colleges turned out in droves to watch their team either fumble to despair or attain noble victory.

These were the days of Knute Rockne's Notre Dame Fighting Irish and their Four Horsemen, and the days when the Rose Bowl was the de facto national championship game.

Not even Rockne could eclipse the nationwide fascination with Harold Grange, the running back who muscled up his physique by hauling ice in his part-time job at $37.50 a week.

The legend of the 6-foot, 180-pound runner-defensive back exploded in the Fighting Illinois triumph over Michigan in 1924 when No. 77 scored four touchdowns in the game's first 12 minutes and five in all. Such was Grange's fame afterward

In preparation for the American Football League, formed by Grange and his manager C.C. Pyle, Grange delivered ice in 1926 as part of his off-season training.

honor in playing the game as an amateur, entirely for the sport of it. It was pure and wholesome. To make a living avoiding would-be tacklers was to cheapen the very morals of sporting competition. Yet Grange knew he was in his prime and did not want to give up playing football at age 22. Besides, he needed to make a living. Zuppke, Grange's once-staunchest supporter, was so angry he refused to give the player an oil painting that was made of the runner.

Pyle stalked Grange one day at a movie theater in Champaign, Illinois, and asked if he would like to make a million dollars. Grange said he would, and Pyle rolled into action.

In the earliest, leather-helmet (or no helmet) days of the NFL, the Chicago Bears were a power. They won the 1921 title and were runners-up as either the Staleys or Bears four of the league's first five years. The United States was still pretty much a nation of farmers and rural communities not quite easily linked to the biggest cities, but that was changing. Many of the numerous enthusiastic attendees at the NFL's organization meeting in Ohio who came from smaller cities were finding the commitment to a professional league to be onerous financially.

There was considerable instability in the ranks. Teams came and went swiftly, one minute appearing on the schedule, the next evaporating into obscurity. The comings and goings of those teams like migrating birds did not help credibility. Nor did the public image of players as hardscrabble, uncouth men of little education who spent most of a day each week grunting and bashing one another in the desire to open a sliver of a hole large enough for a cleated brute to plow through. One thing was certain, the pro game, both in perception and reality, was one of slogging advancement, of trench warfare, with a lack of sophistication in the offense.

Worse to hear for George Halas, and the dedicated builders of the sport, was the oft-uttered

that when he was about to complete his college eligibility in 1925, he was quietly approached by a person who could now be termed either the first sports agent or the midwife in the birthing of the acceptance of pro football by the masses.

C.C. Pyle was a marketing man ahead of his time. He was later teased when some called him "Cash and Carry" Pyle. He promised Grange that if he turned professional and left the career decisions to him, he would make him a rich man. This was touchy because pro football was considered disreputable by the pooh-bahs of the college game, Grange's formidable coach Bob Zuppke included. To Zuppke, and many others, Grange's going pro was akin to selling his soul to the devil. There was

C.C. Pyle and Red Grange in the mid-1920s.

comment that any good college team could beat a pro team. That type of remark drove him crazy. Halas had been an all-around athlete in high school and college, and during his short sojourn with Major League Baseball's New York Yankees in right field he quickly learned the difference between the pros and the amateurs. He batted .091 in the majors. Men were tougher than boys.

Halas and the Bears were a rock of the NFL, along with the Green Bay Packers and Curly Lambeau, and before the end of the decade the New York Giants and the Mara family. The Bears of the 1920s were well stocked with former college stars who wished to continue their football education. Eventual Hall of Famers of Chicago's line included tackles Ed Healey and Roy Lyman and center George Trafton. Healey had been a three-year starter at Dartmouth when the Ivy League was a rugged league, and he became a five-time All-Star in the NFL. "Link" Lyman came out of Nebraska. Trafton was a six-time All-Pro

out of Notre Dame who also boxed and later coached in the Canadian Football League. These men were serious about their football, and many an opponent who doubted it needed to either be carted off or bandaged up.

Halas, who also played through the 1928 season, always had his say, expressing his opinion to officials. He battled for his Bears any way he could. Grange once said that the word to best describe Halas was "Guts. There was not a man on the football field he was afraid of."

★ ★ ★ ★

The NFL skeptics were many in the 1920s, so when Pyle approached Halas with a gleam in his eye and a clever proposal to boost the credibility of the league, "Papa Bear" was keen to listen. Grange was from Wheaton, near Chicago, so his identification with the NFL came through the Bears.

Crowds pack a Philadelphia stadium to watch Red Grange (carrying the ball) and the Chicago Bears beat the hometown Yellow Jackets on December 5, 1925.

Pyle suggested that when the 1925 college and pro seasons ended, the Bears sign Grange for a barnstorming tour.

It was commonplace at that time for Major League Baseball players to band together for post-season tours to the hinterlands in order to show off the best baseball to fans who could not attend big-league games, nor see it any other way since television wasn't around yet. Fans poured in to see the big names in those exhibitions.

Grange, who decades later was called "the greatest open-field runner ever" in a *Sports Illustrated* special issue devoted to college football, scored 31 touchdowns in 20 games as a collegian. His style electrified witnesses. It is unclear just what those admirers thought Grange should do with his talents if not play pro ball.

"There were many who thought I made a big mistake when I turned pro after my last college game in the late fall of 1925," Grange wrote in his autobiography. "Professional football in those days was frowned upon by faculty representatives, coaches, athletic directors and the commissioner of athletics for the Big Ten. It was hard to find anyone in college circles who was for it."

Pro football was not the career Grange's guidance counselor mapped out for him. But he bucked the tide of opinion and struck a deal with Chicago to showcase his professional unveiling. An ambitious schedule was planned, and Halas called Pyle "a born promoter."

When it all ended it was a 19-game, 67-day circus-like excursion that enticed fans out of their living rooms and created great copy for newspaper sports sections. The tour made Grange about $100,000 and exposed pro football to generally large, and frequently new, audiences. At one point, Grange and the Bears played 10 games in 17 days as far south as Florida and New Orleans. Then they went west for games in San Diego, Los Angeles and San Francisco. The game in LA drew 75,000 to the Memorial Coliseum.

Gate receipts were split 50 percent for the Bears and 50 percent for the Grange-Pyle team. Of that share Grange obtained 60 percent. The payouts were about as generous as Pyle promised, and his foresight helped pro football upgrade its stature. The barnstorming tour made the sporting public view pro football in a new way. Having the best-known college star provide his stamp of approval to the fledgling operation allowed many fans to discover it was worthwhile to cheer for another football team beyond the program where they earned their degree.

During some games on the tour Grange rushed for a fair number of yards and scored touchdowns. Other times he had trouble walking because of the beating he took, and he had to sit out some games. Overall, the Pyle-organized journey was a smash hit. It was like taking Broadway shows to outlying regions. Grange proved to have marquee value.

★ ★ ★ ★

When the adventure concluded, Halas wanted to keep Grange for the Bears, but they couldn't agree on money. Pyle, sensing Grange was

THE FIRST AFL

🏈 Just about the entire reason for the existence of the original American Football League was to provide Red Grange, the Galloping Ghost out of Illinois, a place to play pro ball.

In an arrangement orchestrated by agent C.C. Pyle, Grange, the most exciting collegian ever to that point, had turned professional with the Chicago Bears for a barnstorming tour of the nation in 1925.

The tour proved Grange was a major draw, but the Bears and Pyle couldn't agree on what the halfback was worth, so Pyle created a team—and ultimately a whole league—for his star. The AFL launched in 1926 with Grange leading the New York Yankees. Pyle filled the league with teams such as the Boston Bulldogs, Brooklyn Horsemen and Los Angeles Wildcats—many of the franchises coexisted in cities with NFL teams.

However, few AFL teams drew well, and the nine-team experiment failed after one year. Grange and his Yankees were adopted into the NFL in 1927. Grange missed the entire 1928 season because of injury, but from 1929 on he played for the Bears.

still hot, helped form an entire league (the first American Football League) to show off his star. That ill-fated venture ended after one season, and Grange joined the Bears for the rest of his career. Injuries prevented him from being as flashy as he had been at Illinois, robbing him of his slashing ability, but he was a team leader and significant contributor on offense and defense until 1934. Grange scored 32 touchdowns in the NFL and was a member of two Bears championship teams.

Through Pyle's efforts, Grange appeared in movies and piled up endorsements. He could afford a $5,500 Lincoln to drive and an expensive raccoon coat to wear.

For the rest of his life, upon induction into the Pro Football Hall of Fame in its first year of existence in 1963, and as a broadcaster, Grange, who died in 1991 at 87, was perpetually identified with the Chicago Bears. He and Halas remained good friends.

And Grange lived long enough to see pro football first gain a foothold in the American sporting consciousness, watch it take off through the promotion of television and ultimately eclipse baseball as the nation's most popular sport. And none of it would have happened without Grange's talent, star power and willingness to go against the grain.

Chicago BEARS

CHAPTER 8

Bronko and the Champs

The reason Bronislau Nagurski was called "Bronko" was because his elementary school teacher couldn't pronounce his given first name, which was Ukrainian. It was only later, as a college football player at the University of Minnesota and later still as a professional battering ram for the Chicago Bears, that it became apparent how suitable the nickname was.

Irvine "Cotton" Warburton of the Pacific Coast All-Stars is leveled by the Bears' Bronko Nagurski in a 26–7 drubbing Chicago handed the All-Stars in 1935.

That's because Bronko Nagurski was as naturally physically difficult to contain as a rodeo's bucking bronco. On offense Nagurski played fullback, and the running joke that followed him through the defensive line and into legend was that he was so strong he created his own interference. That was the parlance of the day—what it meant was that Nagurski was his own best blocker.

On defense, the 6-foot-2, 230-pound lineman leveled opposing

ball carriers with bone-crushing tackles. Today Nagurski's listed dimensions don't impress as much as they did in the 1930s, but when Bronko lined up, on either side of the ball, he was larger than most NFL linemen of the day. On top of that, his immense strength and massive hands—two attributes that made his work going both ways look easy—magnified his size.

"Just before they got to me," Nagurski said of would-be tacklers, "I'd knock 'em out of the way and keep running." He ran with his head down and led with his shoulder, and that's why many, including Giants coach Steve Owen, said he was essentially his own blocker.

The 1932 World Champion Chicago Bears.

★ ★ ★ ★

Once when Nagurski bulled over the goal line for a touchdown at the almost-too-small Wrigley Field, his momentum kept him going until he was stopped by the retaining wall. "The last guy hit me awfully hard," Nagurski said.

Famed sportswriter Grantland Rice once penned the comment "Eleven Bronko Nagurskis would have beaten 11 [Jim] Thorpes or 11 [Red] Granges." Grange, Nagurski's celebrated teammate, did not disagree. He said, "Tackling Nagurski was like getting an electric shock."

The funny thing, though, is that when he was a youth in International Falls, Minnesota, Nagurski's parents forbade him to play football.

"I guess they thought their little boy would get hurt," Nagurski said.

The story of his discovery is the stuff legends are built on. Allegedly, Minnesota coach Clarence Spears was driving through International Falls, got lost and stopped to ask for directions. Nagurski, who was plowing a field at the time, supposedly lifted the plow and pointed in the direction Spears was headed. The coach, so impressed with Nagurski's strength, signed him on the spot.

Nagurski became a centerpiece of the Bears organization and was one of the cornerstones of the team that broke an 11-year championship drought in 1932. Since the NFL's inception in 1920, the champion of the league was always the team with the best winning percentage at the end of the season. In 1932, although the Green Bay Packers had won 10 games, far more than anyone else, both the Bears and the Portsmouth Spartans (forerunners of the Detroit Lions) finished with six wins and six ties, and a higher percentage than Green Bay. The result was the NFL's first playoff game, the winner of which would be named champion.

The contest was set for December 18 in Chicago. Although Chicago is a wintry place, snow does not always arrive in abundance until Christmas or New Year's. But 1932 was an exception. Snow began falling in the days leading up to the critical game, burying the city. The game was scheduled for Wrigley Field, but the blizzard also delivered ferocious below-zero windchills.

"We couldn't really practice," Spartan Glenn Presnell said a half-century later of the conditions.

It was hazardous to the health to go outside at all, never mind attempt to play football smoothly. People wondered how many spectators would show up and what kind of effort it would take for them to get to Wrigley. So the game was moved indoors to Chicago Stadium, where the hockey-playing Black Hawks contested their home games.

This change of venue required using a field that seemed more suitable for a playground game conducted by teenagers after school. Instead of being 100 yards in length, the dimensions of the building dictated the field could be only 80 yards long. It was narrower as well. Overall, it more resembled the latter-day arena football field than what patrons and players commonly saw. The reduced size of the field resulted in the appellation "the Tom Thumb Game" being applied.

Indicative of how preoccupied Chicago was with the storm and how little pro football still rated in the public mind, Bears owner George Halas later recalled how every day he scoured the newspapers for stories or mentions of the upcoming championship game—and how he rejoiced if he came across 2 inches of copy.

An additional oddity was that Portsmouth's star quarterback Dutch Clark was absent. His day job was coaching the Colorado College basketball team, and the football season was supposed to have ended before the basketball one began. If Clark participated for the Spartans, he would have been fired as the hoops coach.

The game was tight nonetheless, with the score 0–0 at the half. The Bears tallied the winning points on a touchdown pass from Nagurski to Red Grange. Nagurski tossed a jump pass over the line of scrimmage. There was some question whether he adhered to the rules for throwers then in place, but the TD stood and the Bears went on to win 9–0.

The famous 1932 Tom Thumb game between the Portsmouth Spartans and the Chicago Bears. Because of inclement weather, the game was staged in Chicago Stadium on a hockey-rink-sized field.

★ ★ ★ ★

For the next season, the NFL made some much-needed changes. Teams were divided into two divisions, with the winner of each facing off in a championship game. Rule changes by NFL committees, spearheaded through Bears owner George Halas and a few allies, led to more sympathetic passing rules that allowed quarterbacks to throw the ball from anywhere behind the line of scrimmage, as opposed to the previously enforced 5-yard drop back, a holdover from the college game. Also assisting the passing game was the streamlining of the football itself. The narrower ball with more prominently pointed ends made it easier for quarterbacks to toss greater distances.

The Bears defended their title under the new rules, and as kings of the West, they bested their eastern counterparts, the New York Giants, 23–21. It was a typical season for Nagurski, rushing 128 times for 533 yards, the identical totals he accumulated in 1932. Those days there were no work-horse backs who carried the ball on almost every play, and Nagurski was a 60-minute man, playing both sides of the ball. Halas mostly saved him for defense.

And while some said Nagurski alone might

WORKING MEN

In the years before signing with a professional sports team almost automatically made a player rich, athletes, including members of the Chicago Bears, worked in the off-season to supplement their income.

They had to because their salaries were more in line with what the average American earned than with lottery winners.

Some of the most famous Bears players held jobs in the community, selling automobiles or insurance.

Hall of Fame lineman Stan Jones returned to Maryland to teach school each year. Quarterback Sid Luckman (seen here), who had always wanted to go into business, worked part time at Cellu-Craft Products, a packaging company, during the 1940s and eventually became the owner.

Players were usually employed in areas where they hoped to continue working when their gridiron days were behind them. Retiring from football often meant returning to their off-season jobs.

have beaten a team, the big back was far from a one-man show under Halas. Nagurski's reign as the strongest man in football coincided with numerous Bears Hall of Famers, including Grange; Joe Stydahar, a stone-wall lineman nicknamed "Jumbo"; George Musso, who later became a sheriff; lineman Danny Fortmann who became a surgeon; end Bill Hewitt (who never did get used to the idea that he should wear a helmet and was

one of the league's last bareheaded players); and 1920s holdovers Link Lyman and George Trafton.

Fortmann played college ball for little Colgate, hardly a power, and was an undersized lineman at barely over 200 pounds. Scouting was hardly a top priority heading into the first annual player draft in 1936. By the time Fortmann was chosen in the ninth round, the Bears had no idea of the qualifications of players still available. Legend has it that Halas liked the sound of Fortmann's last name, and that's why he grabbed him.

Fortmann was a shrimp, even by 1930s standards, but he had large dual ambitions.

"I wanted to play pro football, but I was also determined to go to med school," he said. Halas gave him permission to miss a couple of weeks of training camp for summer school, and in the long run Fortmann became a six-time All-Star and a doctor.

That same year the Bears made Stydahar their first No. 1 choice in history. As an All-American out of West Virginia and a larger specimen at 6-foot-4 and 235 pounds, he was a better-known quantity than Fortmann. With guys like Lyman, Trafton, Musso, Fortmann and Stydahar around, Nagurski really didn't need to open his own holes. That's mainly what they did for a living when they weren't also playing on the tackling side of the ball.

Halas, who outlived Stydahar, watched him develop into a four-time All-Star, coach two NFL teams and return to the Bears as an assistant coach years later. Halas praised Stydahar as "a man of outstanding character and loyalty."

In 1934, a new Bears running back became the answer to a trivia question, one that not many 2000s fans could probably answer. The question: Who was the first back to gain 1,000 yards rushing in the NFL?

Future surgeon Danny Fortmann of the Chicago Bears, during practice in 1941.

The answer: Beattie Feathers out of the University of Tennessee, who that season rushed for 1,004 yards on a remarkable average of 8.4 yards per carry. And the 5-foot-10, 185-pound runner's season was cut short by injury. Feathers appeared in 11 games. The Bears finished the regular season 13-0 and appeared a certainty to win their third straight title. Heavily favored, the Bears were upset by New York in what became

Beattie Feathers' rush is aided by the blocking of Bronko Nagurski in a game against the New York Giants at the Polo Grounds in New York City in 1936.

known as "the Sneakers Game."

The game was played at the Polo Grounds, and the teams woke up to an icy field. However, the Giants adapted at halftime, finding basketball shoes whose softer treads afforded more traction than the spiky cleats, which were rendered useless by the frozen field, and ran away from the Bears, 30–13, in the second half to spoil the undefeated season.

Feathers was never the same player after his injury, and in an NFL career spanning parts of seven seasons he was unable to double his rookie-year running total. It was 13 years before anyone else ran for 1,000 yards in a season. Feathers' achievement was stunning—ahead of his time—and even more so because of his yards-per-carry mark.

Later, Feathers would credit being tutored by Red Grange and blocked for by Bronko Nagurski as key reasons for that season's milestones. He said as a rookie he was not intimidated because he was already 25. Feathers had dropped out of school a few times, and the only reason he finished college, he said, was because of football.

"I knew I had to pass to play," he said. Meaning he knew he had to get the grades to run. While acknowledging the greatness of Feathers' season 30 years later, Chicago sportswriting legend Bill Gleason opined that Nagurski was so good he probably could have reached the 1,000-yard barrier first, but he "may never had thought of doing it."

Back in that Bears-Giants epic of 1933, which attracted more than 30,000 fans to the championship outdoors, the key play featured Nagurski in a razzle-dazzle maneuver that culminated with a Billy Karr touchdown when New York led 21–16.

Nagurski, who rushed for 65 yards in all, was at the root of the play. Fading back to pass he threw a strike to Hewitt, who on the run flipped the ball to Karr in a lateral for the game-winning score. Karr outran two defensive pursuers over the last 25 yards.

★ ★ ★ ★

Despite Nagurski's general superiority in the sport, he retired to upstate Minnesota after the 1937 season because Halas, gaining a reputation as a skinflint on salaries, refused to pay him sufficiently. Bronko was making $5,000 and wanted $6,500. Nagurski continued rearranging opponents' bones in professional wrestling (he grappled until he was 52) and operated a gas station. In 1943, when the Bears' roster was thinned by World War II, Halas—who had served in World War I and obtained his own commission to serve again—begged Nagurski to return.

Bronko became a Bear again for one more season—at his own price. Chicago won another crown and Nagurski retired again, accomplishing enough to be recognized in the first Pro Football Hall of Fame class in 1963. Then he went back to International Falls, often cited on any given winter day as the coldest non-Alaska community in the United States.

At his Hall induction, Nagurski—up to 270 pounds, or what he said constituted "a modern giant"—was asked how his summer had been.

An action portrait from the early 1930s displays Bronko Nagurski's impeccable form.

"We don't have summer," Nagurski said. "We just have a season in the middle of the year when sledding is poor."

The occasion was a time for storytelling about Nagurski. He laughed at all the tall tales—and conceded that some of them might even be true. What is certain is that the unique power and skills he brought to Chicago helped make the Bears of the 1930s and 1940s one of football's greatest teams.

CHAPTER 9

Sid Luckman and the All-American Massacre

Saved from a sedentary and obscure life in private business by father figure "Papa Bear" George Halas, Sid Luckman became the greatest quarterback in Chicago Bears history.

Needing to be talked into pro football by the silver tongue of the Bears' founder, Luckman led the team to its greatest decade and the most singular victory in professional sport.

New York born and raised, Luckman was an Ivy Leaguer who attended Columbia University, but he found his niche with the Bears when the NFL was just adjusting to life with throwing quarterbacks. The old-style grind-'em-out game was being challenged by a throw-deep mentality for the first time, and Luckman was the right man in the right place at the right time.

He broke in with the Bears in 1939 and was the maestro waving the baton when the Bears crushed the Washington Redskins, 73–0, to win

Second-year pro Sid Luckman shows his passing form in this 1940 photograph. Luckman was named to his first Pro Bowl that season.

the 1940 league title in the most merciless beating ever suffered by an NFL team. Occasionally, a baseball pitcher hurls a perfect game. This contest, however, is the only football game where there was any type of consensus that the winning team could not have performed any better.

It was the ultimate doesn't-figure game. Only three weeks earlier in a regular-season encounter, the Redskins had defeated Chicago 7–3. That victory gave Washington owner George Preston Marshall the forum to gloat, and he rubbed it in

with insults flung at the Bears. Wise man that he was, Halas pinned newspaper clippings of Marshall's ill-advised commentary on a bulletin board to pump up his men.

On game day, December 8, 1940, Chicago needed little encouragement. Even with the incomparable Sammy Baugh at quarterback for Washington, the Redskins were like lost children roaming the gridiron from the opening kick to the last whistle. The Bears scored 11 touchdowns that day and famously, at the behest of officials,

The Bears line up in the T formation (the backs slotted behind the quarterback as opposed to alongside him) prior to the 1942 NFL championship game. The Bears lost the game to the Washington Redskins but had used the formation to humiliate Washington 73–0 in the 1940 championship.

stopped bothering to kick extra points toward the end because they were running short on footballs. Talk about silencing a crowd. The 36,034 fans in Washington's Griffith Stadium might as well have been visiting the Tomb of the Unknown Soldier.

One of the key elements of the blowout was the mechanical expertise brought to the Bears' offense by T-formation genius Clark Shaughnessy. Brought in as a consultant by Halas, Shaughnessy tinkered with the playbook in the weeks leading up to the championship game and introduced new tactics that the Bears could easily incorporate into their regular play-calling.

"That day in football was like going from the Ford Model T to the super deluxe Rolls-Royce," Luckman said.

There has been no NFL game before or since that could compare to the 73-point beat-down. For the rest of his long life, any time the game was mentioned, Halas would smile. And any time he was asked for his biggest thrill in the sport, Halas replied, "The 73–0."

The punctuation mark that would emphasize how thorough a slaughter that game was has yet to be invented, but the triumph did make the point that the 1940s were going to be the Bears' decade. Chicago defended its crown in 1941 and was named champion again in 1943 and 1946. (The Bears also reached the championship game in 1942, losing to, of all teams, the Redskins, their chief rival of the era.)

The 1940s Bears were so loaded with talent that looking back years later it seemed likely they could have won even more crowns if not for the intervention of World War II, which stripped the team of much of its talent for the seasons between their 1943 and 1946 titles.

★ ★ ★ ★

Although Chicagoans have always loved their Bears, the 1940s seemed to bind the team and spectators more tightly. Winning championships will do that. But the bond was more than the sum of their titles. In 1939, the University of Chicago Maroons dropped college football. The team had been called "the Monsters of the Midway" because of its campus location, adjacent to the

Midway Plaisance of the 1896 World's Columbian Exposition.

Almost simultaneously the Bears' defense growled its way to fame and the nickname was transferred to the pro club. The overwhelming 73–0 destruction of the Redskins in 1940 spawned the penning of the team theme song, "Bear Down, Chicago Bears," in 1941. The song is regularly played at home games when the Bears score.

Developments like those embedded the Bears into the cultural fabric of Chicago as they introduced new stars regularly and annually were in the hunt for championships. Unless a football player throws, catches, or runs with the ball, his yardage totals easily catalogued, many of his achievements are doomed to anonymity. That is particularly true for blockers, whose work is obscured in the scrum at the line of scrimmage, and often true for defenders.

Despite the anonymity inherent in those roles, Bears fans—savvier than most—recognized instantly that 1940 rookie Clyde "Bulldog" Turner was a gem at center and linebacker. Turner, who was 6-foot-2 and weighed about 240 pounds, grew up in the same Texas neighborhood as Baugh and played college ball at Hardin-Simmons. As Chicago's No. 1 draft pick, Turner became the equivalent of a truck boring holes on offense and the most agile linebacker of his time on defense. His eight interceptions in 1942 led the league, a stat normally dominated by defensive backs.

In his size, demeanor, force on the field, and ability to wreak havoc on both sides of the play, Turner was the closest thing Bears fans had seen to the second coming of Bronko Nagurski. When Turner signed with the Bears, newspapers referred to him as the highest paid lineman in history. Years later Turner revealed that distinction netted him only a $2,200 salary.

Teammates, coaches and fans definitely understood his value, though, and were especially impressed with the big man's speed. Luke Johnsos, a Bears assistant coach and co-coach of the team when Halas was away during World War II, believed Turner was unstoppable.

Bulldog Turner, shown playing for the Air Force team during wartime in 1945.

"You couldn't possibly block him," Johnsos said. "He'd center the ball and be the first man down field under punts. He was the first center quick enough to block the onside guard on sweeps and the first linebacker to cover receivers coming out of the backfield, and he'd be with them stride for stride."

For many players, Turner was a big brother protector on the field, the one guy on the Bears no opponent wanted to tangle with regardless of circumstances.

"He looked out for all of us," said Luckman, who at 6 feet tall and 190 pounds was more likely to break on contact. "If there was trouble, Bulldog was there."

Turner, the son of a ranch hand, didn't grow fast. He weighed only 155 pounds in high school, and it took extra hard work and a big appetite to turn him into a college scholarship athlete—the only way his family could afford higher education.

Chicago's Joe Stydahar (13) gathers a Sammy Baugh fumble during the Bears' 73–0 championship beat-down of the Washington Redskins in 1940.

He stayed hungry and when the Bears drafted him, Turner found his calling. One day at practice Halas yelled out that he wanted a center. Turner didn't know that the coach would pause and then name someone. During that pause he ran onto the field and stood over the ball. The rest of the Bears were surprised, but no one budged Turner from center for 13 years after that and he almost single-handedly represented all that was good about Bears football.

"When we had those great teams from 1940–46," Turner said, "it was the closest-knit group I've ever seen." Halas didn't want Luckman being too tight with the other players because he wanted him to be an authority figure. "We weren't buddy-buddy," Turner said, "but I thought the world of him and I think he did of me."

★ ★ ★ ★

Chicago thought the world of its team. Luckman was the most prominent, the man out front. Turner was almost like his bodyguard. But George McAfee, who would join both of them in the Hall of Fame, was an all-around threat on offense. McAfee could run, catch passes and return kicks. A product of Duke University, the 6-foot, 180-pound utility man also intercepted 25 passes on defense and scored 234 points in a war-interrupted career.

McAfee, who had a track man's speed, scored 12 touchdowns in the 11-game 1941 season, on a team that many believe was the Bears' best. And, as if to display what kind of all-around athlete the fleet-footed star was, his touchdowns that season were scored by five different methods: receiving, rushing, interception, punt return and kickoff return. Including the playoffs, Chicago finished 12-1 and overwhelmed the New York Giants, 37–9, in the championship game. It wasn't 73–0, but it was a thorough going over.

Another fan favorite, and perhaps the most eccentric of the Bears' bunch was end Dick Plasman. The 1941 campaign was the final full-time playing season for Plasman, who was the last NFL player to compete without wearing a helmet and loved to show off his blond hair as he ran. Plasman did play a few more games after his military service later in the 1940s. By then the NFL had banned bareheadedness, but the league made an exception for Plasman's blond locks.

Decades later a newspaper syndicate caught up to Plasman for an interview and made a big deal of the "hole in his head." More accurately, it was a dent, and it was a permanent reminder of a football injury incurred in a 1938 game. Indeed, a helmet may have prevented it. Still, Plasman was never comfortable with a helmet that slid over his eyes, or any type of headwear for that matter. Even in the Army, he was once nearly court-martialed for being out of uniform. Of course it was because he was minus the regulation chapeau.

With Plasman out, but few other changes to the roster, the 1942 Bears were on a path to eclipse their previous achievements by finishing the regular season 11-0. Yet the Redskins got some measure of revenge for the 73–0 humiliation of two years earlier, defeating the Bears 14–6 in the championship game. Luckman, among others, felt the Bears had gotten complacent and with the massacre fresh in their minds believed they would easily handle the Redskins. They forgot the words to their new theme song and didn't "bear down." Just as the anomaly of the 1940 score struck people, the loss of the unbeaten streak provoked comments like "How did that happen?" The championship-game loss to the Redskins ended a 24-game Bears winning streak.

★ ★ ★ ★

By 1943 the ranks of NFL rosters were thinning as the athletic big men switched uniforms from football teams to those of the Army, Navy, Air Force and Marines. Halas was old enough to stay out of World War II, but he wanted in and prevailed upon his contacts to set him up as a Navy lieutenant commander. At times he was in touch with Bears happenings, and at times he was overseas and completely out of reach.

The greatest single passing day of Luckman's career—and one of the best in league history—came in 1943 when the Bears manhandled the New York Giants, 56–7, in New York. As a native son, the city was proud of Luckman and declared the day of the contest to be "Sid Luckman Appreciation Day." Giants fans would have appreciated Luckman quite a bit more if he had been playing for their team.

That day Luckman threw seven touchdown passes and gained 443 yards through the air. Although the seven airborne scores in one game has been tied a handful of times (most recently by Nick Foles with the Philadelphia Eagles in 2013), no one has been able to exceed the mark Luckman first set.

As soon as the 1943 season ended, however, Luckman became an ensign in the Merchant Marine. He was not stationed overseas, and in 1944 and 1945 he was able to obtain weekend leave to play for the Bears.

WORLD WAR II

President Franklin D. Roosevelt gave Major League Baseball the green light to continue scheduling games during Word War II in order to provide the populace with entertainment. Other professional team sports followed suit. However, no players received exemptions.

According to the Professional Football Hall of Fame, 21 men with NFL connections were killed in action, 19 of them current or former players, plus an executive and a head coach. The most prominent NFL player to die during the war was New York Giants All-Pro tackle Al Blozis.

Numerous members of the Bears' active roster fought during the war. Seen here is George McAfee in 1942. Bears owner and coach George Halas was a Navy ensign in World War I and rejoined as a lieutenant commander in World War II, taking a leave of absence from his team.

As a part-time quarterback Luckman did not practice with the club but instead flew to the game's location each weekend and then hustled back to base. Compared with those under bombardment overseas, Luckman was lucky. It was challenging, and a bit tricky, but a rare have-your-cake-and-eat-it-too situation where he could serve his country and still pursue his civilian career.

Luckman was never Cam Newton, even in his prime. He hardly ever ran with the ball, and so it was an astounding maneuver when late in the 1946 NFL championship game against the New York Giants, Luckman called his own No. 42 for a keeper run. Entering the fourth quarter at the Polo Grounds, the Giants had their 58,436 fans feeling pretty good about a 14-14 score.

The Bears got the ball and methodically churned downfield. With the pigskin resting at the 19-yard line, Luckman knelt in his huddle and told his startled teammates the play. They were caught off guard and he had to repeat it. "I see something," Luckman said of New York's defense.

The Giants did not. Nor did they suspect anything unusual after the hike. Luckman's

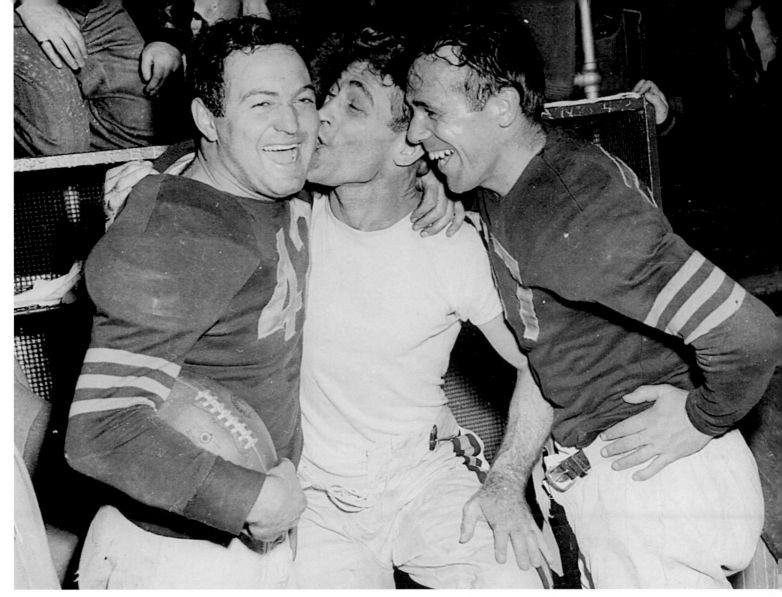

Sid Luckman gets a kiss from teammate George McAfee as Ray McLean watches following Chicago's 24–14 victory over the New York Giants in the 1946 NFL championship. Luckman's 19-yard touchdown run in the final quarter broke a 14–14 tie.

reading of the Giants defense was accurate. He bootlegged around the end untouched for the go-ahead touchdown. Chicago added the extra point and a field goal and won 24-14. Luckman's play-calling adaptability paid dividends.

★ ★ ★ ★

Although the star quarterback played through 1950, the touchdown run to seal the 1946 championship was really the capstone of his career. But Luckman's legacy endured. He is now considered one of the pioneers of the passing game and retired with 137 touchdown passes, which is not a lot by present standards but a huge number for his time. While going head to head with legendary Sammy Baugh, Luckman led the NFL in passing

yards three times and in touchdown passes three times. He was a five-time NFL All-Star and was inducted into the Pro Football Hall of Fame in 1965.

After retiring from football Luckman did go into business, eventually working his way up to president of the Cellu-Craft company, which made cellophane products. He was 81 when he passed away in 1998. Halas and Luckman remained close friends as long as they both lived. Halas' initial judgment was proven correct—Luckman's acumen off the field included the stuff it took to make it big as a pro quarterback.

CHAPTER 10

Chicago BEARS

What Is and What Could Have Been

The Chicago Bears of 1963 were a grizzled bunch. It was a veteran team with a roster featuring many stars. They were led by an aging coach who some believed should retreat to the front office for good, not merely take periodic breaks from the sidelines as he had done a few times over the decades.

Clockwise from the top are long-serving Monsters of the Midway Stan Jones, Joe Fortunato and Bill George, who starred on the league's top-ranked defense in 1963 on the way to claiming the NFL championship.

But there was something special about this group, something in its spirit, its know-how and its experience that owner-coach George Halas was determined to make blossom.

Chicago had not won an NFL crown since 1946—an eternity by Bears standards. Since the retirement of Sid Luckman in 1950, Chicago had played musical quarterbacks with little continuity behind center. There had been great prospects, but unfortunately Halas drove them away before they reached their potential, and they ended up demonstrating

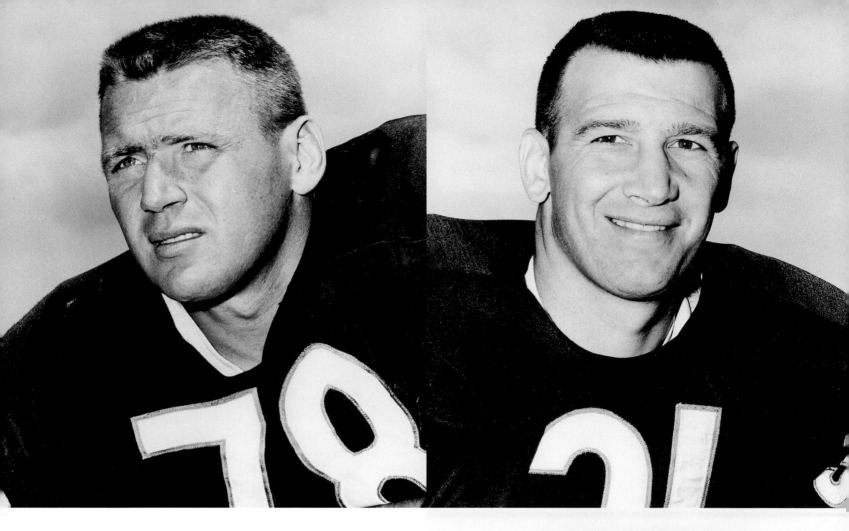

greatness for other franchises in other cities.

The Bears did manage to keep some first-rate talent on the club, like future Hall of Fame linebacker George Connor, who toiled with the post-war Bears and not once played in a title game. In fact, the closest the Bears of the 1950s came to a championship was in 1956, the year after Connor finally said goodbye. Hall of Famer Paddy Driscoll ran the squad that season while Halas was on vacation from coaching. His charges won the Western Division with a record of 9-2-1 but weren't any match for the Giants, who pummeled the Bears 47–7 in New York for the championship.

In a rather amazing coincidence, that lone chance in the 1950s turned into a second sneaker game. It was the same situation that bedeviled the Bears in 1934—an icy field in New York, with the Giants eschewing their cleats that couldn't dig into the frozen tundra in favor of softer-soled sneakers that at least provided a modicum of traction. That made it twice the Bears were

CHICAGO BEARS

George Halas and linebacker Bill George (left) celebrate their crucial 10–3 victory over rival Green Bay on September 15, 1963.

outsmarted by the same gambit.

Halas resumed the head coaching task in 1958, and by 1963 many of the biggest stars of '56 were aging. They were facing their 30s—and perhaps the end of their careers—without a title on their resumes. Accomplished players like Rick Casares, Joe Fortunato, J.C. Caroline, Stan Jones, Bill George and Doug Atkins wanted that championship validation.

There were whispers Old Man Halas had lost his touch with personnel judgments and that the modern game was passing him by. Worse, the archenemy, the Green Bay Packers, under coach Vince Lombardi, ruled the roost. The Packers' 1950s had been more of a lost decade than the Bears', but Lombardi had swooped in after being an assistant coach with the Giants and rebuilt them virtually overnight.

Swiftly regrouping, the Packers reached the NFL championship game in 1960 and then won it all in 1961 and 1962. They were the nation's darlings. But Halas was upbeat. He believed he could coax a title out of this group as long as the Bears could beat the Packers in their home-and-home scheduled meetings. To him, that would

be the story of the season. Beat the Packers both games and everything would fall into place. The Western Division crown would be theirs, and the Packers would be shut out of the playoffs.

"Halas loved that rivalry," Mike Ditka said. "He drilled it into us, 'You've got to beat the Packers.'"

If Halas was right there would be enormous pressure on the Bears all season. Any little mistakes could haunt. Any faltering could allow the Packers an opening. For 14 games, Chicago would have to play at a very high peak. It was a daunting task.

★ ★ ★ ★

Right from the first kickoff, the Halas model played out to form. The Bears traveled to Green Bay for the September 15 season opener and won 10–3. Immediately, they had a big advantage in any tiebreaker. Week after week for the entire season, the Bears played their hearts out and won every time but for a single loss to San Francisco, while eyeing the Packers from afar. When the Wrigley Field rematch came around on November 17, the Bears throttled the Packers, 26–7.

Meanwhile, Green Bay lost to no one else. As the final weeks of the regular season approached, the Bears had to maintain. On November 24, the Bears nearly lost their edge. It took a remarkable tackle-breaking reception and run by tight end Mike Ditka to set up a game-tying 18-yard field goal by Roger LeClerc to salvage a 17–17 result against the Pittsburgh Steelers.

Ditka was in his third season with the Bears, and from the start he was a special player. For most of their existence, tight ends were regarded as linemen and mostly counted on to block and catch a pass every full moon. Ditka possessed the speed and strength to be an offensive weapon as well as a granite blocker. His rookie year he caught 56 passes for 1,076 yards and 12 touchdowns. In 1963 he caught 59 passes and was a rescue outlet for quarterback Bill Wade, a result of the league's still trying to understand how to defend against the new dimensions Ditka brought to the position.

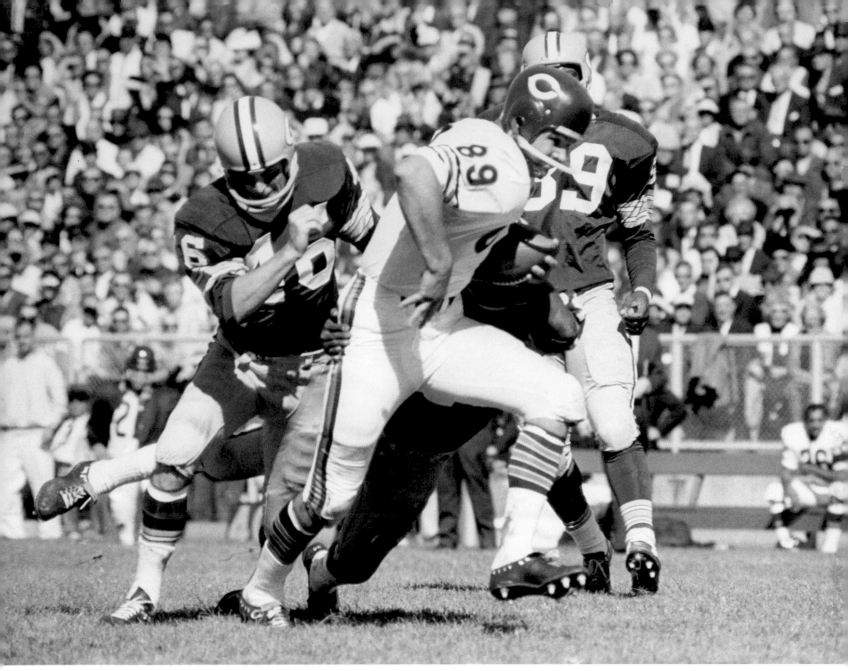

Mike Ditka breaks a Green Bay tackle in the early 1960s.

Ditka swiftly earned the nickname "Iron Mike" for his ability to run over tacklers and to shrug off hard hits. Fans knew that when No. 89 was in the neighborhood, bodies would fly. He played the gritty style that Halas and Chicago fans loved.

"I don't think Ditka has ever felt pain," said Mike Pyle, Bears center and Ditka's roommate. "I don't think he even has a pain threshold."

Ditka was apparently always like that. A University of Pittsburgh teammate, Paul Martha, who also played in the NFL with the Steelers and Denver Broncos, said Ditka was so tough nobody would dare fight him.

"He was just Mike Ditka, and people didn't fool around with Mike Ditka," Martha said.

In the key game, helping pull out the tie against the Steelers, Ditka didn't score a touchdown, but he caught seven passes for 146 yards and saved the day.

The regular season played out just as Halas had predicted it could. The Bears finished 11-1-2. The Packers finished 11-2-1, with both losses to the Bears. The Bears won the West, and that gave them the right to face the Giants. New York had been the victim two years running in

championship-game losses to the Packers and still had some veterans who had thrashed the Bears in 1956.

Chicago had grudgingly yielded each yard all season, and the defensive 11 permitted just 144 points, the fewest in the NFL. The Giants, with Y.A. Tittle at quarterback, Frank Gifford now a receiver and lanky Del Shofner at end, were explosive and scored 448 points, the most in the NFL. The Bears could score when they needed, and the Giants were no slouches on defense, anchored by middle linebacker Sam Huff. It was a great matchup.

In the showdown, the most valuable player was really Chicago's defensive corps. The Bears won 14–10, harassing Tittle all day, even landing a strike that had him hobbling while trying to orchestrate a comeback. All of the Bears' scoring came on short-yardage quarterback sneaks by Bill Wade. Chicago intercepted New York five times, including on the final play when defensive back Richie Petitbon picked the ball out of the air as time ran out.

Linebacker Larry Morris was the individual cited for MVP play. "The Brahma Bull" intercepted a pass and ran it back 61 yards, and he made the tackle on Tittle that derailed him.

"I tackled him and he couldn't walk when he rose," Morris said. "I think I hit him just as he planted his foot."

After the game, the Bears were giddy in the locker room. A mighty cheer went up, "Hooray for George!" Halas always took it to mean his boys were honoring him, although the hoopla may have been for defensive coordinator George Allen.

In some ways it was a last hurrah for Halas as a coach. The Bears reported to 1964 training camp seeking a repeat. But one of the saddest episodes in team history intervened. Running back Willie Galimore and receiver John Farrington were killed in a one-car crash returning to their dorms one evening. The disaster cast a pall over the team from which it never recovered. The Bears finished 5-9, and Green Bay continued its ascent as one of the finest teams in league annals.

There was only one consolation for the Bears— the 1965 draft yielded two of the greatest players in team history in linebacker Dick Butkus of Illinois and running back Gale Sayers of Kansas. Both became Hall of Famers. Yet both also suffered crippling injuries that cut their careers short. The drafting itself was a Halas coup. But what followed was dismaying, as the Bears failed to approach championship-caliber play for the rest of the 1960s and 1970s.

★ ★ ★ ★

Sayers had wheels that would put a Ferrari to shame. His nickname was "the Kansas Comet,"

and along with his speed, his shifting and cutting talents were otherworldly. Sayers stood 6 feet tall and weighed a shade under 200 pounds. He ruined opposing defenses, darting around and past tacklers. He was a human hurricane, havoc on two feet.

Rarely has any rookie season matched Sayers'. He scored an NFL record 22 touchdowns in 1965, and his ability to squirt free meant he was always ripping off chunks of turf the way a hungry carnivore might rip off chunks of raw meat. As a rusher, Sayers averaged 5.0 yards per carry. As a pass catcher, he averaged 17.5 yards a reception. He averaged 14.9 yards a punt return and 31.4 yards a kickoff return. His 2,272 all-purpose yards that season set another NFL record.

There was no sophomore slump. In his second year Sayers led the NFL in rushing with 1,231 yards on an average of 5.4 per carry; he caught 34 passes, led the NFL with a 31.2-yard kickoff return average, and set a new record for all-purpose yards with 2,440. If it seemed that Sayers was a one-man team, it's because he pretty much was. The smartest Bears game plan was to put the ball

in Sayers' hands and watch him work. But teams caught wind and despite Sayers' brilliance, the Bears finished 5-7-2.

After two great years for Sayers and two disappointing seasons for the Bears, Halas sought to diversify the offense heading into 1967. The plan was to incorporate fullback Brian Piccolo to help take some of the burden off of Sayers and make other teams guess a little more as to what the Bears had in store for them. That year, Sayers ran for 880 yards, averaging 26.7 yards a punt return and 37.7 yards a kickoff return. The master plan worked, as Piccolo gathered 317 yards rushing as well as 13 receptions and 103 yards receiving. The Bears finished 7-6-1.

Sayers, potentially the greatest running back of all time, had his career wrecked by knee surgeries that robbed him of his extraordinary ability to change direction and avoid tacklers. In his six

When George Connor was born underweight, doctors believed he was fated to die as a baby. A major portion of Connor's doctor-ordered diet was cabbage juice.

"Boiled cabbage juice and faith are a strange mixture, but they saved my life," Connor once said.

He got a lot bigger. At 6-foot-3 and 240 pounds, Connor became a Hall of Fame defender for the Bears after winning the Outland Trophy as the best college lineman for Notre Dame. He was a two-time All-American for the Fighting Irish.

During his Bears career, between 1948 and 1955, Connor was a four-time Pro Bowl selection. Many felt that during Connor's career he was the toughest Monster of the Midway.

GEORGE CONNOR

years in the NFL, all with Chicago, he managed to rush for nearly 5,000 yards anyway, with a terrific 5.0 per carry average. He achieved so much so quickly that Sayers, albeit because of his early retirement at 34, is the youngest player ever voted into the Hall of Fame.

Chicago's other 1965 draft darling, Dick Butkus, was the prototype Monster of the Midway. At 6-foot-3 and 245 pounds he was a large middle linebacker. Possessing tremendous lateral speed, he could hunt down a ball carrier with a head start and practically rip off his helmet, if not his head, with a ferocious tackle.

Butkus was so good that opponents feared contact with him—so much so that he was often the subject of jokes whose punch lines mostly revealed Butkus to be a member of the wild animal kingdom. Mostly the linebacker laughed off those references, though eventually he got tired of them. Once a story about Butkus appeared with the headline "Nobody Thinks I Can Talk."

Butkus was the perfect fit for the City of Big

Shoulders. His own shoulders were plenty wide, and he used them to good effect when clobbering a ball carrier. He did not make close friends in the running back fraternity.

"If I had a choice, I'd sooner go one-on-one with a grizzly bear," said back MacArthur Lane, who was then a representative of the Packers. "I pray that I can get up every time Butkus hits me."

Unfortunately for Butkus and the Bears, his career, too, was shortened because of knee injuries. An eight-time All-Star, Butkus was finished by 1973 after nine seasons in which he made 1,020 tackles, accompanied by 22 interceptions and 27 fumble recoveries. Considered one of the greatest football players of all time, Butkus was made a member of the Pro Football Hall of Fame six years after he retired, in 1979.

Years ahead of any other controversy over in-house medical care, Butkus sued the Bears, saying team medical officials inappropriately injected him with drugs to keep him playing instead of allowing him to have surgery. It was not a friendly parting with the Chicago club.

Nor did things end happily for Ditka as a player in the Windy City, despite his own obvious greatness. Ditka spent 12 seasons on the field, half of them with the Bears and the rest of his time split between the Philadelphia Eagles and the Dallas Cowboys. Ditka and Halas argued over money, and when Ditka issued the spectacularly insightful yet ill-advised comment that Halas threw money around like manhole covers, he was gone.

Ditka was a Bear who never should have been anything else, but if he had not played and coached in Dallas for Hall of Famer Tom Landry, he might not have gained the requisite experience needed to be ready when the Bears called for help.

While Ditka's departure as a player was on the bitter side, his resurrection as coach nearly two decades later was like welcoming a prince in waiting to the throne. Chicagoans embraced Iron Mike as if he had never been away, although there was always skepticism that he could lead the Bears back to prominence.

Ditka was anointed coach by Halas long after the great owner had left the sidelines and toward the end of his life. Halas' final season as full-time coach was back in 1967, when the club had looked full of promise. He had wanted to go out a winner then, but at 72 years old, he knew he had to pass the baton. Still, he remained owner and chief of the front office. Halas had been voted coach of the year in 1963 and 1965, admission by pro football watchers that even in his advanced age, Halas was still in tune with the game. When he retired at the end of 1967, his regular-season record was 318-148-31, a winning percentage of 68.2. Halas was 6-4 in playoff games. Only Don Shula, with 328 victories with the Baltimore Colts and Miami Dolphins, has surpassed Halas despite the NFL's longer playing seasons now.

When Halas did step aside for the last time, it was no surprise that he kept the coaching job in the Bears family. Jim Dooley, an eight-season end

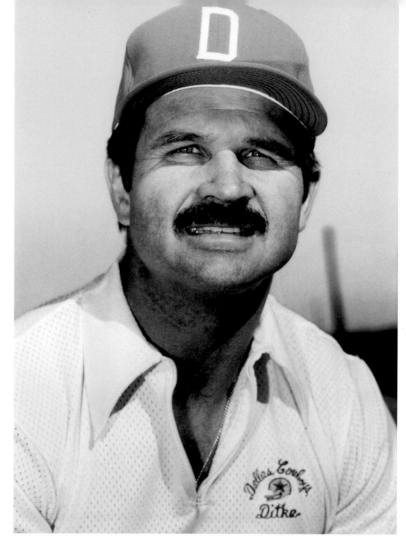

Dallas Cowboys assistant coach Mike Ditka in 1973.

for the Bears in the 1950s and into the early 1960s, got the job. Dooley had a career-high 53 catches in 1953 and grabbed 211 passes for the Bears in all. Immediately following his retirement in 1961 Dooley joined Halas' coaching staff. His last position before being elevated to the boss was defensive coordinator.

Although the cupboard was not bare for Dooley—he had Butkus and Sayers, after all—the best of his four seasons at the helm was a 7-7 record in 1968. His reign also included a Bears all-time worst 1-13 record in 1969. That nightmare season set the stage for the disappointing 1970s when Chicago didn't seem to be going anywhere faster than an L train could travel.

But Ditka's signing in 1982 brought hope to the franchise. For the first time in a long time, things looked bright at Soldier Field. As always, only time could reveal Chicago's football fortunes.

CHAPTER 11

A Special Friendship

The story of Gale Sayers and Brian Piccolo's relationship as backfield mates and roommates with the Chicago Bears is unique. Their connection rose above the pettiness, hatred and racism prevalent in the late 1960s, going beyond the limiting boundaries established during a turbulent time in American history.

Newlyweds Joy and Brian Piccolo celebrate Brian's first NFL contract. After being snubbed in the NFL Draft despite leading all collegiate rushers in 1964, Brian signed a walk-on contract with the Chicago Bears in December of that year.

It is no longer a big deal for whites and blacks to mingle in public, on fields during sporting contests or in any way in American society, but at a time when there were demonstrations in some streets favoring passage of civil rights legislation and riots in other streets instigated by those against equality, it was.

For many Piccolo and Sayers' partnership is the ultimate "we're all the same" tale. It was such a simple thing, an African-American and a Caucasian sharing a hotel room on the road. But it was far from simple. If being roommates was all that the pairing of Sayers and Piccolo

produced, then it would have become a forgotten anecdote of the times. But their tie-in rose to a more far-reaching and enduring level because of the ultimately tragic nature of how their friendship ended. Piccolo, the powerful fullback of the Chicago Bears, was felled by cancer at age 26. The retelling of his and Sayers' defiance of the common conventions of the time, and his sad and untimely death, led to the making of one of the most iconic sports-related movies of all time, *Brian's Song*.

★ ★ ★ ★

Brian's Song, a 1971 made-for-television film starring James Caan and Billy Dee Williams as the two main characters, made a nation weep. The humanity of it touched souls by the millions, and it has remained for decades the gold standard for realistic football movies. Jack Warden played George Halas, and numerous former Bears players, from Mike Ditka, Dick Butkus and

Jack Concannon to Ed O'Bradovich, appeared on screen. The script was adapted from Sayers' autobiography, *I Am Third*.

As the best sports movies often are, this one was more about life and death than sports. The friendship between Piccolo and Sayers was the crux of it, but in their own minds, after perhaps a few initial awkward moments, it was never about black and white, even if those removed from the duo thought it was extraordinary.

Halfback Gale Sayers was a No. 1 Bears draft pick in 1965 and was an instant star. Brian Piccolo was a star running back at Wake Forest but went undrafted because several pro scouts characterized him as being too slow to play NFL football. George Halas signed Piccolo as a free agent, and he played sparingly as a rookie in 1966. Some 25 pounds heavier than Sayers, he emerged as a complementary blocker and runner in the backfield the next season and turned in solid performances.

Brian Piccolo charges through the Minnesota Viking line in 1967, his second year in the league.

Initially, despite their shared backfield and hotel rooms, Sayers was put off by Piccolo's nature. He joked around too much for the quieter Sayers. Sayers was shy, Piccolo gregarious. Sayers was subdued and always serious about himself and football. Piccolo could take a joke and make a joke. Gradually, they warmed up to one another, and eventually Piccolo's ways eroded Sayers'

reticence and brought to the forefront his sense of humor.

Interracial roommates were almost nonexistent in the late 1960s. The country was undergoing tremendous upheaval over race, a long-running battle for fairness for millions of its citizens. The nation had endured the assassination of civil rights leader Martin Luther King Jr. and was slowly adjusting to new legislation passed by Congress. So this odd couple stood

BRIAN PICCOLO AT
WAKE FOREST

Before Brian Piccolo became nationally famous for his inspiring but ultimately unsuccessful fight against cancer, which took his life at age 26, he was a star at Wake Forest University in North Carolina.

As a senior at Wake Forest in 1964, the 6-foot, 205-pound running back led the nation in rushing with 1,044 yards and in scoring with 17 touchdowns. His exploits earned him recognition as the Atlantic Coast Conference Player of the Year. But it still wasn't good enough to get him selected in the NFL draft—teams thought the college star was too slow for the pro game.

The Bears invited Piccolo to try out as a free agent in 1965, and he made the team. He primarily played fullback but also served as a second option for star running back Gale Sayers. The two became unlikely friends in a time of strained race relations—another reason Piccolo is fondly remembered.

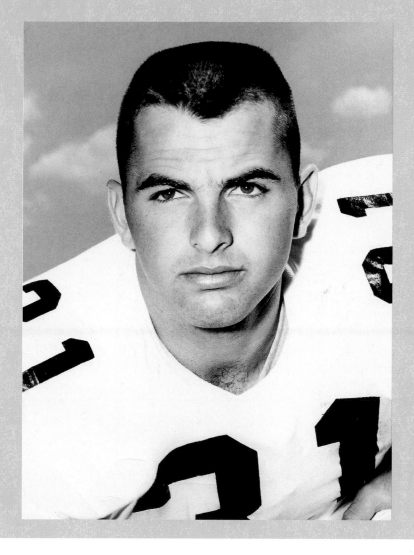

out. Professional athletes in the major sports contested in the United States do not have roommates in the 2000s—they all have single rooms. If not it would hardly be surprising to find the ebony-and-ivory arrangement commonplace during these changed times.

The coupling of the two ball carriers as shared housekeepers on the road was the beginning of their real connection and one thing that brought them media attention. That would have

been enough, but almost as if they were being punished by wrathful, unfair gods, both Sayers and then Piccolo experienced individual and shared heartache that, more than anything else, resonated with a nation of sports fans.

★ ★ ★ ★

This phase of their relationship began with Sayers felled by a terrible knee injury. His natural speed and talent were stifled by torn ligaments in his right knee, which collapsed about two-thirds of the way through the 1968 season, when he had been as brilliant on the field as he had during his first three seasons. In the 1960s, the capability of sports medicine did not approach its present-day sophistication. Often, a serious knee injury would be career ending. Sayers was traumatized by the damage done, but he willed himself to endure extensive and exhausting rehabilitation, determined to return to the Bears' backfield.

Bill Guthrie, president of the Pro Football Writers of America, awards Gale Sayers the Most Courageous Athlete award in 1970. Sayers' emotional acceptance speech honored teammate Brian Piccolo, whom he indicated should have won the trophy.

During this period of excruciating work, Piccolo constantly exhorted and encouraged Sayers. Defying the odds and the pessimism of doctors, Sayers bounced back in 1969 to play a full 14-game schedule and lead the NFL in rushing with 1,032 yards. Never again quite as agile, Sayers nonetheless achieved through sheer perseverance.

Stunningly, however, early in the 1970 season Sayers once again incurred a demoralizing knee injury, this time to his left knee. He again underwent surgery and fought through another round of rehab.

However, by this time Piccolo, whose ordeal began in November of 1969 with a wracking cough, had been diagnosed with a malignant tumor in his chest that was removed in a four-and-a-half-hour operation. Rather than view his illness as a death sentence, Piccolo declared he would soon be cancer free and back playing football. He endured a far more rigorous and physically debilitating regimen of treatment than had Sayers.

Piccolo was married with three small daughters and said the sledgehammer diagnosis altered his way of thinking.

"At one time football was the most important thing," he said, "but when you're lying on your back and you wonder whether you're going to live or die, and you're thinking about your three little girls, you come to discover there are more important things than football."

Piccolo's family and friends rallied to his side, constantly bucking him up. Sayers was often present, offering positive words to help guide his friend through the hardships of frequent setbacks.

Piccolo's problems also made Sayers realize that even a second knee surgery was insignificant by comparison. The word *courage* is carelessly applied to athletic fortitude, and while more attention has been drawn to the notion that real heroism and courage are displayed in war, not on football fields, at the time it was frequently used. In the late spring of 1970, a dinner in New York featured Sayers as an honored guest for being named Most Courageous Athlete by the Pro Football Writers of America. It was a bow to his ability to overcome his seemingly crippling knee injuries.

Sayers did not offer a routine acceptance speech. Instead of issuing platitudes, he talked about Brian Piccolo and his challenges. Piccolo was in a hospital, approaching the end of his doomed battle. Sayers told the assembled listeners that they had given the award to the wrong guy.

"You flatter me by giving me this award," Sayers said, "but I tell you here and now I accept it for Brian Piccolo. Brian Piccolo is the man of courage who should receive the award. It is mine tonight. It is Brian Piccolo's tomorrow. I love Brian Piccolo

Brian Piccolo's Bears teammates carry his casket in Chicago, on June 19, 1970. Left, front to back, are Randy Jackson, Dick Butkus, and Gale Sayers. Right is Ed O'Bradovich.

and I'd like all of you to love him, too. When you hit your knees to pray tonight please ask God to love him too. He has the heart of a giant and that rare form of courage that allows him to kid himself and his opponent—cancer. He has the mental attitude that makes me proud to have a friend who spells out the word *courage* 24 hours a day every day of his life."

Those who heard the words could not hold back tears.

Three weeks later, Piccolo died. He was 26. George Halas said, "He was so young to die, with a future that held so much for him." Halas set up a trust fund for Piccolo's children's college educations. The girls were four, three, and one-and-a-half years old at the time.

Sayers wrote a newspaper story saying Piccolo "was a hero to me. He was a beautiful man."

★ ★ ★ ★

Tastefully and touchingly made, *Brian's Song* appeared on television in late 1971 and strongly stirred viewers. Dramatic and revealing, glowingly reviewed, the movie became a classic. Holding a nationwide audience in its thrall, the movie also demonstrated the power of intelligent storytelling.

The entire country talked about the movie, and the ripple effects were wider than if a boulder had been dropped from a third-story window into a pond. Sayers, who had some minor critiques, was astounded by the breadth and intensity of the reaction.

"I must have received a thousand letters and telegrams after that show," he said months later. "Telegrams that said things like, 'I'm sorry your dear friend passed away.' And letters like, 'I thought a great deal of you as a football player. Now I think even more of you as a man.'"

Years passed and the principals—Piccolo's family and Sayers—went on with their lives. Sayers could not truly overcome his second knee injury and retired at 29. He became a very successful businessman and served a stint as fundraiser for special projects at Kansas University, his alma mater. He is now in his 70s.

The Chicago Bears still honor players with the Brian Piccolo Award. From 1970 to 1992, rookies were cited. Since 1992, a veteran has also been rewarded. The award is given to players who "exemplify the courage, loyalty, teamwork, dedication and sense of humor" that the young fullback from Wake Forest demonstrated in his four pro football seasons and too-short life.

Chicago BEARS

CHAPTER 12

The Greatest Bears of All

There may never have been a season to match it, one that combined dominating excellence and the grandest wink-and-smirk personality of any team in history. The 1985 Chicago Bears rekindled thoughts of the original 1940s Monsters of the Midway while at the same time providing the entertainment value of a Tony-winning Broadway comedy.

The 1985 Chicago Bears— perhaps the greatest aggregate of Bears to date.

And the funniest—and funnest—part of all was that the entire thing was built around Ditka II.

Mike Ditka, the wayward son, was back, this time as head coach of the team he first helped to a championship on the field in 1963. He was anointed by George Halas, in essentially a dying act, as the one to restore

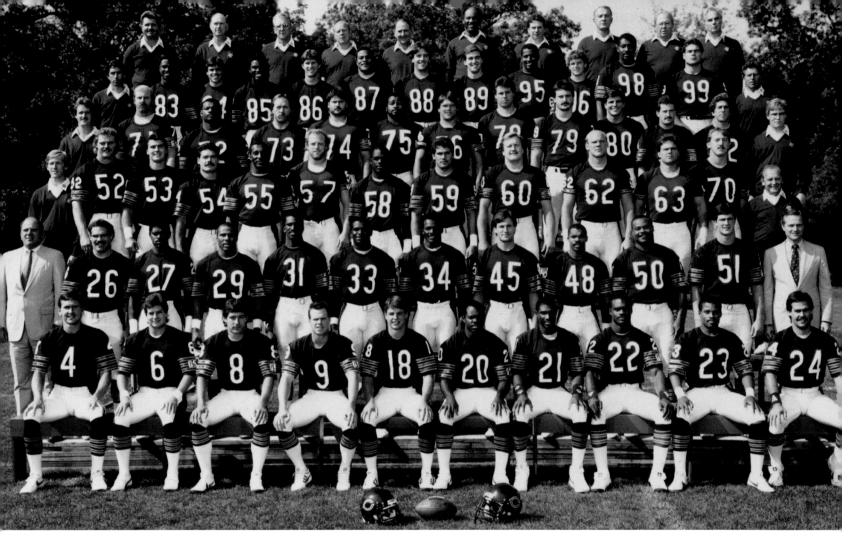

the Bears to their glory years.

For a Bears fan on the south side of 50, the strongest identification with this iconic NFL franchise dates to the 1985 superteam. The last couple of generations of Bears fans may have heard about Sid Luckman and those good old days of the 1940s, but to them that's history book stuff, not a real-life connection.

Another reason the '85 Bears are so cherished is that die-hard Bears fans have had limited opportunity to cheer from the depths of their souls for all of these years since. Only the 2006 bunch, led by future Hall of Fame linebacker Brian Urlacher, has repeated the journey to a Super Bowl, but those Bears dropped the big game to the Indianapolis Colts. It was memorable to get there, but celebration was muted since they came home with the L on their record.

Urlacher collected more than 1,000 tackles during his 13 Bears seasons, but not even being

complemented by the fleet Devin Hester, the NFL's greatest punt/kickoff return man, could carry the Bears to another world championship. And the franchise is still waiting for its modern savior.

✷ ✷ ✷

When Ditka took the reins as coach in 1982, there was a desperate need for a savior then too. Once Halas stepped back from the sidelines after the 1967 season, the Bears seemed lost. They were abysmal in 1969 with that worst-ever 1-13 record. The 1970s were painful years, until near the end, and the Bears ran through four head coaches during the decade.

Halas knew he was dying when Ditka reappeared on the scene, first representing a rapprochement with the Old Man, and then being knighted to lead the crusade. Ditka had

Chicago Bears owner George Halas introduces new head coach Mike Ditka on January 21, 1982.

This was a team so talented, so good, so dominating, that it seemed preordained to capture the Super Bowl. The players thought so too, and before the regular season even ended they recorded "The Super Bowl Shuffle" rap song, which did no damage to poetry, sent proceeds to charity, and made much of the universe laugh out loud. A headline in a national magazine about the team read, "Please Don't Feed the Bears."

"They want a bunch of cookie cutters," defensive tackle Dan Hampton said of football observers before adding, surely unnecessarily, that the Bears did not fit that mold.

★ ★ ★ ★

the misfortune to assume command during the strike-shortened 1982 season. But, after that, he imprinted his personality—and the personality of the old black-and-blue Bears—on the team and watered the crop until it matured.

His was an uneasy partnership with defensive coordinator Buddy Ryan, but for the greater good, Ditka pretty much let his assistant and his troops run wild as they perfected the "46" defensive alignment. Ditka remained the alpha male leader, but the defense was almost an entity unto itself, and the locker room was bursting with colorful killers on that side of the ball. Meanwhile, the offense featured running back Walter Payton, a man known to the world as "Sweetness," and one Ditka called the greatest football player he ever saw. Leading the offensive 11 was quarterback Jim McMahon, who as time went on made headlines with outrageous actions and lips flapping at 100 miles per hour.

There were crazy characters like William "the Refrigerator" Perry, the massive 300-plus-pound draft choice who hit like a truck and smiled like a beauty queen, delivering one of the all-time mixed messages to the sporting world. How could someone so large move so quickly, and how could someone built like a home appliance be so cuddly?

Halas missed it all. He died on October 31, 1983, confident his Bears were safe in the meaty hands of Mike Ditka, but without witnessing the season that made them a nationwide phenomenon.

When Halas passed away, the football world mourned. About 1,200 people attended his memorial service at St. Ita's Church in Chicago, and other than gatherings at the Pro Football Hall of Fame, rarely was seen such a group of the sport's luminaries under one roof. Mourners included NFL commissioner Pete Rozelle, prominent team owners such as the Pittsburgh Steelers' Art Rooney, and the entire active Bears team.

Halas was a walking history book of the NFL, a living monument to its founding, its growing pains, and a chief booster of its elevation to the most popular sport in the land.

"He was a man that stood tall and a man who was magnificent every step of the way," said his old quarterback Sid Luckman.

Quarterback Jim McMahon in action in the 1985 championship season.

CHICAGO'S BIG TEAMS

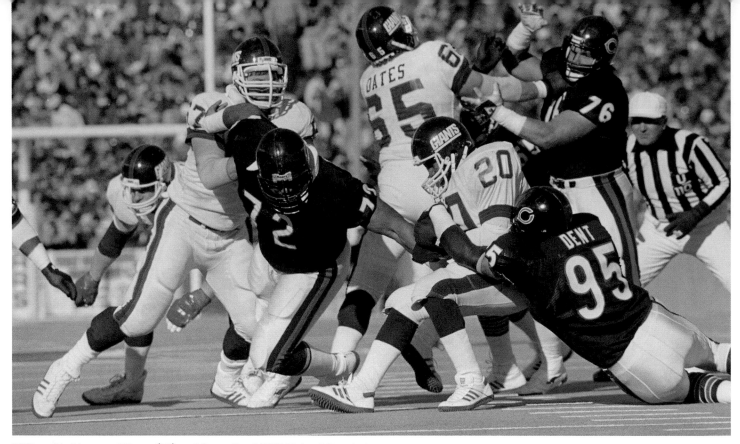

William "Refrigerator" Perry (72) and Super Bowl MVP Richard Dent halt New York Giants running back Joe Morris in the divisional playoffs on the way to the Bears' Super Bowl triumph.

Some had to wonder how Halas would have reacted to the shenanigans of the 1985 team: McMahon defying the commissioner's office, mooning a helicopter hovering over practice; Steve McMichael throwing a chair so hard at a blackboard that its legs stuck; and Ditka alternately charming and snarling behind his big, fat cigars that he ultimately had to swear off when he had a heart attack.

Halas would have grumbled over some of the antics of the 1980s Bears. He would have smiled at others. But overall he would have been pleased because the Bears were winners, and sports fans in every corner of the country couldn't resist talking about them.

★ ★ ★ ★

Ditka was just as ornery off the field as he had been on it. He could still body-block a challenger out of bounds, though now it was done verbally. When a pesky sportswriter doubted his wisdom,

Ditka was not above calling him a jerk. Ditka knew his football. He was a proud man and a forceful leader. But he also proved to be a man of many dimensions. It was difficult to imagine the tight end of 1963 becoming entranced by fine wines, but eventually Ditka had his own label.

The Bears of the mid-1980s were densely populated with great football players. Hall of Famers Mike Singletary; Richard Dent, the sack king; and "Danimal" Hampton anchored the remarkable defense, which allowed just 198 points in a 16-game season as the team cruised to a 15-1 regular-season record in 1985.

McMahon's deep passes to world-class sprinter Willie Gault had the capacity to send voltage through the crowd. Rookie kicker Kevin Butler fit right in. And a gaggle of muscular blockers protected anyone with the ball; much of the time that was Payton, who was a marvel to watch. He rushed for 1,551 yards, and no dilettante either, Payton blocked as if he were an extra lineman.

Payton was a special player. That had been discerned almost instantly in his rookie year of 1975. He was an established star on a weak team, aching to play for a champion, and then it all fell

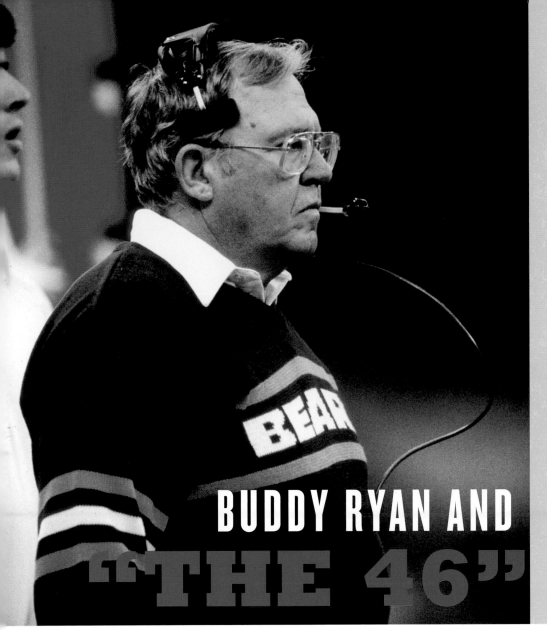

BUDDY RYAN AND "THE 46"

Buddy Ryan reacted to the world the way he wanted his defense to react to ball carriers: show no mercy, and meet any challenges with aggression.

Bears defensive coordinator Ryan and head coach Mike Ditka did not get along during the team's 1985 Super Bowl run, but as the architect of the 46 defense, Ryan knew he played a huge role in bringing that championship to Chicago.

In structure the 46 had six men up front, with four playing as linemen and two standing upright as linebackers. Those six were backed up by two more linebackers and three defensive secondary men. The main goal of the formation was to put supreme pressure on the quarterback and make him hurry his throws. The Bears personnel were a perfect match for the system, and the combination made it a devastating success. The defense was named for safety Doug Plank, who wore 46 on his jersey, although Plank retired before the Super Bowl triumph.

into place. Payton stood just 5-10 and weighed 200 pounds, but he played much bigger and sturdier. In 1977 Payton rushed for 275 yards in a game against the Minnesota Vikings. At the time it was an NFL record. He was selected for nine Pro Bowls.

If there was any question about how much Payton burned to win a title, his thinking surfaced as the Bears began their 1985 playoff run.

"I can't wait another nine or 10 years," he said. "I'll be a two-foot running back by then. For me, the Super Bowl would be the ultimate. Next to my children being born, that's it."

It almost seemed as if the Bears invented swagger that 1985 season. The Bears were 12-0 entering late November before they blew their only game of the year to the Miami Dolphins with laissez-faire play. Then they swept to the end of the regular season 15-1 and roared into the playoffs with a gunfighter's confidence. They manhandled the New York Giants 21–0, crushed the Los Angeles Rams 24–0 and destroyed the New England Patriots 46–10 in Super Bowl XX in New Orleans.

"Not too shabby," Ditka opined.

After the triumph, the city threw a parade for the Bears, and 300,000 people turned out in their thick winter parkas to celebrate.

★ ★ ★ ★

There was only one note of discord following the Super Bowl. Payton had not scored a touchdown in the romp. To make matters worse, Ditka had allowed the Fridge to rumble over on a goal-line carry that should have gone to the stalwart of the backfield. Payton fumed, though he didn't want to rain on the parade. He always looked at that incident as the missed opportunity of his career. At the time Ditka made no apologies, and it served as one more brick in the construction of Fridge lore.

Perry was an affable if especially large kid at 6-foot-2 and somewhere between 308 and 325 pounds. He was a star out of Clemson, but Buddy Ryan didn't think he was good enough for his defense. When Ryan refused to play Perry, Ditka borrowed him for the offense, and the sight of the big man periodically lumbering through the line occasioned eye-opening commentary and chuckles throughout the land.

"He's so wide I can just hide behind him," Payton said.

Nicknamed "the Refrigerator," aptly due to his bulk, Perry was the most popular appliance in the United States during the fall of 1985. He had a down-home wit and seemed to enjoy the jokes about his size as much as those who uttered them. He featured a gap-toothed smile, and corporate America fell in love with him. Perry was not merely big; he looked chubby, not chiseled. Hampton once said that Perry should learn what Diet Pepsi could do for him.

When Perry scored a touchdown against the Green Bay Packers on a short run (all of his runs were short), he spiked the ball.

"I said I wanted to help the team any way I could," Perry said.

The plunge was the first of three touchdowns for Perry that year, and there was something about the way he handled the ball that made people smile. He appeared on David Letterman's show and for a time was a folk hero of sorts.

Later in life Perry contracted an illness that

Walter Payton in action for the Chicago Bears in the late 1970s.

attacks the peripheral nervous system and also dealt with weight control and drinking issues. Whenever he was able to make public appearances he seemed as popular as ever despite being retired since 1994.

The leader on the defensive side of the ball was, appropriately enough for the Monsters of the Midway, a middle linebacker. Following the path first blazed by Bill George and later Dick Butkus, Mike Singletary tore into ball carriers with ferocity. A pious man, Singletary somehow wore his Christianity on one sleeve and the hanging threads of opponents' jerseys on the other. The middle linebacker, who came out of Baylor University, was inducted into the Hall of Fame in 1998 and later coached the San Francisco 49ers. Singletary was alternately called "Samurai Mike" and "the Minister of Defense" during his playing days. He was always viewed as a warrior, and that included his thoughts when he looked in the mirror.

"When I get a chance to land a clean, hard shot on somebody," Singletary once said, "it's scary and exciting at the same time. You're so primed, so pumped, so prepared that you really let a guy have it and you want to shout, 'Yeah!'" Presumably after reading that comment, fellow parishioners might have moved farther down the pew.

The Bears were so good (just ask them) that they seemed likely to jump-start a dynasty after the crowning-touch Super Bowl win. But that core group of players never returned to the big game. They won big in the regular season but were upset in the divisional playoffs. Under Ditka, Chicago won five straight NFC Central Division titles and six in seven years, but after the team slumped to 5-11 in 1992 he was fired.

It was a stunningly bold decision by Bears management, one that clearly upset Ditka, irritated the fan base and for years paid no dividends. More than 20 years later, if anyone in Chicago utters the words "Da Coach," everyone knows

Left: Refrigerator Perry spikes the ball after rumbling in for a short-yardage touchdown in Super Bowl XX. Right: Mike Singletary (50) dives for Los Angeles Rams running back Eric Dickerson during the NFC Championship Game, a 24–0 Bears victory on January 12, 1986.

who they're talking about, and it isn't Dave Wannstedt, Ditka's little-recalled successor. Ditka tried coaching again in New Orleans in 1997, but it wasn't the same. He lasted three years in the Big Easy, posting a paltry 15-33 record.

As owner of a well-liked Loop restaurant, with frequent television appearances as a commentator, and by lending his name to charitable causes, Ditka has remained at least on the periphery of the limelight and is indisputably a Chicago symbol of football greatness. He can be counted on for a brash comment, and more than any other past NFL figure, he has been in the forefront with his time, energy and finances to gain pension and medical benefits for needy former players who never made big salaries or who ran into personal problems.

Ditka was the most vociferous and active lobbyist to gain assistance for those seeking a small slice of the rich NFL pie. He auctioned off his Dallas Cowboys Super Bowl coaching ring and gave the proceeds to the Gridiron Greats Assistance Fund. When the NFL earmarked $10 million to a medical fund for retirees, Ditka was pleased.

"I hope it changes some lives," he said.

★ ★ ★ ★

In the late 1990s, when good Bears news was tough enough to come by, the Bears family received the worst, most shocking news. Walter Payton's health was in serious decline. At 44 he suffered from a disease of the bile ducts and needed a liver transplant. When he went public with the information, Payton said he was confident he would recover, but he also said, "Hell yeah, I'm scared. Wouldn't you be scared?"

Cancer interfered and Payton died in late 1999 at age 45. Payton's passing broadly affected the Bears organization and the Chicago region. It was like Brian Piccolo all over again, though with some distinct differences. Payton was older, but still a young man. Payton was the bigger sports figure. Payton, like Piccolo, was remembered best for his attitude, for his humanity and for being a good person.

"Here's a guy who had the most heart I've ever seen in a football player," said Payton's former teammate Jim McMahon. "He was the greatest."

When it comes to the Bears, and with a nod to all of the greats that played in the early years, Payton may be the single best player the team has ever had. And, with Sweetness in the backfield anchoring the most talented and crazy set of characters the city has witnessed, there was simply none greater than the 1985 Bears.

Chicago WHITE SOX

The SOU

The Chicago White Sox were founded along with the American League in 1901, and the South Side club was a cornerstone franchise for the new league that sought to challenge the established National League. The NL had been around since 1876, and one of the teams it featured was the crosstown rival Chicago Cubs.

More than a century has passed, but the clubs remain constants and Chicago is one of only a few cities able to support two teams in modern Major League Baseball. The White Sox and Cubs have long coexisted in a peace of sorts, less hostile than North Korea and South Korea, but hardly as tight as fraternal twins, either. The Cubs are based on the North Side of the city and the White Sox on the South Side. The South Siders played in the then-monumental Comiskey Park, opened in 1910 at 35th Street and Shields Avenue, and in 1991 a replacement Comiskey Park was erected next door. Several years later naming rights were sold and the park became known as U.S. Cellular Field.

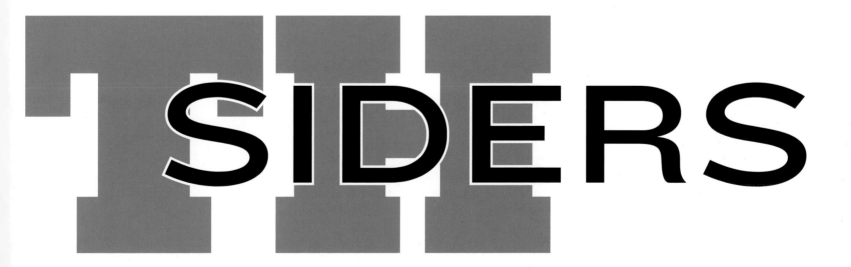

Left: Fans line up at Comiskey Park for the opening game of the 1959 World Series. Right: An aerial view of Comiskey Park during the first game of the 1959 World Series.

Overleaf: Two-time American League MVP Frank Thomas, "the Big Hurt," in 1997.

Technically, the lineage of the White Sox predates the origins of the American League. They grew out of a minor league team called the Sioux City Cornhuskers that competed in the Western League. Charles Comiskey, who played for and managed a few teams between 1882 and 1894, purchased the club and moved it to St. Paul, Minnesota. Comiskey relocated the team to Chicago in 1900, and it became a Major League franchise with the birth of the AL.

Virtually all minor league history of the White Sox has been forgotten, and all record keeping for the club began with its entry into the American League.

In the earliest days of the team, the White Sox were called the White Stockings (which for a time in the 19th century had referred to the Cubs before they changed their name). There is some speculation that White Stockings was clipped to White Sox by newspaper headline writers for their convenience and then stuck.

On the field the White Sox were an early, if not dominant, success. Under the guidance of manager Clark Griffith, a legendary figure from the early days of baseball, the Sox won the very first American League pennant in 1901. However, there was no World Series until 1903 and thus no postseason. Griffith, who later owned the Washington Senators and even had a stadium named after him in Washington, D.C., was the Sox's player-manager in 1901 and 1902.

The Stockings won World Series crowns in 1906 and 1917. The 1906 world championship was especially gratifying because the White Sox upset the Cubs despite being a team so anemic at the plate that it was known as "the Hitless Wonders."

But what happened in 1919 after the White Sox won their fourth pennant scarred the franchise and nearly ruined baseball. Key players on the team were accused of fixing World Series games at the behest of gamblers so the Cincinnati Reds would win. Known as "the Black Sox Scandal," the incident is probably the best-known and worst scandal to afflict a major professional sport in the United States.

The repercussions were massive. Skittish owners who needed to restore the game's good

name appointed baseball's first commissioner, who issued lifetime bans to numerous players.

As a result, the White Sox tumbled from the top ranks and did not truly recover on the diamond for decades. The occasional great player adorned the roster, but the franchise did not win another pennant for 40 years.

During many of those years—and in subsequent decades, as well—the Cubs were Chicago's better team. Although the world-class drought between World Series titles for the Cubs is well chronicled, much overlooked on the national scene was the enormous gap between World Series triumphs for the White Sox. There was no joy on the South Side in grabbing the ultimate baseball prize between 1917 and 2005.

Many a worthy White Sox star wore the uniform during the lean years, from Red Faber and Ted Lyons to Luke Appling and manager Jimmy Dykes, to Minnie Minoso, Billy Pierce, Chico Carrasquel, Nellie Fox, Luis Aparicio, Early Wynn and manager Al Lopez, before a well-known feisty character became owner and enthusiastically and creatively presided over the club's 1959 AL pennant.

Bill Veeck, the same Bill Veeck who introduced the ivy to the Cubs' hallowed Wrigley Field, brought entertainment as well as good baseball to the south side of town. He actually owned the White Sox twice, years apart, before they entered the modern era.

Veeck delighted fans with his promotions, which saw everything from little spacemen landing in the outfield to players being (briefly) forced to wear short pants as part of their uniforms. Lack of deep pockets in 1981 drove Veeck into retirement the second time, and the White Sox flailed somewhat helplessly at the start of baseball's free-spending era. And then they pulled the coup of plucking catcher Carlton Fisk off the market.

Fisk played with Chicago from 1981 to 1993 and while there broke the career marks for home runs and games played by a catcher. He was also instrumental in leading the Sox to the 1983 playoffs. Despite a tenuous relationship with owner Jerry Reinsdorf, who took over the Sox in 1981, Fisk is a fan favorite and is today honored with a statue outside U.S. Cellular Field.

Reinsdorf, who has also owned the Chicago Bulls basketball team for more than a quarter of a century, presided over the 1983 return to the American League playoffs and finally the long-sought World Series crown, in 2005.

Players like Harold Baines, Magglio Ordonez, Ozzie Guillen, Robin Ventura, Jack McDowell and Mark Buehrle shined for the Sox in the modern era, but none of those All-Stars compared in glitter to first baseman and designated hitter Frank Thomas. "The Big Hurt" was a South Side slugger from 1990 to 2005 and is probably the best player in White Sox history. Most of his 500-plus home runs were hit while he wore the Sox uniform.

And, it was Thomas' induction into the Baseball Hall of Fame in his first year of eligibility in 2014 that has most recently given the franchise and its fans something to gloat about. It was an emotional day, especially for those who remember the crack of Thomas' bat striking those long balls. For White Sox fans, there wasn't any sweeter music.

YEAR FOUNDED: 1901

WORLD SERIES CHAMPIONS

1906 1917 2005

AMERICAN LEAGUE PENNANTS WON

 1901  1906  1917

 1919  1959  2005

RETIRED NUMBERS

 2   3    4    9

Nellie Fox   Harold Baines   Luke Appling   Minnie Minoso

 11    16    19    35    72

Luis Aparicio   Ted Lyons   Billy Pierce   Frank Thomas   Carlton Fisk

HALL OF FAMERS

Luis Aparicio

Luke Appling

Eddie Collins

Charles Comiskey (owner)

Red Faber

Carlton Fisk

Nellie Fox

Al Lopez (manager)

Ted Lyons

Ray Schalk

Frank Thomas

Bill Veeck (owner)

Ed Walsh

Hoyt Wilhelm

THEME SONG
"Let's Go,
Go-Go White Sox"

BATTING AVG.
.340
Joe Jackson

HOME RUNS
448
Frank Thomas

RUNS BATTED IN
1465
Frank Thomas

GAMES WON
260
Ted Lyons

EARNED RUN AVG.
1.81
Ed Walsh

STRIKEOUTS
1796
Billy Pierce

Champs from the Start

The No. 1 reason why the Chicago White Sox won the first American League pennant in 1901, finishing 30 games over .500, was the pitching arm and managerial acumen of Clark Griffith, who pulled double duty.

Tobacco cards of early days White Sox stars George Davis and Clark Griffith (pictured during his time with Cincinnati in 1909).

A righty thrower, Griffith, known as "the Old Fox" was well into a Major League career that began with the St. Louis Browns in 1891, and he produced Hall of Fame pitching credentials. Although he gained greater fame as owner of the Washington Senators, Griffith posted a career mark of 237 wins to 146 losses. That first year with the Sox he led the staff with a 24-7 record.

Griffith's great numbers came during the Deadball Era, which ended in 1920. Back then, pitching outweighed big bats, and the White Sox of that time featured some of the finest arms in the game.

In fact, their 1906 pennant, the club's second, was almost entirely the work of the pitching staff. There is no way to be polite about it, but the 1906 aggregation couldn't hit a lick. The team batted a pitiful .230 and still put together a 93-58 season. No wonder they were called

G. DAVIS, CHICAGO AMER.

GRIFFITH, CINCINNATI

"the Hitless Wonders." Probably the best position player on that squad was third baseman George Davis, who managed to drive in 80 runs without a single homer while hitting .277. Davis, who spent seven seasons with the White Sox, is the team's least known Hall of Fame player.

Mistakes in the batter's box in 1906 mattered little, however, as the Sox quartet of "Big" Ed Walsh, Nick Altrock, Frank Owen and Doc White flummoxed batters all season long.

Walsh, a Sox hurler for all but one of his 14 seasons between 1904 and 1917, by most measurements is still the greatest pitcher in franchise history. That

season he went 17-13 with a 1.88 earned run average. Not shabby, but far from his best. No matter, Walsh was picked up ably by the others.

Altrock, later known as one of baseball's funny men for his on-field comic acts, went 20-13 with a 2.06 ERA. Owen, who no one in Chicago remembers today, went 22-13 with a 2.33 ERA. He was out of the majors by age 29 but won 20-plus games three times. In 1904 he threw 34 complete games, and between 1904 and 1906 he averaged more than 300 innings. His arm may have given out.

White, a yeoman twirler for the Sox for over a decade, went 18-6 and his 1.52 ERA led the league.

White Sox star hurler "Big" Ed Walsh, as seen in 1911 when he led the American League with 255 strikeouts.

Two years earlier, White pitched 45 straight scoreless innings for Chicago—five straight shutouts! The Los Angeles Dodgers' Don Drysdale broke the record in 1968, and as he approached the mark, White sent a telegram to Drysdale to wish him luck. White flustered hitters with control and breaking stuff. "He was a cutey on the mound," said his catcher Ray Schalk, and he played the violin, wrote songs and performed some vaudeville in the off-season.

But make no mistake, despite his "down" season, it was Walsh who was the ace of the Sox's staff in 1906. A spitball specialist, Walsh compiled some insane annual innings totals over his career, including the still-standing White Sox record of 464 innings in 1908. Walsh also topped 422 innings and reached 393 innings in other years.

The Plains, Pennsylvania-born Walsh, who was good-sized for the time at 6-foot-1 and 195 pounds, posted full-season ERAs of 1.88, 1.60, 1.42, 1.41 and 1.27 in a row. His lifetime 1.82 ERA is the career all-time Major League record. Walsh's 1908 season was so stupendous it defies comparison. Besides his 464 innings pitched, he led the American League in games (66), complete games (42), shutouts (11), winning percentage (.727) and strikeouts (269). His win-loss record that season was an unheard-of 40-15.

★ ★ ★ ★

Incredibly, even in Walsh's down year, the 1906 White Sox had a team ERA of 2.13. If the pitching staff had even a mediocre level of run support, the squad may have set a record for wins. But runs were scarce, and the 93-win season was a miracle all the same.

It was Chicago's other team, the National League's Cubs, who ended up setting the Major League record for wins, as they marched to the pennant with a 116-36 record and were heavy favorites to waltz away with the World Series title. The crosstown, best-of-seven showdown was so early in the evolution of big-time baseball in Chicago that neither Comiskey Park nor Wrigley Field had been built. The West Side Grounds and the South Side Park, both much less grand structures, alternated as the host sites for the Series. That meant attendance ranged from about 12,600 to a high of 23,200. One reason attendance was low at some games was early-season freezing temperatures. The Series opened on October 9, the 35th anniversary of the Great Chicago Fire—and there were snow flurries in the air.

The White Sox's Nick Altrock won the opener, 2–1, holding down Cubs ace Mordecai "Three-Finger" Brown, giving the South Side the early edge. Each team stroked four hits. The Cubs woke up in Game 2 and knocked out Doc White en route to a 7–1 victory. It was Walsh, hurling a two-hit shutout in a 3–0 game, who turned the momentum back to the South Side. But Mordecai Brown relished a rematch with Altrock and twirled his own two-hit shutout in a 1–0 Cubs victory in Game 4.

With the series knotted at two wins apiece, Game 5 was pivotal and a surprisingly high-scoring one for the Sox. Walsh threw again and was far from his normally commanding self. For once, though, his men swung some serious lumber, collecting 12 hits, with second baseman Frank Isbell doing the most damage with four hits. Walsh was lifted after six innings, and although he walked five, only one of the six runs surrendered was earned. Walsh got the win, but White pitched three effective innings of relief in the 8–6 triumph.

Seeking to shift momentum in Game 6, as part of the pregame festivities, Cubs officials trotted out four baby bear cubs, two borrowed from the Lincoln Park Zoo and two from an amusement park. Since those cubs couldn't hit, it did not affect the outcome.

Charles Comiskey, seen at left in a tobacco card from the late 1880s as a player for the St. Louis Browns, and at right as the owner of the Chicago White Sox in 1914.

Doc White got the call to start Game 6 and the Cubs answered with their ace, Brown. But amazingly the Sox bats stayed lively. Brown did not have his best stuff, gave up three runs in the first and was yanked for Orval Overall as the Sox piled on four more runs in the second inning. The White Sox cracked out a total of 14 hits and won handily, 8–3, to beat their crosstown rivals for their first World Series in franchise annals.

★ ★ ★ ★

Nobody was happier about the victory than White Sox owner Charles Comiskey, who threw his owner's winning share of $15,000 into the players' pool.

Comiskey had batted .264 in 13 Major League seasons between 1882 and 1894, twice driving in more than 100 runs in a season and totaling 416 stolen bases. Adept as a fielder, Comiskey is credited with being the earliest first baseman to play off the bag, shading toward second to better field grounders on the right side. He also managed for 12 seasons before he gained additional fame as owner of the White Sox.

The White Sox were fortunate to obtain Eddie Collins at the zenith of his career in 1915, a year after he won the American League MVP award. One of the greatest second basemen in baseball history, he was available because the Philadelphia Athletics' Connie Mack sold some of his major stars in order to raise capital.

Collins, who played 12 years with the Sox sandwiched between tours in Philadelphia, was chosen for the Hall of Fame in 1939 on the strength of a lifetime batting average of .333 along with 3,314 hits and 745 stolen bases.

Collins was also a university graduate—a rarity for ball players at the time—but afterward spent his entire professional life in baseball. Following a 25-season playing career that did not conclude until he was 43, Collins later managed the White Sox and became the longtime general manager of the Boston Red Sox.

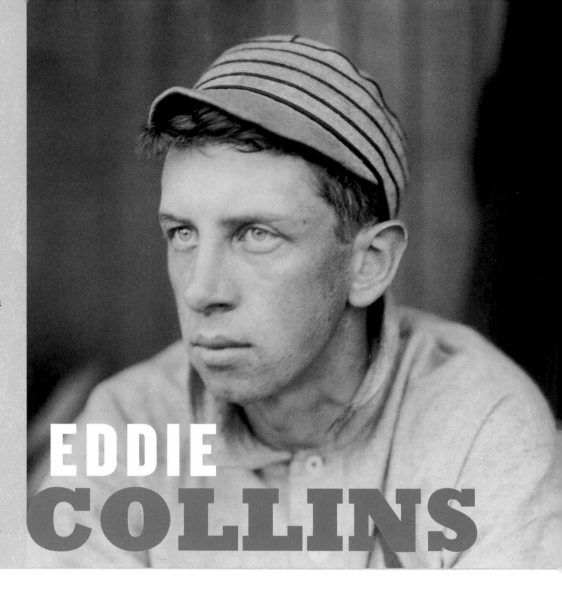

EDDIE COLLINS

Nicknamed "the Old Roman," when Comiskey committed to building the Sox's new ballpark for $750,000, which opened with his name on it in 1910, he suggested it be modeled on the Roman Colosseum. It lasted as the team's home field through the 1990 season. Although there were accusations later that Comiskey was a cheapskate with his players and that this contributed to their betrayal in the 1919 World Series, there are other indications that he invested wisely in building good teams.

One of Comiskey's best moves came at the expense of the Philadelphia Athletics' Connie Mack, who had built a dynasty right after the Sox's early-century success. Mack, furious that his players were tempted by offers from the competing upstart Federal League, declared a fire sale

and parted with many star players. Comiskey snagged the great Eddie Collins, the reigning American League MVP. Collins, who played for 25 seasons, 12 of them in Chicago, had a lifetime batting average of .333. He was just as good for Comiskey as he had been for Mack, one season batting .372 for the White Sox.

Adding a guy like Collins to an already strong team helped put the White Sox back in contention a decade after their World Series triumph over the Cubs.

★ ★ ★ ★

In the meantime, the Boston Red Sox had also risen to prominence. Boston won the first World Series in 1903 when the American and National leagues made a peace treaty. But the Red Sox also won in 1912, 1915 and 1916. By then Boston had a hot-stuff southpaw named Babe Ruth pitching for them. In 1916 Ruth led the American League with a 1.75 earned run average and posted a 23-12 record. Recognizing that the kid, who broke in at 19, could also hit a little bit, the Red Sox began using him as a pinch hitter or outfielder on occasions when he wasn't on the mound.

Ruth made the Red Sox more formidable, but the cast assembled in Chicago was Boston's match. Although Boston won 90 games, Chicago finished 100-54 and took the AL pennant in 1917.

That World Series team had two things in common with the 1906 champs: good pitching and a power outage at the plate. Although the White Sox could hit for average, home runs were as hard to come by as an honest man in Al Capone's gang. Collins, who did bash 12 triples, hit zero homers that season. Nemo Leibold, an outfield starter, also hit none. But outfielder Oscar "Happy" Felsch drove in 102 runs and batted .308. The famous "Shoeless" Joe Jackson, who had already passed through Philadelphia and Cleveland and hit .408 in 1911 for the Indians, had an off year but still hit .301.

Pitching made up for it. The team ERA was 2.16. Eddie Cicotte, credited as the inventor of the knuckleball, was the big cheese with a 28-12 record and a 1.53 earned run average. Red Faber, a future Hall of Famer, went just 16-13, but his ERA was 1.92.

Faber won 254 games in a 20-year career between 1914 and 1933, every minute of it with the White Sox. His real first name was Urban, and early in his career Faber was touted as being an ironman hurler because he alternately started and relieved three times in four days. Faber, like Walsh, relied on a fastball and a spitter to get batters out.

Faber popped up on the White Sox's radar after the Pittsburgh Pirates signed him and assigned him to Dubuque in the Three-I League. There he pitched a perfect game in the minors, and the Sox bought him for $35,000.

Red Faber in 1918, the fifth of his 20 years with the Chicago White Sox.

They invited Faber along on a world tour that pitted the Sox against the New York Giants. Christy Mathewson missed a game, and New York manager John J. McGraw borrowed Faber for a day in Hong Kong to throw against his teammates. Faber was the winner for the wrong side, and McGraw liked what he saw so much he put in a bid to buy Faber. But Chicago turned down the deal.

Sure enough, when the White Sox entered the 1917 World Series, the Giants were their foes. Chicago's rotation was Cicotte and Faber taking turns, and when the White Sox won the crown in six games, 4-2, Faber was the hero. McGraw had to grumble a bit; Faber won Game 2, won Game 5 on two days' rest and won Game 6 on another two days' rest as Chicago claimed their second world championship.

It was a heady time for the South Siders, but it was about to take a dramatic turn.

CHAPTER 14

The Black Sox Scandal

Even the casual fan has not forgotten the most notorious scandal in American professional sports history. That fixed World Series came close to wrecking professional baseball because it broke the fundamental contract of trust between a professional sports organization and spectator.

No team or player is perfect. Winning every game all of the time is an impossible task. But it is expected and understood that every team and player will always try their best and do all they can to win.

The 1919 Chicago White Sox did not. In a messy performance that ultimately played out as courtroom farce, the White Sox were accused of and blamed for fixing the 1919 World Series against the Cincinnati Reds. The charges resulted in an astonishing stink and shame of the

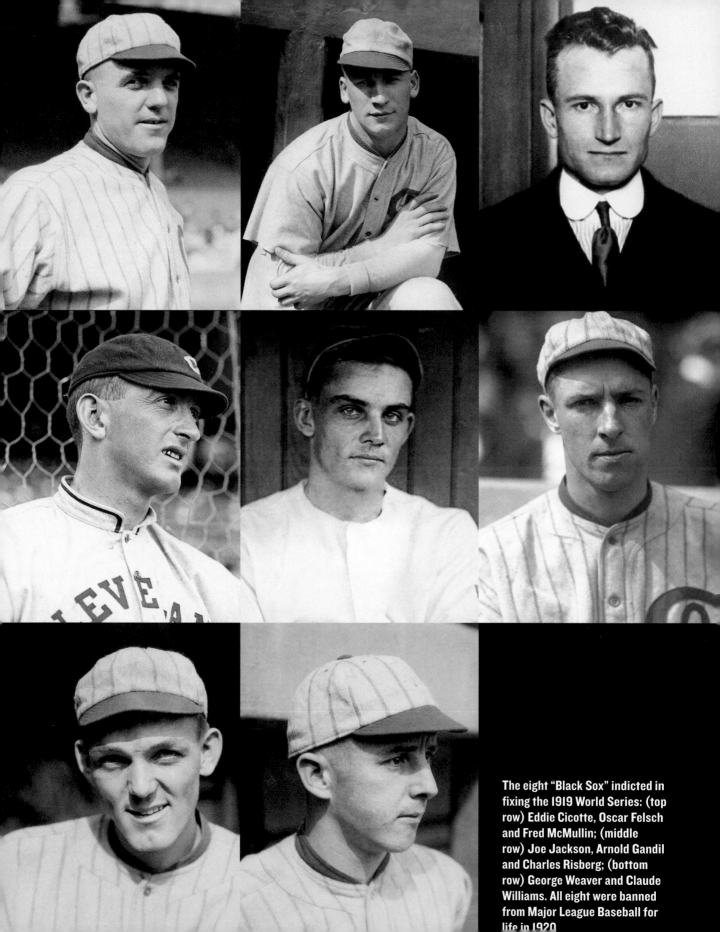

The eight "Black Sox" indicted in fixing the 1919 World Series: (top row) Eddie Cicotte, Oscar Felsch and Fred McMullin; (middle row) Joe Jackson, Arnold Gandil and Charles Risberg; (bottom row) George Weaver and Claude Williams. All eight were banned from Major League Baseball for life in 1920.

Eddie Cicotte, seen here in 1913, signaled the fix was in by hitting the first batter he faced in the World Series.

worst kind. The headline-grabbing drama had far-reaching consequences, and the unfortunate Reds are now mostly remembered as a piece of trivia rather than as a true champion.

Even today, with nearly a century of examination on the books (and in the movies and newspapers, too), there is some murkiness about what happened and who did what and why.

★ ★ ★ ★

What did happen was this: The White Sox, under manager Kid Gleason, won 94 games and the AL pennant. The Reds won the National League with 88 victories. Baseball played a best-of-nine World Series that season, and Cincinnati defeated Chicago 5-3, upsetting predictions that the superior Sox would win the crown.

Chicago's off-kilter performance was blamed

on the efforts of majordomo gambler Arnold Rothstein, a crooked gangster who shocked the world by bribing players to make errors, throw bad pitches and lose games to enhance his bankroll. He paid off enough key men to make certain of the results and then rolled in dough as the players found that going against the grain of their instincts was so difficult that many of those in on the crime felt they either did no harm or could show evidence they tried to win. Other gamblers operated in the shadows, too, complicating matters even more.

Many of the same star players on the White Sox's 1919 roster had banded together to win the 1917 Series. Owner Charles Comiskey had fired manager Pants Rowland after the 1918 season because the White Sox had tumbled to sixth place and finished 10 games under .500 in a season cut short by World War I. Along with peace, 1919 was presumed to bring normalcy to the diamond.

Shoeless Joe batted .351, Eddie Collins hit .319, and Nemo Leibold batted .302. Red Faber missed part of the year because of military service and then battled a sore arm to finish only 11-9. He also suffered from an ill-timed bout with the flu as a worldwide epidemic of the illness was killing people by the millions. Whether it was illness, rustiness or both, he was left off the Series roster. Claude "Lefty" Williams, who won 23 games, and young Dickey Kerr, who went 13-7, made up for Faber's loss. None of them could match Eddie Cicotte, though. He was brilliant, going 29-7 with a 1.82 earned run average. However, Cicotte was in a sour mood. His contract called for a bonus if he won 30 games, and he felt he was withheld from the mound in the closing days of the season on the orders of Comiskey, who, he claimed, wanted to save the money. The record showed Cicotte did get some chances, though, so the story may be apocryphal.

Cicotte, the opening-game starter for Chicago, was an integral figure in the fix. He collected $10,000 the night before the Series started, and he gave the signal to gamblers that the fix was on by hitting Cincinnati leadoff man Morrie Rath with a pitch. Cicotte was shelled that day, losing 9–1. He later admitted he found the envelope with cash under the pillow in his hotel room bed. He got what he wanted, and he cooperated.

Several of the Chicago conspirators were as subtle as they could be, yet in the press box there were rumblings that some things did not look or feel right. Kid Gleason spoke up for his guys but inwardly worried. Some of the "clean" Sox exhorted teammates to straighten up, play hard and perform to their abilities.

There was more background lobbying than at a political convention. Hard discussions became almost circus-like once other gambling rings jumped into the fray and players did not receive promised payments. Shoeless Joe Jackson said he was offered $20,000 for his involvement but collected only $5,000—which he didn't even want because he wanted out of any deals.

Many White Sox played well throughout the Series, even some of those later implicated in the scam. But the Sox did not play well enough to win, and the championship trophy went to the Reds. Comiskey issued a statement in support of his players, indicating he felt they just were outplayed.

* * * *

Hard-nosed investigating by sportswriter Hugh Fullerton led to a series of articles in December of 1919 pointing at gambling as a corrupt influence on baseball. Before the Series even began Fullerton received a tip about the fix, and during the ensuing games he made notes about suspicious plays, consulting with the now-retired Christy Mathewson in the booth.

It took until after the 1920 season had played out, but the bombshell reporting led to impaneling of a grand jury and the indictments and trials of eight players in Chicago. Cicotte confessed.

"I don't know why I did it," Cicotte said. "I needed the money." He had a wife and kids and had just bought a farm in Michigan so was strapped for cash.

Gangster Arnold Rothstein, seen here in 1928, is widely accused of having paid players to throw the 1919 World Series.

Shoeless Joe confessed, too, but during the Series he tried to return the money advanced to him and tried to tell Comiskey what was going on, but he was rebuffed. In the future he denied any wrongdoing, said he played to win and he played well in the Series, batting .375. Jackson, who was illiterate, has been a cause celebre for sympathetic supporters who suggested slick conspirators had taken advantage of him. Somehow, his original confessions were stolen, though then reconstituted for trial.

Claude Williams and outfielder Oscar "Happy" Felsch talked to the grand jury with a level of candor, Felsch to newspapers, as well. Felsch said he collected $5,000.

The eight accused were Cicotte, Jackson, Williams, Felsch, first baseman Arnold "Chick" Gandil, shortstop Charles "Swede" Risberg, backup Fred McMullin and third baseman George

Judge Kenesaw Mountain Landis, surrounded by Major League owners, signs the contract that made him baseball's first commissioner, in 1920.

"Buck" Weaver. Weaver demanded a separate trial—the request was refused—and spent the rest of his life proclaiming his innocence. Gambler "Sleepy" Bill Burns took the stand and issued damning testimony, although he said Jackson was not in the room when he offered his bribes. Some of the other key gambling figures had fled the country to lie low. The jury deliberated for less than three hours, and none of the players were convicted.

However, the owners, dismayed by the horrible publicity and the likelihood of the gamblers' believing they might get away with something like this again, banded together—AL and NL leaders alike—to hire the sport's first commissioner. The man they chose was an iron-fisted judge named Kenesaw Mountain Landis, and they gave him carte blanche authority, as he demanded, to run things as he saw fit and restore public confidence.

Trust was a tremendous problem. Baseball was the national pastime, the game of the masses. Portrayed in stories and film since that time is the sight of a little boy with big eyes beseeching Shoeless Joe Jackson as he stepped out of a courtroom with the comment, "Say it ain't so, Joe." The incident may never have happened, but it might as well have.

Landis surveyed the evidence and the landscape and affixed a hanging-judge penalty. Bringing the hammer down one day after the acquittal, Landis banished all eight players from baseball for life, abruptly ending their careers.

* * * *

The exile of the eight players effectively gutted the White Sox, removing them from the ranks of American League pennant contenders for the foreseeable future. Analyzing the scandal in terms of on-field results, the repercussions were long lasting. The White Sox did not win another pennant for 40 years.

For the better part of a century, historians and newspapermen have been riveted by the ins and outs of the scandal, what really happened, who the guilty parties were and who may have had less culpability. Reds players of the time, including such luminaries as Edd Roush, Heinie Groh, Slim Sallee and Dolf Luque, insisted they won fair and square. They did not want their title tarnished.

Risberg and Gandil are most often portrayed as the ringleaders who brought the others into the orbit of the fix. Cicotte was a critical figure, and decades later he said he had always regretted his participation but led an otherwise clean life. Williams, Felsch and McMullin were lesser players in the events.

Weaver was the most vociferous in proclaiming his innocence. He regularly petitioned for reinstatement and to have his name cleared, right up until his death in 1956. His career ended at 29, after nine seasons. It is agreed that Weaver's only crime was that he did not snitch on his friends, but awareness of the plot was enough in Landis' mind to ban him. For some years after his death, Weaver's descendants continued seeking to have his name cleared by Major League Baseball, but no pardon has been forthcoming.

Jackson possessed one of the most famous nicknames in baseball. He acquired it while playing in the Carolina Association in 1908 after developing serious blisters while wearing new shoes. Jackson planned to ask for the next day off, but his team was shorthanded and he had to play. He went to the outfield in stocking feet, and fans who noticed began yelling at him. After he became famous there was even an advertisement for a shoe company that featured his picture and the words "When 'Shoeless' Joe Jackson wears 'em, he wears Selz shoes." Actually, when Jackson played in Chicago he cavorted about town in alligator shoes. In the bigs he was known for wielding a big bat he called "Black Betsy" more than going shoeless.

Jackson, too, was distressed by his ejection from the sport, but he never applied for reconsideration, although others periodically made his case. The difference between Jackson and the other seven, with the possible exception of Cicotte, was that he was a likely Hall of Famer if ever put on the ballot.

A lifetime average of .356, third highest ever, plus one .400 season probably would have resulted in his receiving the honor. Jackson also batted .395, .382 and .373 in other full seasons. Once banned, Jackson disappeared from the limelight. He played semipro ball in Georgia and South Carolina and once ran a dry cleaning business in Savannah, Georgia. Jackson was born in South Carolina in 1887 and he eventually resettled in Greenville, where he ran a liquor store. Once, the great Ty Cobb, accompanied by famous sportswriter Grantland Rice, turned up there. Jackson only hesitantly greeted them, saying he wasn't sure at first if they would want to associate with him because so many others didn't.

In 1949, Jackson gave a lengthy interview to another famous southern sportswriter, Furman Bisher. The story ran in *Sport* magazine and later appeared in some newspapers.

"I had been acquitted by a 12-man jury in a civil court of all charges and I was an innocent man in the records," Jackson said. "If I had been the kind of fellow who brooded when things went wrong, I probably would have gone out of my mind when Judge Landis ruled me out of baseball. I would have lived in regret. I would have been bitter and resentful because I felt I had been wronged. I thought when my trial was over that Judge Landis might have restored me to good standing.

"Baseball failed to keep faith with me. When I got notice of my suspension three days before the 1920 season ended ... it read that if found innocent of any wrongdoing I would be reinstated. If found guilty I would be banned for life. I was found innocent and I was still banned for life."

In this account Jackson admitted that he knew there was something going on. He was also well aware sportswriters penned tales about him as "an ignorant cotton-mill boy." He said that helped him because it fooled pitchers into thinking he was going to be dumb at the plate.

"I have read now and then that I am one of the most tragic figures in baseball," Jackson said. "Well, maybe that's the way some people look at it, but I don't quite see it that way myself. I can say that my conscience is clear and that I'll stand on my record in that World Series."

THE 1920 SEASON

In some ways the 1920 season was the most peculiar in the history of the Chicago White Sox. Even as the year played out with fine results—a 96-58 record—the team was under suspicion for its actions (or inactions) during the 1919 World Series.

It was remarkable that the White Sox did not win the American League pennant. Chicago had four 20-game winners in their rotation, while Shoeless Joe Jackson batted .382, Eddie Collins .372 and Buck Weaver (seen here) .331. As a team they played phenomenal baseball despite whispers of crookedness.

It was only in the closing days of the 1920 season that a grand jury convened to investigate. Eight players were suspended for the last week of the season. With the pennant race on, the Cleveland Indians went 4-2 to wrap up their season while the White Sox went 1-2. As a result, the Indians finished two games ahead of Chicago for the AL pennant and won their first World Series that year.

Left: "Shoeless" Joe Jackson, business owner, in 1935. Right: Jackson, during his time in Cleveland between 1910 and 1915, where he was widely considered to have the best bat in baseball.

Jackson died of a heart attack at 64 in 1951. However, the saga of Shoeless Joe did not die with him. A book about the Black Sox scandal called *Eight Men Out* was published in 1963 and was made into a movie in 1988. Author W.P. Kinsella wrote a novel called *Shoeless Joe*, published in 1982, and it was made into the movie *Field of Dreams* in 1989. The player is a character in all of them.

In 1998, the legendary Hall of Famer Ted Williams began campaigning to open the doors to Cooperstown for Jackson. Williams delivered a speech in May of that year at a Joe Jackson Symposium in Florida. The first words of his talk were "I want baseball to right an injustice." Williams continued, "It's about time we say he's paid the price, served his sentence—served his sentence for a crime no court of law ever found him guilty of."

Williams passed away in 2002, and lobbying in Jackson's favor subsided after that. In 2011 an auction house sold the bat purported to be Jackson's Black Betsy for $537,750, although there had been other bats in the memorabilia market with the same designation.

Jackson's Black Betsy was retired by Judge Landis at the beginning of the Lively Ball Era.

The increase in offense, along with the rise of Babe Ruth, was credited with restoring baseball's luster and regenerating public interest. It is worth noting, however, that Ruth modeled his swing after Jackson's perfect form.

Charles Comiskey, who always professed to know nothing about the fix before newspaper revelations began to tell the story, died in 1931. Many believe that Comiskey did his best to cover up the facts he did know—Jackson's attempt to inform him is one example. Today a statue of the former owner resides in the concourse at the team's new home, U.S. Cellular Field.

The White Sox struggled mightily between 1921 and 1959, when they next won a pennant, finishing as far back as 56½ games in 1932. The demons were finally exorcised in 2005, when the club broke through for their latest World Series championship, 88 years after the 1917 triumph. The lessons learned for baseball—and all pro sports, for that matter—will never truly disappear. For as long as there is a World Series, the scandal will always be part of its history.

Chicago WHITE SOX

CHAPTER 15

From Oh-No to the Go-Go White Sox

The star catcher on the 1919 Black Sox club, Ray Schalk, always bemoaned the fate of that team. It seemed that the wrath the commissioner visited upon the White Sox—banishing eight players from the sport and gutting the lineup—forced the club to wander baseball's desert. And they did, finishing fifth or worse in the American League for 15 straight seasons starting in 1921, when the ban was enacted.

"Old Aches and Pains" Luke Appling poses at third base during spring training, late in his career.

There were highlights, however. Schalk convinced management to sign Baylor University star Ted Lyons in 1923. The right-hander spent 21 seasons pitching for the Sox and won 260 games, three times collecting seasons of 20 wins or more. Lyons' one bit of good fortune was overlapping with Hall of Famer Red Faber in the rotation for 10 years, but they both often faced the same plight—a shortage of scoring assistance.

Faber's best two years were arguably 1921 and 1922—directly in the wake of the Black Sox Scandal. Remarkably, Faber won over 20 games in each campaign and led the league in ERA both seasons. And on the heels of Faber's retirement in 1933, the additions of position players Jimmy Dykes and Al Simmons, as well as the emergence of Luke Appling, gave fans a reason to come to the ballpark, even if it was a losing cause.

Dykes and Simmons were champions in Philadelphia before being shipped to Chicago in 1933. Both brought winning attitudes with them to the South Side, and while they performed admirably, their addition to the clubhouse wasn't enough to make the Sox a contender. They did, however, represent the White Sox in the inaugural All-Star Game in 1933, which took place at Comiskey Park. The game was so popular that the league began its annual midsummer tradition.

Dykes became a long-term skipper for the club, managing 13 nonplayoff seasons. Simmons, later inducted into the Hall of Fame, did fine in Chicago but didn't have the same surrounding cast as he did in Philly. Simmons spent three years with the White Sox and then completed his career elsewhere.

Shortstop Luke Appling made a cameo with

the White Sox in 1930 and then stayed around through the 1950 season—a long time for someone nicknamed "Old Aches and Pains" on account of his chronic complaints about his health. Over his 20-year stay in Chicago, he collected 2,749 hits

Minnie Minoso takes a practice cut for the camera at Comiskey Park.

and pitcher Thornton Lee posted the league's best ERA in 1941. But, for any player who came in during the post–Black Sox era, the reality was that the team could never put it all together on the field. But that started to change in the 1950s.

★ ★ ★ ★

Minnie Minoso, the first black player for the Chicago White Sox, immediately made himself popular with the fans at Comiskey Park in 1951. The Cuban-born acquisition from the Cleveland Indians was still a rookie, and it might be said that English was his third language, behind Spanish and baseball.

But the flashy and speedy Minoso declared his arrival rambunctiously. On May 1 he blasted a 439-foot home run off New York Yankee hurler Vic Raschi. The fans swiftly changed their assessment of Minoso from "Who is this guy?" to "We like this guy!"

He gave the Comiskey spectators many reasons to like him. Minoso finished second in the American League Rookie of the Year voting on the strength of a .326 average and league-leading triples and stolen bases totals.

"I am the first black player for the White Sox," Minoso said years later, "but it had to be somebody. It is a good thing, but I am not a special person because of that."

But Minoso was a special person in many ways, and he became one of the symbols of the new-look White Sox that wheeling and dealing general manager Frank "Trader" Lane was

on a career batting average of .310. He was chosen for seven All-Star Teams, and when times were toughest for the Sox, Appling was sometimes the only shining light. He won two batting titles, the first with a .388 average in 1936.

Appling was not a bragging man, and when he was asked how he hit .388, he said he didn't know, he had to have been "just plain lucky."

Naturally, there was more to his hitting—and his Hall of Fame career—than that. And there was more to the postscandal White Sox than Lyons, Faber, Dykes, Simmons and Appling. Players like Rip Radcliff and Mike Kreevich won All-Star nods, hustling to build during his seven years at the helm (1948–54). These Sox were to be the team that would finally pull the franchise out of the doldrums of the 1930s and 1940s.

The first building block acquired for the White Sox's long-term success of the era was southpaw Billy Pierce. Swapped to Chicago from Detroit in 1949, he became a popular and effective hurler. In 1955 Pierce won the league ERA title with a 1.97 mark. Overall, he won 211 games in his career.

The White Sox's first Hispanic star was shortstop Chico Carrasquel of Venezuela. He came to the club the year after Pierce and became a four-time All-Star—and the first Latin American player to start in an All-Star Game. The only reason Carrasquel didn't stay with the White Sox past 1955 was because of future Hall of Famer and fellow Venezuelan Luis Aparicio.

Aparicio, the 1956 AL Rookie of the Year, won nine straight American League stolen bases titles and nine Gold Glove awards from the start of his career. His keystone partner was second baseman Nellie Fox, who won an MVP award and also was enshrined in Cooperstown.

The talent in Chicago was obvious and abundant, but the team struggled to leapfrog the dominant New York Yankees and the upstart Cleveland Indians. The Yankees, under manager Casey Stengel, won nine pennants in the 10 years between 1949 and 1958. The only skipper to edge him out was Al Lopez, with the Indians in 1954. Lopez was a savvy catcher-turned-manager, and the Sox lured him to the South Side in 1957 with a pennant on their minds.

The final piece of the roster puzzle was the acquisition of a supposedly over-the-hill pitcher of dubious temperament and stuff at age 39.

Early Wynn fooled them all. First, the Washington Senators gave up on him and he became a Cleveland Indian hurler on their marvelous 1954 team. He was sent to the White Sox in 1958 and was so-so with a 14-16 record and a 4.13 earned run average. None of that heralded Wynn's spectacular 22-win season of 1959 when he won the Cy Young Award.

Nellie Fox, left, and Luis Aparicio pose at spring training in 1961; both were named All-Stars that year.

A fastball specialist, Wynn had the reputation of a mean man on the mound. He would deck a batter with an inside pitch if he so much as looked at him wrong. The joke that followed Wynn around was whether or not he would hit his own mother with a pitch in the batter's box. Wynn's comment was, "Only if she dug in too close."

＊＊＊＊

First with Minoso and then with Aparicio doing their things on the basepaths, the White Sox of the 1950s earned the reputation of a team with speed that could win close games. In Chicago they were called "the Go-Go White Sox." Eventually, as the team won more often and played an exciting brand of baseball, it was serenaded with a song, "Let's Go, Go-Go White Sox."

The tune was introduced during the 1959 pennant run, fell into disuse for a while, and then was revived in the 2000s when the Sox made another pennant run.

To some extent the 1959 White Sox resembled the Hitless Wonders of 1906. Nellie Fox hit .306 en

White Sox slugger Ted Kluszewski shows off his biceps in his sleeveless uniform as he hits a home run during Game I of the 1959 World Series.

route to winning the Most Valuable Player award, but he was the only .300 hitter on the team. Wynn was the broad-shouldered leader of the pitching staff. Youngster Bob Shaw won 18 games, and the veteran Pierce followed with 14 victories. Any science involved in relief pitching was still in its infancy, but manager Lopez counted on the two-headed system of Gerry Staley and Turk Lown to finish off opponents. Using veteran arms to shut down foes in the late innings was Lopez's forward thinking.

The White Sox clinched the pennant on the road in Cleveland and returned late to Chicago. Air raid sirens were set off in celebration, and some Chicagoans feared the Russians were invading. The daytime celebration was better received.

"When it happened, it was fabulous," Lown said. "The great parade is something I'll never forget."

The World Series opponent was the Los Angeles Dodgers, who won their first pennant since moving to the West Coast from Brooklyn. The Dodgers were playing in the Los Angeles Coliseum while their permanent home in Chavez Ravine was being built. The Coliseum had been built for football and was the home of many events in the 1932 Summer Olympics. But it was not easily nor logically reconfigured for baseball, with a 40-foot-high mesh screen placed on top of the left-field wall, which was just 250 feet from home plate.

The White Sox had brought in a late-season power addition in Ted Kluszewski. "Big Klu" was from the Chicago area and had some of the largest muscles east of the Mississippi River, and he showed them off in sleeveless uniform jerseys.

When Kluszewski smashed two long blows in the opening game of the Series, which the White Sox won 11–0, it looked as if the acquisition might be a difference maker. But the Dodgers regrouped and won the Series 4-2.

The 1959 AL pennant represented the end of one era and the dawn of another. For Pierce, it was a long ride from his White Sox debut to the pennant, but winning it was very satisfying for the 32-year-old hurler.

"It was an all-around team," Pierce said. "We won the close ball games. We won the one-run games."

Pierce pitched for five more seasons, snagging one more All Star appearance in 1961. The pennant was Wynn's last great hurrah, too, as he struggled on for another few seasons to obtain his 300th victory before retiring and earning his pass to the Hall of Fame.

And 1959 was the beginning of the Bill Veeck era. Veeck, who always wanted to own a team in Chicago, bought controlling interest in the White Sox from Charles Comiskey's granddaughter Dorothy. Charles Comiskey II, the grandson, owned a substantial stake and wanted to keep the team in the family. But Veeck had the law on his side and became team president and presided over the pennant win.

THE ALL-STAR GAME

Major League Baseball can thank *Chicago Tribune* sports editor Arch Ward for its Midsummer Classic.

Ward invented the All-Star Game at the behest of *Tribune* owner Col. Robert McCormick, who wanted a glittery sporting event that could tie into the 1933 World's fair taking place in Chicago. Conceived as a one-time event, Ward's brainchild was so popular it became a staple of the sport. Ward pumped up the event as "the Game of the Century" in his columns and helped sway the decision to play the contest at Comiskey Park because it was larger than Wrigley Field. He also devised the system of fan balloting that continues in similar form today.

On July 6, 1933, the game was contested before 49,200 fans. The American League won, 4–2, and fittingly Babe Ruth hit the first home run in All-Star Game history. White Sox Al Simmons and Jimmy Dykes represented the home team.

Ward went on to launch many other events, as well as the All-America Football Conference—a serious competitor of the NFL between 1946 and 1950.

★ ★ ★ ★

Veeck had spent most of his life in baseball, starting with an apprenticeship under his father, who worked with the Chicago Cubs. He owned a minor league team in Milwaukee and then hit the jackpot after purchasing the Cleveland Indians in 1948. That club won the World Series and set a Major League attendance record.

A promotional genius who believed most baseball team owners were stuffed shirts and absurdly conservative, Veeck became known as the fans' owner. He desired to win, but he also wanted to ensure a family-friendly good time at the ballpark so fans would come anyway, win or lose. Characteristic of Veeck's spirit and sense of humor, he even made his maladies a gag. After losing a leg in WWII and needing a wooden leg to get around, he had an ashtray built into the appendage.

Veeck moved on from Cleveland to own the St. Louis Browns. While nothing could save the Browns, either in the standings or at the gate,

Eddie Gaedel stands in the batter's box for his one and only plate appearance for the St. Louis Browns in 1951.

Veeck's all-time gimmick took place when he signed 3-foot-7, 65-pound Eddie Gaedel for one game. Gaedel, wearing No. ⅛ on his uniform, made one plate appearance in a pinch-hitting scenario for the Browns during the second game of a doubleheader. With his strike zone so small, he earned a walk.

In Chicago, Veeck held Ladies Day, giving free tickets to women and flying in orchids from Hawaii for those attendees. Once he allowed fans to manage a game by holding up placards with their recommendations in key situations. He secretly had shorts designed as a Sox uniform option, but that idea was a flop. More popular was his "exploding" scoreboard. Fireworks were ignited whenever a Sox player hit a home run. Once "Martians" sought to kidnap Aparicio and Fox.

In a serious pioneering role in his early days, Veeck brought Negro League star Larry Doby to the Indians, breaking the color barrier in the American League a few months after Jackie Robinson made his debut in the National League with Brooklyn. Veeck also brought in 42-year-old Satchel Paige to the majors to pitch relief. He and Doby became the first African-Americans to win the World Series when Cleveland won in 1948.

But there would be no World Series champi-onship for Veeck in Chicago. He sold the team in 1961 to focus on his ailing health, and bought them back in 1975. A highlight of Veeck's second-time-around ownership was the memorable "South Side Hitmen" group of 1977. Veeck stocked up on what were essentially rent-a-players with expiring contracts planning to look for a big payday on the open market a year later. No one expected much from the thrown-together group, yet the Sox won 90 games, mostly on the strength of a rocking batting order.

Ralph Garr batted .300. Richie Zisk hit 30 home runs and drove in 101 runs. Oscar Gamble hit 31 home runs and drove in 83. Eric Soderholm hit 25 homers. Chet Lemon hit 19 homers. Jim Spencer hit 18 homers. Jorge Orta drove in 84 runs. Man, could those guys hit. It was a fun summer at Comiskey Park.

Zisk, Gamble and Spencer were gone after that year. And none of the others except Lemon hit as well in 1978.

The 1970s also showed that not every Veeck promotion was a wild success. "Disco Demolition Night" on July 12, 1979, may be the most infamous promotion in Major League history.

Anyone who brought a disco record to Comiskey for the scheduled doubleheader with the Detroit Tigers would be charged just 98 cents. Between the games, the offending records would be destroyed. Local DJ Steve Dahl heavily promoted the event on the air. The White Sox were stunned by the turnout of more than 47,000 people who apparently hated disco. During the intermission, after Detroit won the opener, it was time to kill the records. Only instead, thousands of fans stormed the field. An overwhelmed police force arrested 37 people, and the second game was forfeited.

The field needed $75,000 worth of repairs. One attempt to minimize the mayhem was turning

Fans storm the field at Comiskey Park on Disco Demolition Night after the first game of a doubleheader between the White Sox and Detroit Tigers.

broadcaster Harry Caray loose with his microphone to sing "Take Me Out to the Ball Game." For once, that didn't get enough people's attention. Caray had begun singing the tune for the seventh-inning stretch under pressure from Bill Veeck earlier that season. A year later he was working for the Cubs, and Caray's singing became a hit and a tradition across town.

Eventually, the changing landscape in free agency convinced Veeck that it would be too expensive to compete. He sold the team to Jerry Reinsdorf, who still owns it, in 1981.

★ ★ ★ ★

It was 1983 before the White Sox had another banner year. The All-Star Game came back to Comiskey Park, the same place where it started 50 years before. The American League won 13–3. The lone White Sox representative on that team was Ron Kittle, who was also Rookie of the Year that season.

The hoopla in Chicago didn't end with the midseason classic. The White Sox, under guidance of future Hall of Fame manager Tony La Russa, who was in his first job as a skipper, won 99 games and won

their division by 20. World Series fever gripped the South Side. LaMarr Hoyt won 24 games that season and the Cy Young Award in a career year. Star rookie Kittle smacked 35 homers and knocked out 100 RBIs. Harold Baines—a Sox fixture as a player and a coach and whose number is now retired—collected 20 homers and 99 RBIs. And future Hall of Fame catcher Carlton Fisk belted 26 home runs.

Fisk, although more commonly remembered as a Boston player because of his iconic, waving-it-fair home run in the 1975 World Series, actually played more years in Chicago (13) than he did in Boston (11).

Fisk's nickname was "Pudge" and his demeanor was pugnacious. He was a holler guy and a clutch hitter who always had a dirty uniform. But even Fisk's leadership couldn't get the White Sox over the hump, and the World Series favorites lost the American League Championship Series to the Baltimore Orioles.

And so the 1980s closed and the 1990s came and the White Sox were still after that curse-breaking World Series crown. It had been a long time since the 1917 championship.

CHAPTER 16

The Big Hurt

On the diamond they called Frank Thomas "the Big Hurt" because he was football-player big at 6-foot-5 and 250 pounds, built much like the tight end he had been at Auburn University. He also put a pretty good hurtin' on a baseball when his bat connected with it, sending it into roughly the same orbit as America's space satellites.

Frank Thomas, "the Big Hurt," in 1997; that year he won the American League batting crown with a .347 average.

Thomas, born in 1968 in Columbus, Georgia, was a White Sox first-round draft pick in the 1989 amateur draft, seventh overall. By 1990, he was in the majors, appearing in 60 games. After that Thomas was a regular, although there was nothing regular about his game. He was extraordinary, initially as a first baseman and eventually as a designated hitter.

Thomas spent 19 seasons in the big leagues, from age 22 to 40, the first 16 of them with the White Sox. It was longtime White Sox broadcaster and former player Ken "Hawk" Harrelson who bestowed Thomas with

Two-time AL MVP Frank Thomas in 1999.

numbers, his plate presence was augmented by a glittering smile that could light up an entire clubhouse.

★ ★ ★ ★

Thomas' 521 homers tied him with Ted Williams and Willie McCovey on the all-time list. But he was an all-around hitter who, despite his awesome power, was discerning at the plate. He walked 1,667 times in his career—which put him 10th all time—and his lifetime on-base percentage was a marvelous .419. That mark is 19th on the all-time list. Barry Bonds, in sixth, is the only player higher on the list who played since Mickey Mantle retired in 1968.

"My goal was always to be an all-around hitter," Thomas said, "but my size created an image for some people who felt I should mainly be a home-run hitter. There were some people who looked at me and my physique and said, 'He's a big guy and he should be able to hit the ball 500 feet.'

"I never really went to the plate thinking about a home run," Thomas continued. "I was always taught that the home run happens."

his nickname, and no one ever argued that it didn't fit. He clubbed 521 home runs, batted in 1,704 runs and has a lifetime average of .301. Thomas won a batting title, took home two American League Most Valuable Player awards and was a five-time All-Star. And although it could not be measured in

Thomas could hit the ball 500 feet, but he let the game come to him, so those occasions only occurred once in a while. He topped 40 homers in a season five times and went over 30 four other times. He exceeded 100 RBIs in a season 11 times.

"He wanted to be known as the best hitter in the game," said former teammate Robin Ventura,

BO
AND THE
BIG

HURT

When choosing between Frank Thomas and Bo Jackson for who had more impact on the diamond, Thomas wins by a landslide. But Jackson—who made waves as one of only a few modern athletes to successfully play meaningful minutes in two major sports (NFL football and Major League Baseball)—is an icon in his own right.

The two stars had some fascinating overlaps in their athletic careers, including playing football together at Auburn University. Jackson was the more celebrated athlete there, winning the Heisman Trophy as a running back. Thomas was a tight end who did a lot of blocking. Auburn's football coach said Jackson and Thomas rank No. 1 and No. 2 as the best athletes he coached, and it was a close call between them.

Jackson's career in both sports was derailed by injury, but not before he and Thomas were White Sox teammates in 1991 and 1993. Thomas played 19 years of pro baseball and became a Hall of Famer in 2014.

CHICAGO WHITE SOX

who rose to become manager of the White Sox. "He was driven to be that. Everyone wished they had a guy in the middle of their lineup like him."

Thomas said that former White Sox hitting coach Walt Hriniak offered him key guidance when he was a young player. It was Hriniak who impressed upon Thomas how important walks could be.

"He taught me discipline at the plate," Thomas said. "He said, 'Do you want to be good or do you want to be great? Be a true professional and do it all.'"

The White Sox were not a great team during Thomas' years on the squad. Amid middling seasons they did, however, twice finish in first place in the 1990s. In 1993 they fell victim to the reigning world champion Toronto Blue Jays, and in 1994 the club lost its opportunity when the season ended early because of a player strike. There were other good players on the roster with Thomas, but he was looked to as the one who could be an offensive force, and he took on the pressure of being the Man.

"Every day he stepped out on the field he wanted to be the best," said White Sox outfielder Aaron Rowand. "He threw a lot of weight on those big shoulders, carried a lot of guys on his back for a long time."

✳ ✳ ✳ ✳

Being naturally big during baseball's steroid era was a blessing and a curse for Thomas. He didn't stand out like other boomers who had bulked up through artificial means, but his biggest obstacle was being outdone in key hitting categories by those who took performance-enhancing drugs.

"I do feel I was overshadowed by some of those guys," Thomas said.

But Thomas was never really ever under suspicion. Playing during the heart of the era when home runs were cheapened by players later shown to be users, Thomas spoke out vociferously against the drugs, and when officials asked active players to show up and testify about the problem, Thomas was a rare participant who asked for tougher testing standards.

"Fans got caught up in the idea that home-run hitters had to hit 50 or 60," Thomas said. "I just never lost focus on what I was doing. I didn't focus on what everybody else was doing. It was kind of sad when things unfolded and we started hearing about guys taking steroids and performance-enhancing drugs."

After Thomas retired in 2008, fans frequently approached him, telling him he was a surefire Hall of Famer. But Thomas quickly steered the conversation in another direction. He was superstitious, he said, and didn't want to dwell on that topic.

He had a right to be nervous. Thomas was burned during his career by others' actions—most notably when he was runner-up in 2000 to Jason Giambi (who later admitted to steroid use) for the American League MVP—and may have feared that Hall of Fame voters would honor those other men first.

That did not occur. In 2014, Thomas joined fellow players Greg Maddux and Tom Glavine and retired managers Joe Torre, Bobby Cox and Tony La Russa on the inductees' list. Mentioned somewhat casually about Thomas' induction was that the Big Hurt's election marked the first time a player who competed so often at designated hitter had been chosen.

Upon hearing the news, Thomas flashed that winning smile in the broadest possible fashion and did so again and again. It was a very special moment for him—and one he believed he earned. Thomas thought he should be a first-ballot Hall of Famer, and the voting members of the Baseball Writers' Association of America agreed. He was named on 83.7 percent of the ballots.

"What I did was real," Thomas said, "and that's why I've got this smile on my face right now, because the writers, they definitely got it right."

Thomas said he always had high goals, from the first minute he put on a White Sox uniform.

"When I got into the league I told people I wanted to do very special things in my career," Thomas said. "People thought I was crazy at

National Baseball Hall of Fame inductee Frank Thomas wipes away tears during his induction ceremony in 2014.

times … [but] I really wanted to do something special."

He did. And on July 27, Thomas was enshrined in the Hall of Fame in Cooperstown with more than 48,000 fans cheering at the ceremony. Wearing a black suit and speaking for 18 minutes, a grateful and emotional Thomas more than once brushed away tears during his acceptance speech. He interrupted himself a few times and even said he was speechless because of the honor. But he wasn't really. He thanked his late father, Frank

Sr., for pushing him and helping him as a youth, and he delivered a message to today's youth who might dream of following in his footsteps—or who choose any path, really.

"There is no shortcut to success," he advised kids to recognize. "Hard work. Dedication. Commitment. Stay true to who you are."

Frank Thomas was true to himself—and look where he ended up.

Chicago WHITE SOX

CHAPTER 17

The South Side Rules

The wait ended in 2005. For the first time since 1917, the Chicago White Sox were World Series champions. After an 88-year dry spell often overlooked by the more publicized Cubs championship drought, the Sox took center stage in Chicago and in the national baseball consciousness with their triumph. The town went nuts.

Chicago White Sox' Pablo Ozuna (38), Bobby Jenks, center, and catcher A.J. Pierzynski celebrate after sweeping the Houston Astros for the 2005 World Series.

The final was even a sweep, a 4-0 blitz of the Houston Astros. These Sox were led by MVP outfielder Jermaine Dye, slugging first baseman Paul Konerko, spirited catcher A.J. Pierzynski, designated hitter Carl Everett and the speedy Scott Podsednik—along with strong pitching from Jon Garland, Mark Buehrle, Jose Contreras, Freddy Garcia and closer Bobby Jenks.

But for decades leading up to 2005, many Chicagoans wondered if they would see a White Sox World Series triumph in their lifetimes. For good reason, many also wondered if the White Sox would even continue playing in Chicago. In the late 1980s, officials in St. Petersburg, Florida, made a very determined bid to steal the White Sox. At the same time, owner Jerry Reinsdorf was deeply concerned about the team's need for a new ballpark. In the end, Comiskey Park II (now U.S. Cellular Field) was constructed, and the Tampa Bay area got the expansion Devil Rays as a consolation prize. It was a close call.

Perhaps if the White Sox had been able to grab a championship earlier there would have been less threat of their being poached. Mostly, though, for many years after the club's surprise march to the 1983 American League Championship Series, the Sox were just a middling team with the occasional eye-opening highlight or star player. In the 21 years from 1984 to 2004, the Sox only twice made the playoffs (1993 and 2000), and they also had a great season scuppered by the 1994 player strike.

Closer Bobby Thigpen was one of those star players who made the losing bearable. In 1990, he had the season of his life, recording a 1.83 earned run average and collecting 57 saves. That stood as a Major League record for 18 years.

"I could have had 60," said Thigpen, who is still No. 2 on the all-time list. "I blew eight saves and five of them were with a three-run lead."

In 1997, the White Sox splurged and signed slugger Albert Belle to a big-money contract. Controversy followed Belle wherever he parked his car; he got into arguments and sought to be a clubhouse loner, but he could smash the ball. During the first of two years with the organization, Belle unloaded 30 home runs with 116 runs batted in. The next year he cracked 49 homers and drove in 152. Big-money investment in Belle or not, he chose to take his talents to the Baltimore Orioles.

Somewhat quirky, but usually in a friend-lier way, the guitar-playing, musically inclined

VENTURA

Current White Sox manager Robin Ventura probably wishes he could forget his on-field heavyweight bout against pitcher Nolan Ryan on August 4, 1993, but thanks to the Internet, he will always be followed by the skirmish.

In the top of the third inning in Texas as the Sox took on the Rangers, future Hall of Famer Ryan hit Ventura, a lefty-hitting All-Star third baseman, in the back with a pitch. Ventura took off his helmet, took a couple of steps toward first base and then veered to the mound and charged Ryan.

Ryan captured Ventura in a headlock and unloaded several punches before the scrum resulted in a Ventura tackle and a bench-clearing ruckus. Still, advantage Ryan, who was 46 at the time. The pitcher's already hardy image was solidified with a "Don't mess with Texas" label as a result.

VS. RYAN

pitcher Jack McDowell was a core member of the pitching rotation in the early 1990s. A member of a band, the right-hander played gigs when convenient while with the White Sox. McDowell won 22 games and the Cy Young Award in Chicago's great run to the ALCS in 1993. The defending World Series champions from Toronto ultimately trumped the White Sox, and McDowell was charged with the loss in the final game of that series. But, like always, if McDowell was getting hit hard he tried to lose himself in music.

"It has always been a nice outlet for me," McDowell said. "I don't take baseball home with me a whole heck of a lot because I'm so focused with what I do with music."

McDowell toured for years with his band, stickfigure, after he retired from baseball in 1999.

Robin Ventura, one of the greatest college baseball players of all time—he batted .428 in three seasons at Oklahoma State and drove in 302 runs in 210 games—looked as if he was going to be a White Sox lifer. He broke into the majors with the team at 21 in 1989. A six-time Gold Glove winner at third base and a two-time All-Star, Ventura was an all-around player. Nine times he hit more than 20 homers and three times drove in at least 100 runs. A clutch hitter, Ventura is tied for fifth on the Major League all-time list with 18 grand slams.

Frank Thomas, another big hitter, labored with the Sox for 16 seasons between 1990 and 2005. A five-time All-Star and two-time AL MVP, Thomas was the main draw to the park on many nights. In 2005 "the Big Hurt" was often on the disabled list, and injuries limited him to 34 games that season. He didn't even get a chance to suit up for the playoffs that year. Instead, in one game he got to throw out the ceremonial first pitch. Not the most satisfying of roles for Chicago's big slugger, but at least he participated in some way.

* * * *

Ozzie Guillen was brought in as manager for the 2004 season to give the club a fresh voice. Guillen had played 16 years of shortstop in the majors, winning a Rookie of the Year award and making three All-Star Teams. His first 13 seasons were spent with the White Sox, so he was considered family when hired as skipper. As a player, Guillen had been brash, outspoken, flashy and loud. As a manager he was the same. He was a talking machine, a funny man, clearly passionate about the sport. Sometimes he talked too much and said the wrong things. It was no accident that Guillen was fined and required to take sensitivity training. He was definitely not politically correct. But if you could overlook the frequent profanity and navigate around his insensitive comments, he did deliver some profound messages about the sport in his colorful rants—and with some of the best stand-up comedy this side of late-night TV. Sportswriters loved him for a good sound bite, but White Sox management worried about him stepping over the line.

Even so, there was no doubt that Guillen was a winner who made the White Sox winners in the broadest possible sense. He lifted up a team that had been down for a long time and who had recently showed promise, and he led it to the ultimate prize in the sport.

Under Guillen's guidance, the 2005 edition of

Mark Buehrle delivers a pitch during the first inning of Game 2 of the 2005 World Series, a 7–6 win for the White Sox.

the Sox, figuratively and literally, shot off fireworks every step of the way. Colorful explosions were fired after home runs and victories—an homage to Bill Veeck's exploding scoreboard from the 1970s—as well as in postgame press conferences with Guillen and in the standings. The team was never at, or below, .500. They won the season opener 1–0 over the Cleveland Indians behind lefty starter Mark Buehrle, and they kept on winning.

It was a great start and nobody caught them. The White Sox were in first place in the American League Central Division for the entire season.

Buehrle, who later in his stint with the White Sox pitched a no-hitter in 2007 and a perfect game in 2009, has always been a fast worker. He does not dally on the mound, and a couple of weeks into the season he pitched a complete-game three-hitter with 12 strikeouts against Seattle that

Outspoken White Sox manager Ozzie Guillen provides sound bites to the media prior to Game 3 of the 2005 World Series.

and never won another. Buehrle, Garland, Garcia and Contreras, in that order, won the rest of the games—all of them complete games. It was the first time that four different pitchers for one team had thrown complete games in a row in the postseason since the Cubs of 1907.

★ ★ ★ ★

Although the White Sox swept the World Series, all four games against Houston were close, 5–3, 7–6, 7–5 and 1–0. Contreras and Garcia picked up victories, but two of the Series wins were earned by relievers Neal Cotts and Damaso Marte.

Outfielder Jermaine Dye set the tone for the series by hitting a home run for Chicago in the first inning of Game 1. Paul Konerko hit a seventh-inning grand slam off the first pitch thrown by Houston reliever Chad Qualls in Game 2, and the contest ended with Scott Podsednik— better known for his base stealing (he did not hit a single home run during the regular season)— knocking a deep blast off Astros closer Brad Lidge. His walk-off shot gave the White Sox a 2-0 Series lead.

Game 3 was an epic. It lasted 14 innings, equaling the longest World Series game ever. And Buehrle, of all people, got the save as he came in to relieve the relievers after Guillen worked his way through the bullpen. The game took a record 5 hours, 41 minutes to play, and the 17 pitchers used and 43 players involved also set records.

Geoff Blum, in his only White Sox season— and after appearing in only 31 games—became a White Sox franchise hero by belting the winning home run in the 14th. It was Blum's first at-bat of the entire postseason.

Game 4 was a 1–0 triumph that ended on an infield grounder nabbed by shortstop Juan Uribe, who threw to Konerko covering first.

"In sports I haven't had a greater feeling," said general manager Ken Williams.

Dye, who batted .438 to win the Most Valuable Player award, had played in a World Series as a wide-eyed rookie nine years earlier with the

took just 1 hour and 39 minutes to finish. That was a Deadball Era kind of time.

At the All-Star break the Sox were 57-29. In the second half the Sox were ahead by 15 games after another Buehrle win, and they won the divisional crown by six games.

There was no stumbling in the American League playoffs, either. Chicago ousted the defending World Series champion Boston Red Sox, 3-0, in the Division Series, with Contreras, Buehrle and Garcia each winning a game and Jenks picking up two saves. Feisty catcher A.J. Pierzynski, who came to town with a bad rep as a clubhouse malcontent, proved he was a tough leader in Chicago. He smacked two homers in the 14–2 White Sox first-game win.

The Los Angeles Angels didn't give the Sox much more trouble in the American League Championship Series. Chicago won that series 4-1. The Angels won the first game off of Contreras

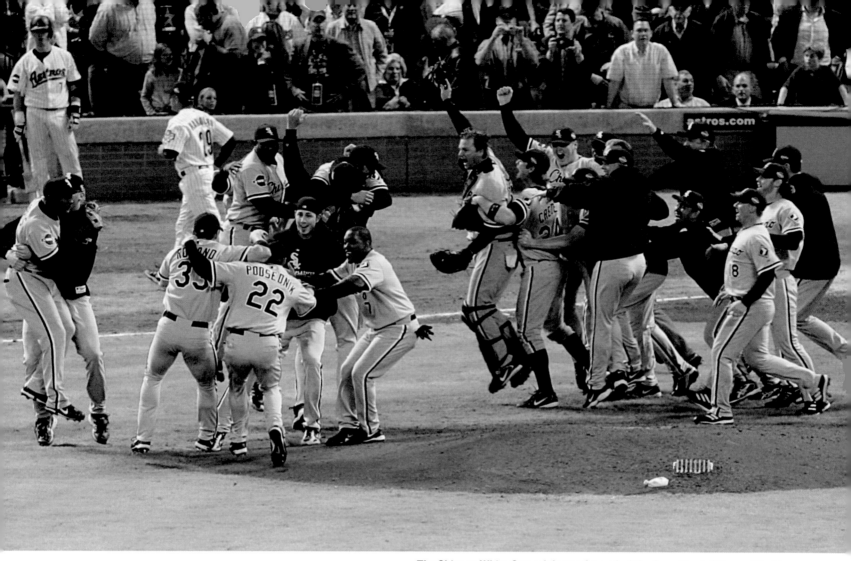

The Chicago White Sox celebrate the end of the franchise's 88-year World Series drought after sweeping the Houston Astros for the championship in 2005.

Atlanta Braves. Winning this one for Chicago felt much different.

"It means a lot," Dye said, "not only to guys in the clubhouse, but to the organization, the fans, and the city. I'm happy to bring a championship to Chicago. It is really special."

Soon after the Series was clinched in Houston, a grand parade took place through Chicago's streets. Paul Konerko, playing off of Chicago's old nickname, said, "Chicago, second city no more." Konerko also kept possession of the ball from the last out in Houston, and he presented it to a grateful Reinsdorf.

Guillen, already a renowned figure in his native Venezuela, brought the championship trophy home to show it off, as if it were the Stanley Cup.

The satisfying regular season, the whirlwind playoffs and the breathless celebration raised the White Sox to a high point of popularity. In 2006,

the season after the championship, attendance hit a record 2,957,414. The Sox were a hot ticket.

However, they could not repeat on the field, not even with the addition of All-Star designated hitter Jim Thome, who smashed 42 round-trippers. Nearing the end of a career that will inevitably place him in the Hall of Fame, Thome followed up with 92 more homers in parts of three seasons with the Sox.

The eight-year Ozzie Guillen era ended in Chicago in 2011, and now the White Sox dream of replicating the glory of 2005 is alive with another Sox legend-turned-manager at the helm in Ventura.

Here's to fireworks exploding nonstop, punctuating another splendid and sublime run to the top.

HERE COME THE HAWKS 157

18 GARDINER GETS THEM
Out of the
GATE 162

19 *The* STANLEY CUP
CHAMPS
of 1961 168

HERE COME THE WHKS

When old-timers talk hockey, or television networks try to drum up nostalgia, they often lean on the Original Six.

That's because from 1942–43 until 1966–67, the world's most prominent hockey league included just six franchises, representing six cities: the Chicago Black Hawks, Boston Bruins, New York Rangers, Detroit Red Wings, Montreal Canadiens and Toronto Maple Leafs.

Although nearly a half-century has passed since the NHL landscape changed for good with the first of many expansions in 1967–68, a certain cachet remains attached to the Original Six franchises, and that is certainly true of the Blackhawks.

Founded on November 17, 1926, by Major Frederic McLaughlin, the team was originally the Black Hawks (two words) and named in honor of the major's Army unit. The franchise closed the compound in 1986 to become the Blackhawks. To those in the city, calling them the Hawks is fine and dandy, and with the backlash happening in collegiate and professional

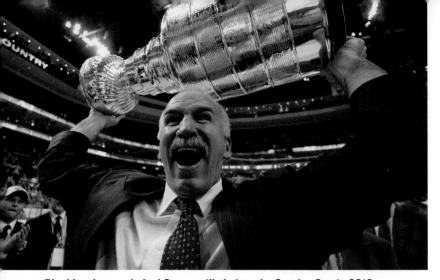

Blackhawks coach Joel Quenneville hoists the Stanley Cup in 2010.

Overleaf: Jonathan Toews (19) and Patrick Kane (88) have led the Chicago Blackhawks back to the top of the NHL.

sports over Native American–themed nicknames, the Blackhawks name may not be much longer for this world. For now, though, the Blackhawks logo is widely considered to be the most handsome in hockey, and the organization is working to build an education initiative about Native Americans through their use of the name.

Of all the Original Six teams, only Montreal, Toronto and Boston have histories that predate the Hawks, who share their founding year with New York and Detroit (then the Cougars). But it is the Wings, by far, that still draw ire from Hawks fans when they come to town. Since Detroit was the only other city in the Midwest during the Original Six era, the rivalry had an extra special focus. Chicago beat Detroit for their first Stanley Cup victory in 1934, and then Detroit laid it on for years when Chicago was almost perennially bad from the mid-1940s to the late-1950s. In fact, aside from the Canadiens and Bruins, it is Chicago and Detroit that have played each other the most in NHL history, a whopping 810 times come the end of the 2015 regular season. A realignment of divisions has separated the clubs; they now play only twice a year in the regular season, and the only time they can face one another in the playoffs is when the Stanley Cup is on the line.

But there are other rivalries too. Expansion brought St. Louis to the table, and the Blackhawks–Blues rivalry has always been hot, especially as of late with some tough playoff battles. The late

1980s and early 1990s also saw heated exchanges in the playoffs with the Minnesota North Stars.

The Blackhawks have been part of the Chicago sports landscape for a long time, but it hasn't always been a glorious time. There have been long droughts between championships, long periods of time when the club was down. Overall, the Hawks have won the Stanley Cup six times (1934, 1938, 1961, 2010, 2013 and 2015) and are top-flight contenders in the modern NHL.

Waiting 49 years between the 1961 and 2010 Cups was the second-longest championship gap for any team in NHL history.

A major turning point for the modern Blackhawks was a change in leadership at the top. Rocky Wirtz, the third-generation owner, has controlled the team since 2007. From the moment Wirtz assumed command from his deceased father, Bill, a new and forward-looking atmosphere permeated the club, and the Blackhawks were swiftly built into champions and perennial contenders.

An important aspect of Wirtz's regime was reconnecting with the past. Because the Blackhawks had been without a Cup title since 1961 and counting when he took over, one of Wirtz's efforts was reaching out to players who were living symbols of that long-ago crown. He not only invited Hall of Famers like Bobby Hull and Stan Mikita back into the fold, he actively courted them and made them team ambassadors. Of all Wirtz's many moves to boost attendance and rekindle success, that was one of his most popular.

One example of Wirtz's innovative thinking emerged when the Blackhawks moved into the Stanley Cup Final in 2010. He entertained the notion of throwing open the United Center for fans to watch road playoff games against the Philadelphia Flyers together as part of "viewing parties."

Wooing fans back to see games live was a first step, and making sure the team was exciting enough to keep winning was critical. The arrival of young stars like Patrick Kane and Jonathan Toews and their emergence as the go-to guys on the ice has helped Chicago maintain its high position in the standings year after year. Chicago also seemed to have the perfect matching coach in Joel Quenneville, who has directed the Blackhawks to three championships.

The second of these came in 2013. The feeling of winning the big one apparently makes athletes greedy. Toews, the captain, made it sound that way.

"Once you win the Cup once, you feel like it's yours," he said. "You don't want to give it up."

And if you do, you want to win it back.

Quenneville asks a lot from his skaters, and he expects players to live up to the recent standards set in what has become an exceptional era of Blackhawks hockey.

"I think you get rewarded when you do a lot of things right," Quenneville said.

In the volatile NHL, where owners seem to have even less patience than they do in other professional team sports, Quenneville is a long-term success story. By the end of the 2013–14 season he had moved into third place on the league's all-time list for regular-season coaching victories. He's now within striking distance of Al Arbour, sitting second with 782 wins—catching Scotty Bowman (a senior advisor to the Blackhawks for several years), who has 1,244 wins, is something else altogether.

At 56, Quenneville is in his 18th season as an NHL head coach. The only Blackhawks coach with three Cups on his resume, Quenneville felt lucky to have been able to coach so much talent in Chicago and also with the St. Louis Blues and Colorado Rockies.

"I've been fortunate," Quenneville said. "I'm very happy with the way things have gone in the places I've been."

Unless his luck turns, it is quite likely that Quenneville will preside over a fourth Cup in Chicago before he is finished.

Thousands of fans pack the streets of Chicago to see the Stanley Cup after the Blackhawks won the trophy for the first time in 49 years; the Cup is hoisted here by captain Jonathan Toews.

CHICAGO BLACKHAWKS

YEAR FOUNDED: 1926

Founded as Chicago Black Hawks, changed to Blackhawks in 1986

STANLEY CUP CHAMPIONS

1934   1938   1961   2010   2013   2015

RETIRED NUMBERS

1
Glenn Hall

3
Keith Magnuson

3
Pierre Pilote

9
Bobby Hull

18
Denis Savard

21
Stan Mikita

35
Tony Esposito

PRIMARY HALL OF FAMERS

- Ed Belfour
- Doug Bentley
- Max Bentley
- Chris Chelios
- Roy Conacher
- Art Coulter
- Phil Esposito
- Tony Esposito
- Bill Gadsby
- Charlie Gardiner
- Michel Goulet
- Glenn Hall
- Bobby Hull
- Tommy Ivan (builder)
- Dick Irvin
- Ted Lindsay
- John Mariucci (builder)
- Frederic McLaughlin (builder)
- Stan Mikita
- Bill Mosienko
- James D. Norris (builder)
- James E. Norris (builder)
- Pierre Pilote
- Rudy Pilous (builder)
- Bud Poile (builder)
- Denis Savard
- Earl Seibert
- Arthur Wirtz (builder)
- William Wirtz (builder)

GOALS

604
Bobby Hull

ASSISTS

926
Stan Mikita

POINTS

1467
Stan Mikita

GOALIE WINS

418
Tony Esposito

SHUTOUTS

74
Tony Esposito

THEME SONG
"Here Come the Hawks!"

Chicago BLACK HAWKS

CHAPTER 18

Gardiner Gets Them Out of the Gate

Hockey is a Canadian game, invented by Canadians and exported by Canadians. But without the United States, the sport would have never thrived professionally.

The National Hockey League was formed from the ashes of the National Hockey Association on November 22, 1917, and until the 1924–25 season when the Boston Bruins made their first foray on wobbly legs, it was a Canadian-only affair.

Tex Rickard, the famous boxing promoter and owner of Madison Square Garden, established the New York Rangers for the 1926–27 season. It was at his prompting that Major Frederic McLaughlin created Chicago's Black Hawks to join the Rangers in the NHL that year. Along with the Pittsburgh Pirates and Detroit Cougars (later Red Wings), who also joined that season, the NHL boasted 10 teams in 1926–27—only four of which were Canadian.

McLaughlin, whose family gained wealth through the coffee business, was granted an NHL franchise for the fee of $12,000. However, he had no players. To rectify that shortcoming, the Major bought the existing Portland Rosebuds of the Western Hockey League for $200,000,

Chicago Black Hawks goaltender Chuck Gardiner makes a diving save against the Detroit Falcons in 1931. Gardiner was the recipient of the Vezina Trophy at the conclusion of the 1931–32 season.

and those players became the foundation of the first Black Hawks team.

The Rosebuds nickname was central to the Portland area and not a favorite of McLaughlin's, so when it came time for him to name his Chicago squad he settled on Black Hawks, in homage to his 86th infantry Army division. That group was nicknamed the Black Hawks after Sauk Indian Chief Black Hawk, and McLaughlin was a commander with Black Hawks 333rd Machine Gun Battalion.

The iconic Indian head design on Chicago's jerseys was created by McLaughlin's wife, Irene Castle, an actress. McLaughlin owned the team until his death in 1944.

✷ ✷ ✷ ✷

The club's first great star was goalie Charlie Gardiner. Gardiner, also called Chuck, was born in Scotland in 1904, but his family moved to Canada when he was a youngster. He grew to 6 feet and 180 pounds as he gained experience on the ice in junior hockey in the Winnipeg area.

Gardiner became a goaltender because he was a late starter on skates and wasn't as steady on his feet as his friends were. In true roots-of-hockey fashion, most of Gardiner's early experience was on frozen ponds, and the weather was so cold he developed the habit of moving constantly in the net to avoid frostbite. That led to an unorthodox,

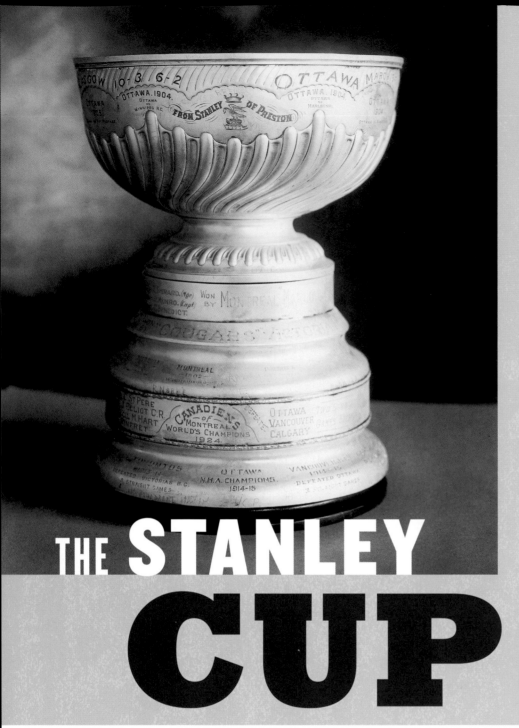

THE STANLEY CUP

The Stanley Cup long predates the existence of the National Hockey League, which formed in 1917.

Lord Stanley of Preston, then Governor General of Canada, wanted a trophy that truly represented the national hockey champion of the nation. So in the beginning, the Cup didn't belong to any league. It was first awarded in 1893 to the Montreal Amateur Athletic Association for being the top-ranked amateur team in the country. After that it became a challenge cup; any team making a legitimate claim that they deserved to vie for the hardware was given a chance to snatch it from the reigning champion. The Cup went pro in 1906 and ceased its challenge status in 1914. It became solely emblematic of NHL championship success in 1927 (the Cup, as it looked in that era, is seen at left).

Unique to the Cup is that names of the members of the winning team are engraved on it, and in the modern NHL, members of the winning team each gain possession of the trophy for one day.

The Chicago Blackhawks have won custody of the Cup in 1934, 1938, 1961, 2010, 2013 and 2015.

somewhat gymnastic style of blocking the puck rather than simply playing the position in a stand-up manner.

Gardiner broke in as a rookie with the Black Hawks for the 1927–28 season, and his timing was a blessing. Chicago was a terrible team their second year in the league. In the 44-game NHL schedule, the Black Hawks finished an awful 7-34-3. Gardiner played 40 of those contests and posted a 2.83 goals against average. Those numbers today befit a backup goalie, but back then the NHL was a low-scoring league—the combined average of the other nine starters was 1.70. But, when you consider that Chicago's other goalie, future Hall of Famer Hugh Lehman, was two goals per game worse than Gardiner in the four games he appeared in, the rookie's brilliance starts to become obvious.

The next season was only marginally better for Chicago despite Gardiner's continued excellence. He dropped his goals against by nearly one goal per game (1.85), but the Black Hawks' offense was pitiful. Just about every game was a low-scoring loss; in fact all games were low scoring, as the 1928–29 season is the lowest-scoring season in NHL history. The Black Hawks team record was 7-29-8, and in an astounding mark of futility, the club scored just 33 goals in 44 games. Perhaps even more mind-boggling is that five of Chicago's seven wins came by way of a Gardiner shutout.

Yet Chicago, with Gardiner as its backbone, turned around the offense just one season later, in 1929–30.

The biggest reason for the change of luck was more than likely to do with a rule change that permitted players to pass the puck forward in the offensive zone. This previously outlawed tactic opened up the game, and goal scoring increased league wide by nearly 50 percent. Chicago went from 33 goals in 1928–29 to 117 goals in 1929–30, and that was only good for the sixth-most goals in the 10-team league. Another reason for Chicago's change in fortunes was the addition of rookie Tom Cook, who led the team in points, as well as the continued emergence of second-year star Johnny Gottselig, who was the Hawks' leading goal scorer, with 21.

Gottselig was the first genuine scorer in team history, and he spent his entire 16-year career with Chicago. In 1929–30, paired with Cook at center and the no-nonsense Mush March on the right side, the trio proved to be a boon to the Hawks. Still it was on the strength of Gardiner's goaltending that they became winners. With a 21-18-5 record, they stood second in the American Division behind only the indomitable Bruins, who set the still-standing NHL record with a .875 win percentage. Chicago's positive turnaround ended in the playoffs, however, as the Montreal Canadiens trumped the Black Hawks in the quarterfinals.

That season set the stage for success in Chicago. The next year the Black Hawks marched all the

Black Hawks scoring star Johnny Gottselig in 1935.

way to the Cup Final, only to be dismissed by Montreal a second straight time. The season after that was also promising, until it ended in play-off defeat by the Toronto Maple Leafs. Then there was the lost season of 1932–33, when the Black Hawks inexplicably fell out of contention for the postseason.

But through it all, the one thing the Black Hawks and their fans knew they could count on

Mush March provides an obstacle for the fleet-footed Tom Cook in practice in 1935.

was the backbone of the defense. Year after year nothing distracted Gardiner. He was named an All-Star in 1930–31 after leading the league with 12 zeros; he won the Vezina Trophy in 1931–32, and even in the horrible year of 1932–33 he was nominated to the Second All-Star Team.

It took every bit of Gardiner's brilliance in the nets for the Black Hawks to contend, but in the 1933–34 season they finally made a breakthrough. As the runners-up in the American Division, Chicago topped the Montreal Canadiens, the Montreal Maroons and the Detroit Red Wings in the playoffs to earn the franchise's first Stanley Cup championship. Gardiner again won the Vezina and led the league in shutouts, this time with 10. In the Stanley Cup series, twice Gardiner had to endure overtime sessions. The Cup winner came off the stick of March, who scored in double overtime. Of his two goals in the playoffs, both were series winners, as he also knocked off the

Canadiens in overtime of the quarterfinals.

Celebration was short-lived, however. What few people knew initially was that Gardiner was experiencing health problems. Sometime in December of 1932, he developed tonsillitis. He kept his affliction quiet. In a game near the end of the year he made 55 saves, yet he actually had collapsed in the dressing room between periods from a fever running over 100 degrees.

Gardiner was briefly hospitalized, but from there his health declined. The goalie developed uremia and did not shake his tonsil infection; he even occasionally suffered from spots in his vision. The Black Hawks knew their leader was suffering, but he kept fighting through his problems, and when Chicago had Detroit on the ropes in the Stanley Cup Final he asked his teammates to get him just one goal and he would provide the rest. He did.

"Without Gardiner we wouldn't have made it," said coach Tom Gorman. "He's the greatest goalie that ever donned the pads."

Although Gardiner played phenomenally throughout the championship season, two months later at the age of 29 he died from a brain hemorrhage that was linked to the original tonsil infection. In 1945 Gardiner was part of the inaugural class of the Hockey Hall of Fame.

✳ ✳ ✳ ✳

The Black Hawks mourned the loss of their star, and although they could replace his spot between the pipes, they could never truly replace the confidence he gave the team. Chicago also moved forward the next season without coach

Gorman. Despite his success, McLaughlin fired the Stanley Cup–winning skipper after the season. It was a typical move by McLaughlin, who made 18 coaching changes in his 18 seasons as boss. Gorman went on to lead the Montreal Maroons to the Stanley Cup the next season.

In a blockbuster trade at the beginning of the 1934–35 season the Black Hawks acquired aging goaltender Lorne Chabot and scoring star Howie Morenz from the Montreal Canadiens for future Hall of Fame defenseman Lionel Conacher.

Morenz was on the back end of a career that had seen him named the league's most valuable player three times. In Chicago he contributed 34 points in 1934–35 but was not the same player he was from his All-Star days with the Canadiens.

Chabot, however, was another story. At 34 he was eight years into a 10-year career that saw him pull duty for six different teams. Expectations certainly weren't high for the veteran. In fact, few if any thought he'd be able to play up to the standard Gardiner had set. And yet Chabot proved them all wrong by posting his best year ever in the NHL. He played in all 48 of Chicago's games, recorded eight shutouts and was named a first All-Star and the Vezina winner with a sparkling 1.80 goals-against average.

But goal scoring was again a problem for the Black Hawks. In the two-game "total goals" quarterfinals that year against the Montreal Maroons, the Black Hawks failed to score a single goal while Chabot allowed only one against. The first game ended in a 0–0 tie. You can't expect to win if you don't score, as they say.

That would be it for Chabot. A knee injury cost him much of the next season, and Chicago moved

The Chicago Black Hawks hoist coach Bill Stewart on their shoulders after defeating the Toronto Maple Leafs for the 1938 Stanley Cup.

him for cash in 1936.

Two goalies and two years later, the Black Hawks pulled off perhaps the unlikeliest championship in NHL history.

Following a horrible regular-season mark of 14-25-9 in 1937–38, Chicago managed to qualify for the playoffs by 2 points. With captain Johnny Gottselig and Paul Thompson—a 31-year-old veteran who posted a career-high 22 goals and 44 points—leading the way, the Black Hawks came alive in the playoffs. After having scored the fewest goals in the entire league over the course of the regular season, the Hawks blitzed their playoff foes, outscoring them 26-21 in the postseason.

Chicago's second Cup stunned the league, but the next season their luck in net fizzled and their lack of goals caught up to them. Thus began the lost years for the Black Hawks, in which they missed the playoffs 14 times in 20 seasons before the ship was righted with the emergence of stars Bobby Hull, Stan Mikita and Glenn Hall.

The Stanley Cup Champs of 1961

Bobby Hull. Stan Mikita. Glenn Hall. The overlap of some of the greatest players in the history of the Chicago Black Hawks paid dividends with the franchise's first Stanley Cup triumph in 23 years. It was a long wait.

Bobby Hull shouts to the Detroit audience in the closing moments of Chicago's 5–1 Game 6 victory over the Detroit Red Wings to clinch the Stanley Cup. At right is Eric Nesterenko.

Between 1940 and 1959 the Black Hawks put some of their worst teams on the ice. The championship drought was headed for a quarter of a century before the 1960–61 club's surprise emergence. Chicago finished third in the regular-season standings with a 29-24-17 record. The key to their newfound success was the trio listed above.

Hull and Mikita were organizationally grown talents. Both plied their skill in the junior ranks with the Chicago-affiliated Teepees out of St. Catharines, Ontario, where star defenseman Pierre Pilote, the heavy-hitting Elmer "Moose" Vasko and two-way winger Ab McDonald also honed their game.

Hull was by far the most prodigious prospect the franchise had seen in

a long time. In his first year he finished runner-up for the Calder Trophy as the league's best freshman. By his third year he'd already led the NHL in scoring.

Mikita was less of a known quantity in 1960–61. His quick temper had him land inside the league's top 10 most penalized players in his first few seasons, but he was also a difference maker. The 1960–61 season was his breakout campaign as he broke the 50-point threshold for the first time; he was ninth in the league in box time and 16th in total points, only a few behind Hull.

Hall, meanwhile, cut his teeth with the Red Wings organization and was traded to Chicago in 1957. The trade shocked the league, as the former rookie of the year had just come off an All-Star season in Detroit. Speculation had it that he was traded along with Ted Lindsay for supporting the rugged winger's attempt at starting the first players' union. Chicago was so bad at the time of the trade that banishment there was seen as the worst punishment that could befall a player. Detroit's loss was Chicago's gain, however, as Hall

PIERRE PILOTE

Sometimes overlooked because of flashier company in the lineup, defenseman Pierre Pilote was a rock on defense for the 1961 Stanley Cup champion Black Hawks.

Pilote played 890 career games spread over 13 seasons (12 with Chicago). He stood 5-foot-10 and weighed 180 pounds, but he played bigger than his roster size; his reputation for big hits was backed up by his top-10 penalty minute totals.

Even with his rough play, Pilote's 59 points (14 goals and 45 assists) in 1964–65 was an NHL record for defensemen in the pre-expansion era. He was voted a first- or second-team All-Star for eight straight years and was awarded the Norris Trophy as the league's best defenseman three times (1963 to 1965).

kept up his All-Star form for the majority of his 10 years with the Black Hawks.

★ ★ ★ ★

The Montreal Canadiens of 1960–61 were in the midst of a dynastic run. The Canadiens had appeared in the NHL Final 10 straight years and won five straight Stanley Cups. Not since the early days when the Stanley Cup was a challenge-based trophy had there been a team so dominant.

Chicago had been eliminated in the first round of the playoffs for four straight years, and when the Black Hawks drew the Canadiens in the first round in 1961, the hockey world expected more of the same.

But these Hawks were different. Chicago may not have been as good as Montreal man-for-man in a long season, but in a short series the Black Hawks were dangerous. Coach Rudy Pilous, who had taken over for the 1957–58 season, had been slowly remolding a team that had been a steady loser. Under Pilous the club matured, improved and was sturdy up and down the roster. Aside from "the Million Dollar Line," featuring Hull, Bill Hay and Murray Balfour (who together certainly did not make a million bucks), and superb two-way play of "the Scooter Line" featuring Mikita, McDonald and Kenny Wharram, the team boasted other solid contributors such as Eric Nesterenko, Ed Litzenberger, Elmer Vasko, Reg Fleming and most importantly, Pierre Pilote.

One of the most intriguing aspects of this club was the way the younger players afforded special respect to the veteran Litzenberger. For three straight seasons in the late 1950s as the new guys came aboard, Litzenberger was the squad's leading scorer. However, in January of the 1959–60 season he was in a serious automobile accident and did not return to the lineup until March. His wife was killed and Litzenberger was struggling, but his teammates insisted he keep wearing the "C" on his jersey as captain.

Glenn Hall sprawls to make a kick save against the New York Rangers in 1962.

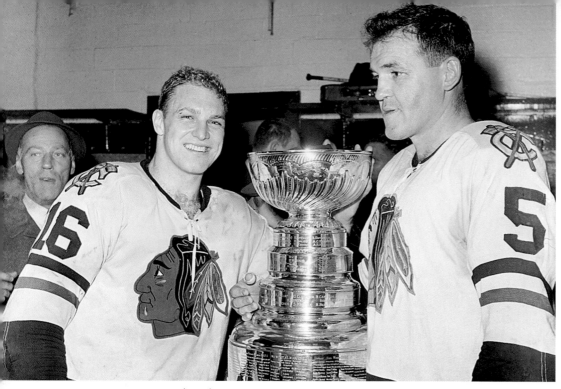

Bobby Hull and Jack Evans (No. 5) pose with the Stanley Cup after defeating the Detroit Red Wings for the Black Hawks' first Cup title in 23 years.

At times in that game Hall was under siege, but he deflected all Montreal chances in overtime, regularly provoking roars from the 20,000 fans in Chicago Stadium. It was Balfour who notched the winning goal.

"That was the greatest moment of my life," Balfour said of the game-winner that brought down the thunder.

The epic series shifted to Montreal, and while another team may have been crushed by such a demoralizing defeat, the Canadiens, as only the Canadiens could, promptly bounced back with a 5–2 win to tie the series, blasting a remarkable 60 shots at Hall.

Showing their own resilience, however, the Black Hawks, on the road at the Montreal Forum, blanked the Canadiens 3–0 in Game 5. Hall made 32 saves for his first career playoff shutout, and just how slick he was in net was noted by a Montreal sportswriter who wrote, "Glenn Hall was so good he could have stopped the Johnstown Flood for 60 minutes." Hockey fans might have suggested that stopping the Canadiens during an hour's worth of play was tougher.

If Montreal had not recognized the threat to maintaining its position on the throne before, it had to be apparent by Game 6 in Chicago, trailing the series 3–2. The Million Dollar Line had a banner night as Hay, Hull and Balfour all scored, and the result was an instant-replay 3–0 triumph. It was a second straight shutout for Hall and the Black Hawks' first trip to the Stanley Cup Final since 1944.

The king was dead and the throne was vacant for the taking.

Chicago also looked to Hall for inspiration. This was the fourth straight season in which Hall had played every game in net for the Black Hawks. That was part of the reason he had been nicknamed "Mr. Goalie."

Another reason the Black Hawks did not fear Montreal was the results of head-to-head match-ups during the regular season. The teams played 14 times. Each won five times and there were four ties. So that was good ammunition for an armchair psychologist like Pilous (who had once handed out miniature Stanley Cups to his players before the second game of a playoff series to get them to think big).

Still, the opening game was inauspicious. Montreal won 6–2, shaking loose after a 1–1 first period, and fans thought, "Here we go again." Montreal after all was loaded with stars like Bernie "Boom Boom" Geoffrion, Jean Beliveau, Henri Richard, Dickie Moore, Tom Johnson and Doug Harvey—Hall of Famers all.

But the Black Hawks rebounded with a 4–3 win in Game 2. Knotting that series seemed to be a coming-of-age moment for the team, and a 2–1 triple overtime victory in Chicago the next game was a statement win.

★ ★ ★ ★

The path to engraving names on the Stanley Cup ran through Hall's old club in Detroit. It would have been easy for the Black Hawks to suffer a letdown after trumping Montreal because the Red Wings were much like Chicago—unheralded underdogs that had overachieved.

But Detroit, led by the inimitable Gordie Howe, Alex Delvecchio and goalie Terry Sawchuk, was on its own mission after topping Toronto 4-2.

It took six hard-fought games for the Black Hawks to outlast Detroit. And in a bit of a comeuppance for the Red Wings, the series unexpectedly became a goaltenders duel: Hall in net for the Black Hawks against Hank Bassen, the goalie included in the 1957 swap that saw Hall land in Chicago.

The Black Hawks took the opener, 3-2, at Chicago Stadium. It was a good start in pursuit of the club's first Cup since 1938. For the first four games the series was low scoring and the results seesawed back and forth, with the series tied 2-2 after four games.

Sawchuk started the series but was hurt after a collision with Balfour in the first period of Game 1. Bassen stepped in admirably and spelled Sawchuk for Games 2 and 3, splitting the contests. Sawchuk returned to the goal, with Detroit no worse off from his absence. However, he played poorly in Game 5 and the Black Hawks ripped the Red Wings, 6–3. It was a hard choice to make, but Bassen was put back in net for Game 6 with the Cup on the line and Detroit down 3-2 in the series.

Chicago had its own injuries to deal with, as Balfour was out with a broken arm after a nasty run-in with the Detroit net in the previous game. Reg Fleming, known for his hard checking, but not his sharp shooting, took his place on the A line with Hull and Hay.

Detroit led 1-0 in the second period when Fleming scored the tying goal with his team shorthanded and opened the floodgates on the Red Wings' net.

"I saw my chance and threw it in the short side," Fleming said. "Bassen, the Detroit goalie, just stood there and watched it go in."

Detroit GM Jack Adams summed up the rest of the contest in his postgame remarks: "They had too

Glenn Hall is paraded around the ice after the underdog Black Hawks captured the 1961 Stanley Cup.

many big guns and too much muscle for us ... that goal by Fleming while we had a man advantage killed us. We didn't have enough left to match them when they accelerated after that break."

The final score was 5–1 Chicago.

As is traditional when the Cup is awarded, the Black Hawks skated around the rink with it held high. As is less traditional, the skaters also picked up Hall and skated him around the rink on their shoulders.

"It was the final result of what you had been looking for all of your life," Hall said.

Really, overall, the Black Hawks had done it as a team. Of all people, defenseman Pierre Pilote's 15 points led the team in playoff scoring, with Hull just one point behind. Mikita wondered if they were building a new NHL dynasty, although that never happened.

"At my age then, 20," Mikita said, "you figured it was going to happen every year. But it's not that easy. You never know when you're going to get another chance."

For Bobby Hull, the victory made him a Stanley Cup champion at 22. Both he and Mikita were emerging as star players for the Hawks, and the next season Hull's legend truly began building.

Chicago's Great One-Two Punch

We'll never know if Bobby Hull's slap shot was as fast as a Nolan Ryan fastball (which once topped 108 mph), but there are goalies, especially those who didn't wear protective masks and played in the NHL at the beginning of Hull's career when he was young, who would no doubt attest to it.

Toothless grins all around after the Black Hawks' 6–2 victory over the New York Rangers saw Bobby Hull (left) notch the 200th goal of his career, while teammate Stan Mikita netted his 100th during the game.

A bigger-than-life personality, Hull broke into the NHL with the Black Hawks as an 18-year-old for the 1957–58 season. He scored 13 goals and added 34 assists, good for runner-up in rookie-of-the-year voting, the honor of which went to future Hall of Famer Frank Mahovlich.

Hull's breakthrough season came two years later when he scored 39 goals to lead the league, added 42 assists and led the NHL with 81 points. He was selected for his first of 12 NHL All-Star Teams.

By the time the Black Hawks won the Stanley Cup in 1961 Hull was an

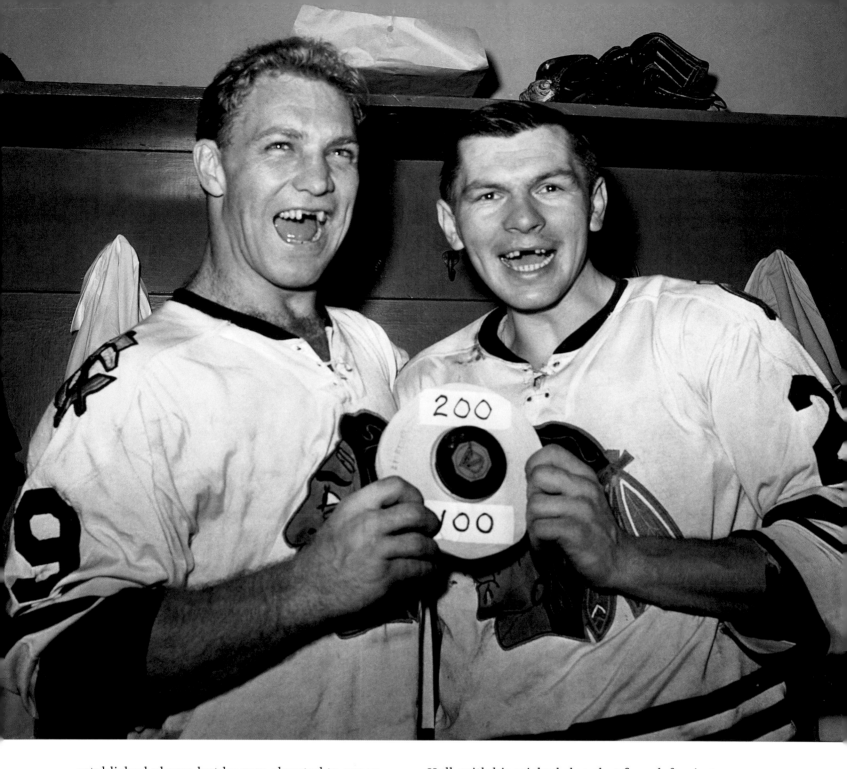

established player, but he was elevated to superstar status (before the word was commonly used) during the 1961–62 season, when he reached the 50-goal plateau. To that point in league history, the 50-goal milestone had been touched just twice, first by Maurice "Rocket" Richard, who had scored a magnificent 50 goals in 50 games in 1944–45, and by Bernie "Boom Boom" Geoffrion, who tallied the total the year before Hull.

Hull, with his wicked slap shot from left wing, topped 50 goals in a season three more times before anyone else managed 50. He led the league in goal scoring seven times. At the height of his game in the 1960s with the Black Hawks, Hull also won the Hart Trophy as most valuable player twice and the Art Ross Trophy as the regular-season top point-getter three times. There was no shortage of hardware in Hull's collection.

Glenn Hall, "Mr. Goalie," was the backbone of the great 1960s Black Hawks teams that starred Hull and Mikita. Sent to Chicago by the Detroit Red Wings for the 1957–58 season, Hall had an immediate impact, as he shored up a position some argue hadn't been capably filled since the days of Chuck Gardiner.

Hall's biggest contribution to hockey was his pioneering butterfly style of protecting the net, which has been refined over the decades and is now the main technique of all NHL goalies. But he is best remembered for the one record that will certainly never be broken: from the first game of the 1955–56 season until the 13th game of the 1962–63 season, Hall played every minute of every contest—502, to be exact, or 551 including playoff appearances. And, as the story goes, he puked before every one of them. "I always felt like I played better if I was physically sick before the game," he said. "If I wasn't sick I felt as if I hadn't done everything I could to try to win."

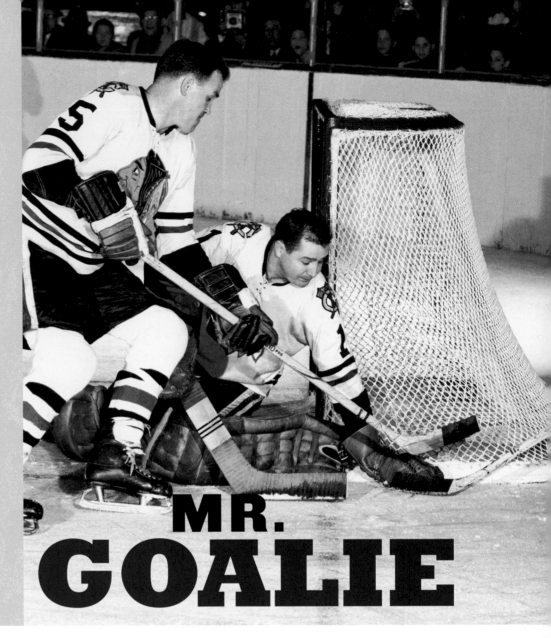

MR. GOALIE

At 5-foot-10 and 195 pounds, Hull was built like a rock, and besides his speed (and hair), which contributed to his nickname of "the Golden Jet," he had sharp elbows in the corners that helped gain him control of the puck in scrums.

"Bobby's the strongest forward in the league," said Leo Boivin, a defenseman who saw his fair share of Hull over their time as rivals in the Original Six days. "You try to get him to go over to the boards, but it isn't easy. He's like a bull. You hit Hull and bounce off of him. He's so fast he's hard to keep up with, and so strong you can't push him out of the way if you catch up to him, and so tricky it's hard to hit him clean."

Hull, who attributes his legendary strength to the time he spent working and bailing hay on his family's farm in rural Ontario, said of the early days of his career that he was full of "hiss and vinegar." But he was really a fan's player. Renowned for his showmanship and care with fans, he was flamboyant on and off the ice—as ready to beat you with a wicked slapper as he was to win you over with his million-dollar smile. With one Stanley Cup and all his personal hardware to go along with his physical play, it wasn't long before Hull was acclaimed as the finest Black Hawks player in history. One-time Chicago coach Billy Reay summed it up succinctly: "He's the greatest hockey player I've ever seen."

Hull's star rose at the same time as fellow forward Stan Mikita. The two were as dangerous a one-two punch as there was in the league, and although Mikita was less flashy than Hull, the duo quickly became the face of the franchise, along with "Mr. Goalie," Glenn Hall, of course.

★ ★ ★ ★

Stan Mikita was born Stanislav Guoth in what is now Slovakia. At 5-foot-9 and 170 pounds, he was hardly the biggest man on the ice, but he was always one of the slickest, and after he got his temper under control, the center became one of the most revered players in franchise history.

Mikita was born in 1940 during World War II when Germany was overrunning Eastern Europe. Germany surrendered when he was turning five, but the Soviet Union's Communist regime replaced the Germans. Joe and Anne Mikita, relatives who lived in Canada, arranged a visit to their homeland when Stan was eight. Mainly due to the bleak conditions in Czechoslovakia, Stan's parents reluctantly agreed to have him adopted by his aunt and uncle and taken to Canada. Stan was young and innocent and did not truly understand the world around him, but he was old enough to have the plan discussed with him and he accepted it at first, although later he shed tears in Prague when the train pulled away and left his parents behind.

Joe and Anne raised Stan in St. Catharines, Ontario, which eventually became home to the Black Hawks' junior hockey affiliate, the Teepees.

Mikita's pull toward hockey began after joining some boys outside his house to play pickup. They welcomed him and he learned the sport and English roughly simultaneously. He was a natural, and by 13 his hockey rights were claimed by the Teepees. He spent three seasons as a star there. Coach Rudy Pilous loved his game, and after Pilous stepped behind the Black Hawks' bench, Mikita was not far behind.

Mikita played three games in the 1958–59 season, and he fondly remembers his debut.

The 1967–68 scoring race featured Hull and Mikita neck and neck. Hull won the goals title while Mikita finished first in overall points. Here they ham up their battle for the media.

Centering a line between future Hall of Famer Ted Lindsay and Black Hawk legend Eddie Litzenberger, Mikita faced off against another future Hall of Famer, Jean Beliveau, and his Montreal Canadiens.

"It had to be the greatest night of my career," Mikita said.

It was the first of Mikita's 1,394 NHL games— all played with Chicago and the most played by anyone in a Hawks uniform. Over the course of his 21 seasons, Mikita was a nine-time All-Star, but early in his career he was better known for following the advice of his linemate Lindsay, a similarly sized player known for his bite.

Lindsay suggested that Mikita hit first and earn respect with his toughness, otherwise risk getting run out of the league. The result was that Mikita played an ornery, aggressive style and averaged 114 penalty minutes per season over his first six years.

Hall of Fame defenseman Bill Gadsby, who had previously played for the Black Hawks but

Bobby Hull with the WHA's Winnipeg Jets; Hull signed a million-dollar contract to move to the rival league.

The other indelible image of Mikita's early Hawks days was the establishment of the "Scooter line." The line of Mikita, Ab McDonald and Kenny Wharram was a top-notch two-way trio. They checked hard and had an offensive flare that often picked up the club when Hull's Million Dollar Line fell silent. The Scooter Line had an instinctual connectedness that allowed them to understand where the others would be on the ice. Mikita always summed it up as making "the obvious plays."

Maybe so, but they had to see those plays unfolding in their minds to make them a reality.

★ ★ ★ ★

To some extent, Mikita's career was often overshadowed by Hull's flashier play. By show business standards Hull was first banana, though in reality they were a tandem. Mikita always refuted newspaper reports that suggested he was jealous of Hull for getting more attention. The pair always got along well, he said.

Hull, too, never paid much attention to the press, and certainly not the numbers. "I left it to others to talk about the 'facts' that I could skate at speeds up to 30 mph and that I could shoot the puck at 120 mph."

But the one number Hull resented was the one on his paycheck. After numerous contract debates, Hull had become the first $100,000 Black Hawks player, but the negotiations were bitter, and while being the star of a franchise was one thing, being fairly compensated was another.

When the World Hockey Association came into focus in the early 1970s, the brass of the rival league intended to give their new darling some legitimacy by luring NHL talent to highlight their rosters. Money was the prime motivator, and Hull was the poster boy. The Winnipeg Jets forked over an up-front $1 million signing bonus and another $1.75 million spread over 10 years for Hull's services. He was the world's first million-dollar athlete, and his departure stunned Chicago and the NHL (the irony of the heart of the Million

was with the New York Rangers during Mikita's early days in the league, called him "a miserable little pain in the butt… I nailed him dozens of times, but I've got to give him credit. He always got back up."

It wasn't until Mikita's four-year-old daughter questioned him about his penalties, however, that he began to understand that "it takes an awfully long stick to score from the penalty box," as he recalled.

What transpired next was one of hockey's great transformations. In 1966–67, Mikita's eighth season, he cut his penalty minutes to 12 and was awarded the Lady Byng Trophy as the league's most gentlemanly player for the first time. Moreover, that season he also became the first player to be awarded three major trophies in a single season, snagging the Art Ross and the Hart Trophy in addition to the Byng. Just to show it wasn't a fluke, he repeated the trifecta the next season.

Hull, left, and Mikita stand in front of their United Center statues after their unveiling on October 22, 2011.

Dollar Line leaving for a million dollars was not lost either). Hull's defection raised the ante in the battle between the two leagues and forevermore made him a symbol as a breakthrough athlete who rocked the establishment, just as Joe Namath had with his $400,000 football deal with the New York Jets.

Hull turned 34 during the 1972–73 season and was the biggest star in the WHA, once again topping 50 goals. He was vilified in Chicago, accused of being a traitor. His invitation to compete for Canada in the Summit Series against the USSR was rescinded.

"Pioneers always suffer," Hull said later. "I don't care who is the first to embark on things. For instance, settlers that settled the West ... they went through hell doing it, but it had to be done."

In Hull's absence, Mikita became the de facto No. 1, and he answered the bell by ringing up three straight seasons of 80 points or more.

In the WHA Hull scored more than 50 goals in a season for five straight years, with the 1974–75 season being almost too spectacular for description. That year Hull scored 77 goals and added 65 assists for 142 points. His total was only 10 points shy of Phil Esposito's NHL record, but with accusations that the WHA was a lesser league, not many were singing Hull's praises.

Both Hull and Mikita hung up their blades in 1979–80. Hull at this point was back in the NHL after the older loop absorbed the WHA. But he remained a pariah to many powerful NHL figures and estranged from the Black Hawks. Mikita, on the other hand was the first Black Hawk to ever have his jersey retired, which happened in 1980.

In recent years, both players have become ambassadors for the franchise. When Rocky Wirtz took over ownership of the club in the wake of his father Bill's death, a major effort to entice famous greats of the past into the fold and make sure they made Chicago ice their home again was started. Hull and Mikita were top of the list.

What followed was the return of the exiled son. Fans who had never seen Hull up close were treated to the sight of him waving to packed houses in the United Center. In October of 2009, Hull, then 70 years old, strapped on skates for the first time in 18 years and helped christen the new NHL season with an on-ice appearance.

Hull admitted he was shaky on his skates because of old injuries but was pleased to be aided by his old pal Mikita. He stayed upright and the fans cheered as if it were 1961 all over again.

In 2011 the Blackhawks made one final show of appreciation, erecting statues of the duo outside the United Center.

"It hasn't sunk in yet, and I don't think it ever will," Mikita said of seeing his likeness readied for permanent display. "I've never been called beautiful, but I'm going to call myself beautiful tonight."

For Blackhawks fans, though, both are beauties, bar none.

The Big Streak

It is hard to argue that having the reputation as a rough and tumble team is anything but a positive in the NHL. The Philadelphia Flyers will forever be labeled "the Broad Street Bullies" in homage to the mid-1970s goons who mugged Stanley Cups away from the Boston Bruins and the Buffalo Sabres. Likewise, the Bruins were viewed as one step above scalawags during the tyrannical reign of Eddie Shore.

Similarly, the Chicago Black Hawks had their time as "the Big, Bad Black Hawks," when visiting teams were wise to supplement their lineups with extra brawn and double down on the protective padding.

Chicago has always been viewed as a rugged, salt-of-the-earth city with an appreciation for bodily contact in its sports. The famed poet

Chicago and Montreal mix it up as Bobby Hull (9) slugs it out with John Ferguson in 1968.

Carl Sandburg referred to Chicago as "the city of big shoulders." Chicago was considered as a city made up of laborers who built things with their hands, who put in an honest day's work and were never scared to get dirty.

Much of the reputation was gained in the stockyards. "The Yards" was the meatpacking district and a central identification of the city beginning in 1865. Chicago was "hog butcher for the world" and the cornerstone of the American meatpacking business. The men employed in the Yards were burly and strong and reveled in the physicality of sport. Many of them were of Eastern European decent and paid in sweat for whatever they earned.

They became Chicago Bears football fans and Chicago Black Hawks hockey fans, and they very much enjoyed a teeth-rattling bodycheck. And if an opponent didn't get up to skate again immediately, it resonated in the same manner as a hard tackle on an opposing running back.

With the inherent physicality of hockey there were always tough guys on Chicago's rosters, but the Hawks specifically became one of the roughest and most penalized teams in the NHL from the mid-1970s through to the late-1990s. Almost always in the top 10 for power play chances against during this streak—and often in the top 5—the club relished being tough to beat both on the scoreboard and in the corners.

Franchise savior Tony Esposito gave Chicago much-needed consistency between the pipes for 15 years between 1969–70 and 1983–84.

the semifinals and three times they played for the Cup. The club's one shortcoming, however, was failing to win it all during that otherwise successful stretch where, for 28 seasons, Chicagoans were blessed with a tough and talented club—and for more than half that time, they looked to one man to make the difference.

✳ ✳ ✳ ✳

Tony Esposito was a small bet that paid off big for the Black Hawks. Claimed with the second selection in the 1969 Intra-League Draft from the Montreal Canadiens, Chicago had relatively little riding on Esposito's success. Plucking him from the Canadiens' unprotected list cost them nothing but career backup netminder Jack Norris and $25,000.

Seldom do rookie goalies come into the league at such an advanced age. Esposito was 26 when he first laced up his skates in Chicago. The Canadiens had signed him as a free agent in 1967 after his starring turn with the Michigan Tech Huskies, where he backstopped the program to an NCAA Division I title in 1965. But Montreal was crowded in the crease and Esposito was never given much of a shot with the club, appearing in only 13 games in 1968–69.

So, with little NHL experience and a porous Chicago net, Esposito was given the task of righting a Black Hawks ship that was in deep trouble. The 1968–69 season saw Chicago finish last in the East Division, missing the playoffs for the first time in 10 years—and the beginning of the 1969–70 season felt like more of the same.

It wasn't until Esposito shut out the Canadiens in Chicago's seventh game of the season that the Black Hawks scored their first win. It was a momentum changer for the club as they lost only two of their next 14 games and went from worst to first in the regular season. And Esposito was the biggest reason for the Hawks' turnaround. He won a league-high 38 games, capturing both the Calder as top rookie and the Vezina as top goalie, as well as a first-team All-Star berth. He almost snagged the overall league MVP award

And despite the constant flow of players to the penalty box, the era of the big, bad Black Hawks ran concurrently with one of modern sport's most remarkable streaks: between the 1969–70 season and the 1996–97 season Chicago recorded 28 consecutive playoff appearances. That's more than any other team in the National Basketball Association, Major League Baseball or the National Football League, and is second only to the Boston Bruins' mark of 29 straight, which began two years before the Hawks' run.

Nine times during the streak Chicago reached

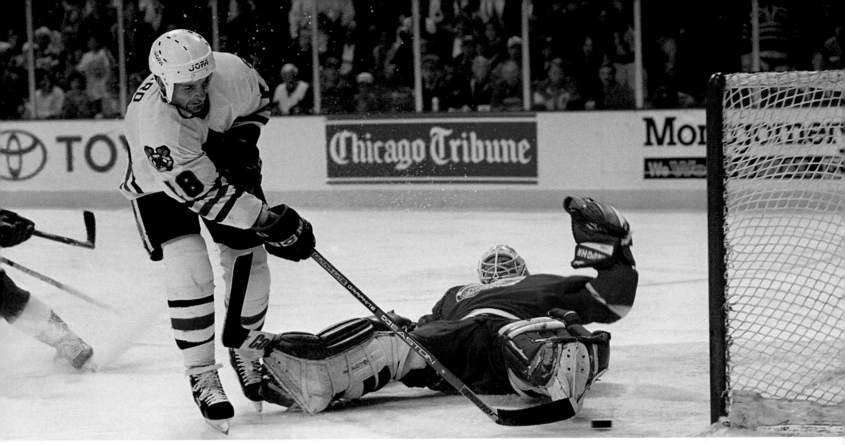

Denis Savard scores a highlight-reel goal against the Detroit Red Wings in 1995.

too, finishing second to Bobby Orr in voting. Most impressive though was the 15 shutouts "Tony O" compiled, which is still the modern-day record.

"I didn't want to win 5–3," Esposito said. "I wanted to win 5–0."

During his career Esposito notched 76 shutouts and won two more Vezina Trophies and three more All-Star selections, all while employing the then-rare butterfly method, which was pioneered by Hawks great Glenn Hall.

Esposito played his entire 15-year career (minus his 13-game call-up with Montreal) in Chicago. And those 15 years of service, which propelled the club to 15 consecutive postseason appearances, remains the hallmark of his Hall of Fame career.

★ ★ ★ ★

Another hero of the Hawks' long playoff run was Denis Savard. It was counterintuitive to think of him as a Chicago deity. He stood just 5-foot-10 and weighed 170 pounds and was French Canadian. Yet his scrappiness, his desire and his goal scoring won over those hard-to-please Chicago fans.

Savard played his first 10 years with the Hawks,

five times notching more than 100 points. At the tail end of his Hall of Fame career, he returned for three more seasons in Chicago. In 1998, the Blackhawks retired his No. 18 jersey.

Savard was famous for his devastating spin move, "the Savardian Spinorama," which paid with goals and was credited with bringing fresh excitement to the team upon his arrival on the roster in 1980. Savard was not really a big, bad Black Hawk, but one the enforcers sought to protect. His swiftness and his playmaking certainly helped sell tickets.

"Denis is not only one of those players who is a great hockey player, but a player with charisma," said former Blackhawks general manager Bob Pulford. "He's got that quality that keeps people coming out to see him play."

Fans were outspokenly unhappy when Savard was traded to Montreal for defenseman Chris Chelios in 1990. Although Chelios too became popular in Chicago it was for completely different reasons.

Of Greek heritage but a Chicago native, Chelios'

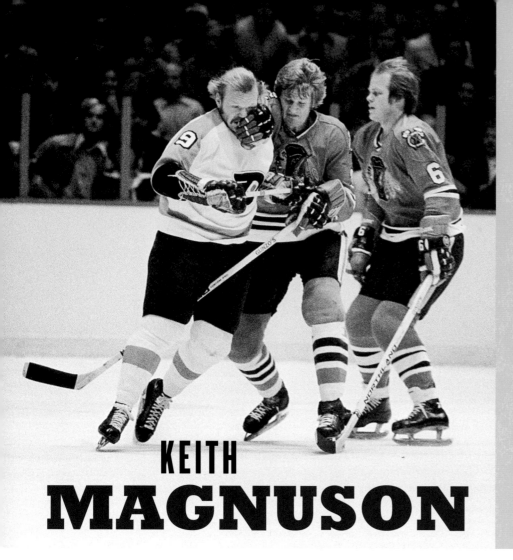

KEITH
MAGNUSON

Keith Magnuson was the biggest and baddest of the Black Hawks when he suited up for his 589 games between 1969 and 1979.

A two-time All-Star, Magnuson had the word "rugged" written in front of the word "defenseman" to describe him a thousand times. He was an integral part of the 1971 and 1973 teams that reached the Stanley Cup Final, and he even finished third in rookie-of-the-year voting in 1969–70. That season he led the league in penalty minutes, same as he did the next year. Never much of a scorer, Magnuson notched just 14 goals in his career, but he added 125 assists and innumerable bodychecks.

On December 15, 2003, Magnuson, 56, was killed in an automobile accident while a passenger in a car driven by another former NHL player, Rob Ramage, who was convicted of dangerous and impaired driving.

given name was Christos Kostas Chelios. He was bigger and stronger than Savard, and he took no guff from opponents.

Chelios was often whistled for being a tough guy while maintaining his All-Star caliber of play. He collected mind-boggling season penalty minute totals, three times exceeding 200 minutes, with a high of 282 in 1992–93. It was that season that he also snagged his second of three Norris Trophies as the league's best defenseman. The Norris is typically given to defensive choirboys who put up points and good plus–minus ratings while managing to stay as far away from the box as possible. It is not rare for the winner's point totals to exceed his box time. To put Chelios' 282 penalty-minute Norris win in perspective, the next highest penalty minute total by a Norris winner in his winning season is 162, set by another

Chicago bone-crusher, Pierre Pilote, in 1964–65.

To say you didn't mess with Chelios was putting it lightly.

Those early 1990s Chicago squads had many like-minded players, and it started from the crease out. Goalie Ed Belfour was a live wire. Another in the fine line of Blackhawks' All-Star netminders, he didn't take kindly to enemy skaters blocking his view or giving him any bumps in net. Goaltenders don't normally accrue many penalty minutes, but Belfour was an exception, as he hacked his way to 240 minutes over eight seasons in the Chicago net.

Belfour was an undrafted player whose time in Chicago started with shades of Tony Esposito. Belfour, like Esposito, won the Calder and the Vezina in his freshman year. He also took the Hawks to the Stanley Cup Final, and he continued to collect personal accolades, even though he couldn't get the Blackhawks over the hump.

Known as "Crazy Eddie," he argued with coaches and threw temper tantrums; but when he was on there was seldom anyone better.

"[Belfour] was the person who showed me that goalies could be temperamental, eccentric personalities," teammate Jeremy Roenick said. "It was common for him to stay after a game until one in the morning, trying to sharpen his skates the way he liked them. Eddie was crazy about many aspects of his game preparation. If he came off the ice and his chewing gum, water or tape wasn't where it was supposed to be, he would start throwing items and yelling at the trainers."

Not that Belfour was the first or last athlete to demonstrate such idiosyncrasies. Roenick, for one, was a bit of a loose cannon himself, famously partying so hard one night in Calgary that he ended up sleeping on the couch of a perfect stranger who happened to recognize him after he had fled the scene of a single-vehicle accident.

The best years of Roenick's career, and his longest stay with one team, from 1988 to 1996, were as a member of the Blackhawks. And boy did young Roenick shine as a swashbuckling, hard-shooting center.

The 6-foot-1, 200-pound Roenick never shied away from contact and he never shied away from the spotlight, frequently sounding brash and outspoken when quoted. He became the third American-born player to collect 500 goals, ending his career with 513 goals and 1,216 points.

Called up as a 19-year-old for the last 20 games of the 1988–89 season, Roenick impressed upon the Blackhawks that he was ready for the big league by scoring 18 points in his audition. He added another four points in 10 playoff contests and was in the NHL to stay for the 1989–90 season.

Roenick was the right addition to the Blackhawks at the right time, and his potential prompted the Savard for Chelios trade. The brash centerman's stick ably replaced the goals Savard had previously supplied, and he scored as

many as 53 in the 1991–92 season, including 10 game-winners.

Those Blackhawks were full of promise. The lineup was dotted with stars like Roenick, Chelios and Belfour, as well as less heralded but vitally important players like Steve Larmer, Michel Goulet and Steve Smith.

Mike Keenan, the iron-willed coach whose temperament Roenick described as being like "camping on the side of an active volcano," had a mandate to bring Chicago a Cup. He came close. His charges were tough and skilled—a Keenan calling card—and just about pulled it off.

If not for the indomitable Mario Lemieux and the very talented Pittsburgh Penguins, Chicago may have claimed the Cup in 1992. After dropping only two games throughout the first three rounds of the playoffs, Chicago came up empty in the final series, failing to take a single game from Pittsburgh, who rolled to their second straight championship.

It was the closest Roenick ever got to a Stanley Cup. Belfour wound up winning his with the Dallas Stars; Chelios, already a winner with Montreal, went on to win more with Detroit, and Keenan left Chicago for New York and led the Rangers to their long-awaited title.

Despite Chicago's nearly three-decade string of playoff appearances, the Blackhawks, like all teams, eventually met their match. As star players began departing in the mid-1990s, the franchise fell on hard times. The last postseason appearance of the streak was a harbinger of things to come. In 1996–97, Chicago narrowly qualified for the playoffs with a losing record and was unceremoniously dumped in the first round by the Colorado Avalanche. So dispirited was the Blackhawks' effort that twice they were shut out in the series, each time conceding six or more goals.

The heady times were followed by some of the worst, as Chicago missed the postseason nine of the following 10 years. Not until the emergence of the current crop of Blackhawks superstars had the franchise any hope for change—and as is often the case, the revolution was a rapid one.

CHAPTER 22

Three Cups and Counting

As good and important as the legendary duo of Bobby Hull and Stan Mikita were to Chicago hockey in the 1960s, there is a new tandem in town giving the old boys a run for their money.

They arrived in Chicago together as 19-year-olds for the 2007–08 season, one a No. 1 overall pick and the other a No. 3 overall pick. Expectations that the pair would shine were high, especially with draft positions like that, but what Jonathan Toews and Patrick Kane have helped the Blackhawks accomplish has been altogether extraordinary.

Before the boy wonders arrived on the scene, Chicago was in a free fall, only once in nine seasons qualifying for the playoffs. The club had cycled through eight coaches in that time, and while the franchise had picked up a few key pieces through the draft that would eventually pay dividends—notably defensive stalwarts Duncan Keith and Brent Seabrook, as well as current franchise goalie Corey Crawford—the team was a middling group. Aside from skill players like Tony Amonte and Alex Zhamnov who spent considerable time in the Windy City,

Patrick Kane hoists the Stanley Cup during the Blackhawks' championship parade in 2010 after winning the franchise's first Cup in 49 years.

AL
MACISAAC   STAN
BOWMAN   KEVIN
CHEVELDAYOFF   JAY
BLUNK   PATRICK
KANE
'88   JONATHAN
TOEWS
'19

BUD
LIGHT

THE CI

Jonathan Toews battles with Carolina Hurricanes Winger Andrej Nestrasil in 2015.

the roster was always turning over with rentals, cast-offs and legends on their last legs.

The club still missed the playoffs in Kane's and Toews' debut season—albeit by 3 points—but the youth movement had rejuvenated the Hawks. Kane was named rookie of the year, and both Kane and Toews were selected to the year-end All-Rookie Team. The never-ending rebuild was finally coming to a close.

★ ★ ★ ★

A born leader, the 6-foot-2, 205-pound Toews, who was born in Winnipeg, was named Blackhawks captain at age 20—the third-youngest captain in NHL history. Tough but agile, Toews does the

things that help hockey teams win: he's equally comfortable and adept at making plays in open ice or digging for pucks in the corner. He can hack and grind with the best of them and hold his own in front of the net, and his silky hands and accurate shot keep goalies and defenders honest.

But the biggest contribution the centerman makes to the Blackhawks is also the most intangible: his great capacity to lead. Toews fits the role of captain so well because of his maturity, which is beyond his years—something he says runs in his family. And so the nickname "Captain Serious" was born—and yes, even that rankles him.

"I've taken a lot of heat from some of my teammates for being so serious," Toews said. "I think my parents are both serious people who value hard work and not taking anything you've been given for granted, and that's the way it's always been."

STAR-SPANGLED BANNER

Any hockey fan will tell you that the anthem at an NHL game is a different experience from most pro sports. The close confines, exuberant fans and sheer volume are big reasons, but so are the singers themselves. Almost all NHL teams have a dedicated singer, and they sing loud, proud no-nonsense versions of the anthem.

For decades the Chicago Blackhawks have been known as the professional sports team with the most impressive "Star-Spangled Banner" singers, first Wayne Messmer and then Jim Cornelison. Their deep-throated versions of the nation's anthem shake the rafters and provoke so much enthusiasm in the listening audience of about 20,000 fans in the United Center that it is almost impossible for the team to do anything to match their vocals.

Messmer began singing the anthem before Hawks games in 1980 and kept it up until 1994, when he had a falling out with the team and took his voice to other sporting events in town.

Matching Messmer's emotionally stirring sound is Cornelison, who first sang the anthem for the Hawks in 1995 and has been delivering his rendition full time since 2008.

Patrick Kane jumps Antti Niemi as Patrick Sharp comes to join the celebration after Kane scored the Stanley Cup-winning goal in 2010.

No one ever accused Toews of being a shirker. His star really began to rise during his two-year tour at the University of North Dakota where he helped lead the Fighting Sioux to two Frozen Four appearances. Both seasons he took time off over Christmas to participate in the World Junior Championships for perennial favorite Canada. Twice he came away with a gold medal, but his signature pre-NHL moment came during the semifinals in 2007 against his future teammate Kane's American side. Tied after overtime, international rules dictate that the game be decided by a shootout. With a trip to the gold medal game on the line, Toews was called upon to shoot for Canada three separate times. He scored on each try, including the game-winner.

That same season Toews, who had still not played a single game in the NHL, was invited to play in the senior world championships, where he helped the Canadian side to a gold medal. To top off his international career, Toews earned gold medals with Canada at both the 2010 and 2014 Olympics.

In a good bit of joking among teammates, Toews is happy to hold bragging rights over Kane in international competition, where his Canadian teams have four times bested Kane's American squads. But Kane, from Buffalo, has his own list of highlights, including scoring the Stanley Cup–winning goal for the Blackhawks' first championship in 49 years.

Kane, at 5-foot-11 and 180 pounds, is an explosive scorer and talented playmaker whose quick feet and amazing puckhandling skills are among

Bryan Bickell (29) celebrates his game-tying third-period goal against the Boston Bruins in Game 6 of the 2013 Stanley Cup Final. Chicago would score again moments later to win the game and the Cup.

the very best in the league. His personality is more happy-go-lucky than Toews', and that has led to some TMZ moments for the right winger. But similar to great Hawks forwards before him like Bobby Hull and Jeremy Roenick, Kane's outgoing personality and proclivity for fun make him exciting to watch. He wears the flashy No. 88 and admittedly gets a rise out of pleasing the crowd.

"You try to make the fans come out of their seats," Kane said of his playing style, "and you put a couple of moves together to do that."

An example of Kane's crowd-pleasing ways came at the 2012 NHL All-Star Game where, during the "trick-shot competition" he donned a pair of Clark Kent spectacles and a Superman cape for a shootout attempt that saw him sliding (flying) belly first on the ice and unleashing a deke that went glove to stick for the goal. It was impromptu

prop comedy and creativity on a large stage, and Kane was voted the winner by the fans.

But Kane's bread and butter is his ability to get to the soft spots on the ice and elude defenders to either set up a scoring chance for himself or dish a pass to one of his teammates. He's often a bigger threat to pass than to shoot, and even though he is viewed as a goal scorer, teams know his playmaking ability is a one-two punch when coupled with his great shot and his knack for finding shooting lanes.

And the Philadelphia Flyers are well aware of that.

★ ★ ★ ★

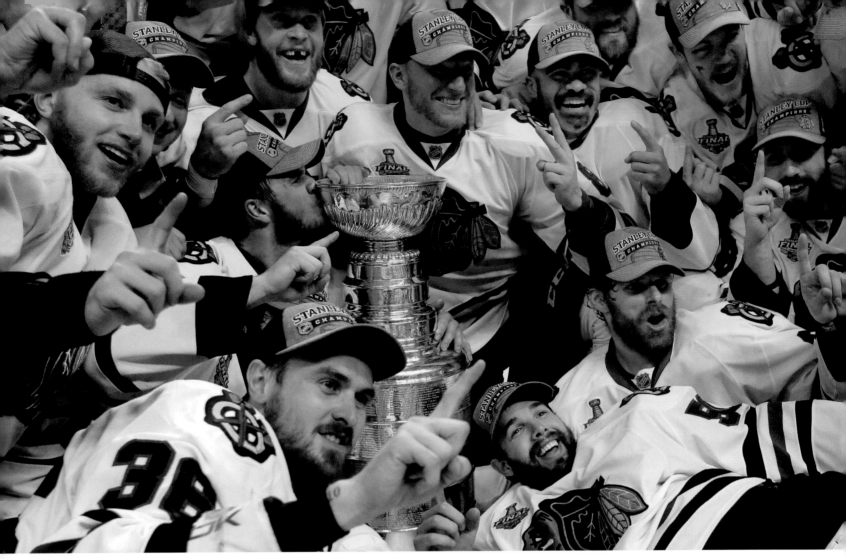

The Chicago Blackhawks celebrate their 2013 Stanley Cup championship; Marian Hossa, holding up two fingers, is all smiles after winning his second Cup with the franchise.

The 2009–10 season was the coronation of the new-look Blackhawks as a serious power in the NHL. The upstart squad captured the Central Division crown and then defeated Nashville, Vancouver and San Jose to land in the Stanley Cup Final for the first time since 1992.

Kane led the team with 30 goals and 88 points during the regular season and was second to Toews for the team lead in playoff points with 28. But more importantly he scored the goal that mattered most.

With Chicago needing one win to claim the Cup, Game 6 in Philadelphia was a freewheeling one that saw the Blackhawks control much of the action. In total they hit the Philly net with 39 shots in regulation but still needed overtime to decide the game.

And that is when Kane made the Flyers guess. After receiving the puck high along the boards to the left of the Philly net, Kane shook off coverage from defenseman Kimmo Timonen and drove hard below the circle and toward the goal. Now almost as low as the goal line, Kane let go a low bad-angle snap shot that caught Flyers goalie Michael Leighton out of position.

"I thought [Kane] was going to pass it," said the Flyers' netminder, highlighting the notion that Kane would choose to be the playmaker in the situation. "But he threw it at my feet and it went underneath me."

The goal was so unexpected, so awkward, that no one on the ice but Kane reacted. There was no horn, no goal light—even the Blackhawks weren't sure it went in. But Kane was, and he raced down the ice throwing his gloves in the air in celebration.

"I knew it went in right away," he said. "What a

CHICAGO'S BIG TEAMS

feeling. I can't believe it. We just won the Stanley Cup."

Toews was named most valuable player of the playoffs and was equally stunned. "I just can't believe it's happened."

But perhaps the most stunned, and grateful, was right winger Marian Hossa. He had been in three straight Cup Finals with three different teams—and Chicago was his first win. "I'm so happy I finally did it," Hossa said.

His gratitude was echoed by team president John McDonough. For 24 years he had worked for the Chicago Cubs, the kings of futility. Only after a handful of years with the Blackhawks did they become champions.

"I have been working in Chicago sports for 30 years and the feeling, the exhilaration, I feel tonight is indescribable," McDonough said.

McDonough had a large cast of contributors to thank for his elation: Antti Niemi, Dustin Byfuglien, Patrick Sharp, Kris Versteeg, Troy Brouwer, Andrew Ladd, John Madden, Brian Campbell, Duncan Keith and Brent Seabrook were just some of the difference makers, as well as coach Joel Quenneville.

But the celebration was short-lived. The painstakingly put-together team had to be broken up over money. Not everyone could be signed to new contracts. It was of primary importance to hang on to Kane and Toews indefinitely, but some integral parts of the championship team, like Byfuglien, Versteeg, Ladd and Madden, would not be back.

* * * *

Chicago barely faltered on the ice but was dismissed in the second round of the playoffs for two straight seasons. However 2012–13 would see a return to the Cup Final. That campaign was shortened to 48 games by a labor lockout. The team that adapted best to the shortened season was going to have the advantage in the playoffs.

The Blackhawks were almost surreally good, finishing 36-7-5. They got off to a quick start when labor peace broke out and never slowed down,

running away with the Presidents' Trophy for most points accumulated in the standings.

The Blackhawks then marched all the way to the Cup Final against the Boston Bruins. There was a second-round scare as old rival Detroit had the Hawks on the ropes, up 3-1 in the series. But Chicago came all the way back to win the seventh game 2–1 in overtime. The final against Boston was another tense series, and it ended almost as unexpectedly as their previous Cup Final against Philadelphia had.

Up 3-2 in the series and trailing Game 6 in Boston by a score of 2–1, Chicago pressed the Bruins. With less than two minutes left to play, Toews eventually worked the puck free from the corner and centered a pass to Bryan Bickell, who potted the tying goal with 1:16 left on the clock. Then, less than 20 seconds later, Chicago's Johnny Oduya kept the puck in at Boston's blue line by sending a desperation slapper toward the Bruins net. Surprisingly the shot hit the post and Dave Bolland banked in the rebound. Disbelief swept both benches and the stadium, and the Blackhawks hung on to claim their second Stanley Cup in four years.

Although a short time had passed between Cup victories this time, 18 members of the Blackhawks were first-time winners. It was obvious the team had been completely rebuilt, of course, around Toews and Kane.

In 2010, Toews won the MVP. In 2013, it was Kane's turn. He was only the fourth American to win the Conn Smythe Trophy.

After the championship was in the bank, owner Rocky Wirtz issued a statement of philosophy.

"We want to be positioned to win every year," Wirtz said, "and we're going to do that every year. We know we can't win it every year, but if we get in position, that's our job."

Prescient words.

Fast-forward two seasons and the Hawks again claimed the Cup — their third in six seasons and the first on home ice in 77 years. Duncan Keith was the rightful MVP, and Kane and Toews were pivotal when it counted most.

"It doesn't feel real right now," Toews said. "It's unbelievable."

Chicago BULLS

An HEIR for HIS

AIRNESS

The word *dynasty* is thrown around carelessly in professional sports. But if there were ever a modern team that epitomized the term, it would be the Chicago Bulls of the 1990s—not since the Boston Celtics of the 1960s had a team so thoroughly ruled the NBA.

Led by Michael Jordan and the coaching of Phil Jackson, the Bulls won six NBA titles in eight seasons. They won three in a row from 1991 to 1993, and then a seemingly burned-out Jordan walked away from the game, choosing to try minor league baseball for what turned into a sabbatical.

Scottie Pippen anchored the Bulls in Jordan's absence, and the team played excellent basketball, but they couldn't gut out a championship without "his Airness." And, as soon as Jordan was back in the fold, the Bulls won three more titles (1996 to 1998)—a dynasty interruptus, if you will.

The Bulls are the third Chicago franchise in NBA history. The Stags, who played in the Basketball Association of America (and later, the NBA) called the Second City home from 1946 to 1950. The Packers (later the Zephyrs) played two seasons in the NBA (1961–62 and 1962–63) before moving to Baltimore and becoming the basis for what is now the Washington Wizards franchise. The 2016–17 season will mark the 50th anniversary for the Bulls, who were a part of the NBA's rapid growth during the 1960s, which saw the league jump from eight to 14 franchises during the decade.

Oft-injured franchise star Derrick Rose breaks out of the backcourt with star defender Joakim Noah.

Overleaf: Derrick Rose looks on during a game in his injury-shortened 2013–14 season.

One of the pillars of early Chicago basketball was John "Red" Kerr. A terrific center in the NBA in the 1950s and into the 1960s, Kerr retired before the Bulls came into existence. He coached the team during its first two seasons and served as a broadcaster for what seemed like forever, up until his death in 2009.

Kerr grew up in Chicago and played his high school ball in the city before suiting up for the University of Illinois. He cared about Chicago basketball.

"I was here when this franchise was born, and one of the reasons why I so desperately wanted to be the Bulls' coach," Kerr said, "was that I wanted to make sure the franchise came into the world in the right way, so I could come back 10 or 20 years later, and still watch an NBA game in Chicago, even if I had to buy a ticket."

Kerr ended up having a free ticket for the rest of his life.

One of the first great Bulls, Jerry Sloan, learned at Kerr's heels as a young player in the league. Sloan, a superb player and eventually a better coach, was 6-foot-5. He was considered too small to be a forward and not fast enough to be a guard. Yet he succeeded for the Bulls in every way.

"Size doesn't make any difference," Sloan said. "Heart is what makes a difference."

Sloan was four times named to the NBA All-Defensive First Team and twice to the Second Team. His trademark hustle propelled him there.

There were other great early-era Bulls, though the numbers are limited. Bob Love was one of the great scorers in team history, and Norm Van Lier was one of the fiercest and best defenders—a player like Sloan who was willing to give blood in order to win.

But it was Jordan who put Chicago on the NBA's map. Drafted by the Bulls third overall in 1984—with special thanks to the Houston

Rockets and Portland Trail Blazers—the budding star made an immediate impact, leading the league in total points and being named Rookie of the Year.

However, it did take the Bulls seven years to assemble a team around Jordan that was good enough to win the first title. They have never quite been able to assemble a second collection of players good enough to win a crown without Jordan. Unlike the New York Yankees, who figured out a way to replace Babe Ruth and keep winning, or the Montreal Canadiens, who managed to continue winning Stanley Cups without Maurice "Rocket" Richard, Chicago has had no such luck.

Life without Jordan has looked like this: as of the 2014–15 season there has been one 60-plus-victory season and two sub-20-win seasons; there have been seven other 50-plus-victory seasons and six other 20-something-win seasons. Those seasons represent the highs and lows for Chicago basketball; everything else has been average good or average bad.

The exhilaration of the six titles captained by Jordan still lingers in the air among the banners at the United Center. The statue of Jordan out front testifies to his lasting importance.

"Overall, I think Michael Jordan is the greatest athlete in any particular sport," said the late sportscaster Will McDonough. "He dominated the game for the Chicago Bulls and brought the NBA to its greatest peak of popularity."

Jerry Krause, the GM during the Bulls' title run, who made trades, selected draft picks and tried to keep replenishing the cast surrounding Jordan and Scottie Pippen, was later vilified for saying that "organizations win championships," as opposed to its players. However, for as much as it rankled people, there was truth in it. As the All-Star Chicago players departed, and the great coach Phil Jackson left, it was the organization that dropped the ball and failed to rebuild adequately, letting the franchise become moribund before rising again.

In the second decade of the 2000s, there is a

Michael Jordan celebrates the Bulls' fourth NBA title, in 1996.

feeling in Chicago that the Bulls are in position to win their first NBA championship since the Jordan era. The focus is on point guard Derrick Rose, who is probably the greatest talent who has suited up for Chicago since the six titles.

Indiana Pacers coach Frank Vogel definitely became a fan when he first viewed Rose's skills.

"He's got Allen Iverson's speed, Jason Kidd's vision, Chauncey Billups' shooting and Michael Jordan's athleticism," Vogel said.

He does not have Jordan's rings, however, although the responsibility for leading Chicago to that next elusive crown has fallen on Rose's shoulders.

"All the days that you wake up, you've got one job, and that's to get better every single day," Rose said.

Winning one more is what Chicago hungers for—Bulls fans are no longer spoiled. They have waited as long as many other teams for a title. So they turn their eyes to Rose.

YEAR FOUNDED: 1966

NBA CHAMPIONS

1991   1992   1993   1996   1997   1998

RETIRED NUMBERS
And Honor Banners

4   10   23   33

Jerry Sloan   *Bob Love*   *Michael Jordan*   *Scottie Pippen*

PHIL JACKSON   **JOHNNY KERR**   **JERRY KRAUSE**

Coach   *Coach, Broadcaster*   *General Manager*

HALL OF FAMERS

Artis Gilmore

Michael Jordan

Scottie Pippen

Dennis Rodman

Nate Thurmond

Chet Walker

MICHAEL JORDAN NBA RECORDS

FINALS MVP AWARDS:	6
SCORING TITLES:	10
CONSECUTIVE SCORING TITLES:	7
CAREER POINTS PER GAME:	30.12
CAREER PLAYOFF POINTS:	5987
CAREER PLAYOFF POINTS PER GAME:	33.45
SINGLE SEASON PLAYOFF POINTS:	759 (1992)
SINGLE SEASON PLAYOFF POINTS PER GAME:	43.67 (1986)
SINGLE SEASON FINALS POINTS PER GAME:	41.0 (1993)
SINGLE GAME PLAYOFF POINTS:	63 (1986)

POINTS
29277
Michael Jordan

POINTS PER GAME
31.5
Michael Jordan

REBOUNDS
5836
Michael Jordan

REBOUNDS PER GAME
15.3
Dennis Rodman

ASSISTS
5012
Michael Jordan

ASSISTS PER GAME
7.0
Ennis Whatley

CHAPTER 23

Chicago BULLS

Humble Beginnings

They say the third time's a charm, and for pro hoops in Chicago it's certainly true. As a 1966–67 expansion team, the Chicago Bulls were a precocious bunch.

Jerry Sloan drives to the hoop against the New York Knicks in 1966–67, his first All-Star year.

Playing under Johnny "Red" Kerr, the former star center of the NBA's Syracuse Nationals, Chicago finished with a 33-47 record. Their .413 average was hardly news in and of itself, but it remains the best first-year record ever posted by an NBA expansion team. On top of that, the 1966–67 Bulls squad is the only first-year club to ever make the playoffs.

The postseason didn't last long, however, as the Bulls fell 3-0 to the Western Division's second-seeded St. Louis Hawks.

But the Bulls succeeded at something far more important. They managed to carve a niche in a major Midwest market that had seen professional basketball come and go. As one of the nation's largest cities, Chicago is always considered prime turf for any new pro venture, and the failure of basketball twice in the city left many scratching their heads.

Between 1946 and 1950, it was the Stags that called Chicago home. They played four respectable professional seasons across their time in

the Basketball Association of America, and later the NBA. Never posting a losing record, the club seemed to have a bright future. The team featured 6-foot-2 Max Zaslofsky, who made all-league four times and was one of the top early NBA players.

But as center Chuck Halbert lamented, "[We were] disappointed with the number of fans that we had." Mickey Rottner, a Stags guard, summed up the local indifference by acknowledging the newness of the sport. "It didn't catch on the way we all hoped it would."

After the club folded, the players were dispersed around the rest of the league. Zaslofsky was off to New York, and Chicago lived without pro basketball from 1950 to 1961 when the expansion Packers were founded for the 1961–62 season. That team won just 18 games but featured star center Walt Bellamy, who claimed the Rookie of the Year award and an All-Star berth. The next season the Packers changed their name to Zephyrs and improved by seven wins, but the team still floundered at the box office and relocated to Baltimore, hoping to find friendlier confines. Today the franchise is the basis for the Washington Wizards.

The 1966 expansion Bulls, playing in the modest International Amphitheatre, represented hope for Chicago hoops fans.

It was Kerr who was the main catalyst for success. His hometown was Chicago and he had starred in college at the University of Illinois

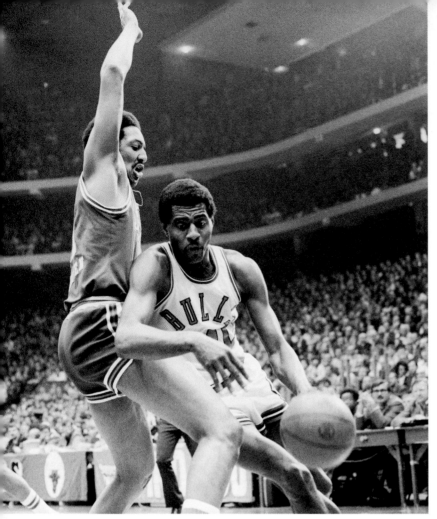

Bob Love drives around Kansas City's Ron Behagen in the 1975 Western Conference semifinals; Love and the Bulls defeated KC to advance to the Western Conference finals.

before his distinguished NBA playing career; the coaching gig felt like a perfect homecoming. He had not considered coaching at all until he began reading newspaper stories that suggested he was a bright guy who could do it.

"I figured that guys dumber than I was had coached in the NBA," he wrote in his autobiography.

Although most people believe the main task of a coach is to win—and Kerr's 1966–67 Coach of the Year award is a testament to that—Kerr said a major portion of his responsibilities with the club was public relations. The Bulls were trying to fill a vacuum and make more friends than the Packers/Zephyrs had.

"My biggest job that first season was selling the Bulls," Kerr said. "I went to every banquet and talked to every organization that would listen."

Kerr helped lay the foundation and coached the

Bulls in their first two seasons before a falling out with management sent him to the Phoenix Suns. He returned to the Bulls to work in the front office in the early 1970s and stepped in as a broadcaster in 1975. He remained in the booth until 2008. If there was one man in Bulls history that essentially saw it all, it was Kerr, who died in 2009.

Forward Bob Boozer out of Kansas State, who was also an Olympic gold medalist, led the offense in that expansion season. He averaged 18 points per game that year and 14.8 over his career. Point guard Guy Rodgers, a four-time All-Star and one of the league's premier assist men of the era, echoed Boozer's production, also averaging 18 points per game—he also led the entire league with 908 assists.

Jerry Sloan introduced himself to Bulls fans that year as well. He scored 17.4 points per game and earned an All-Star berth. There were some well-known players on the club too, such as George Wilson, Keith Erickson and Len Chappell. But they were largely outshined by lesser-known double-figure contributors Erwin Mueller and Don Kojis.

That the Bulls qualified for the playoffs in their first year of existence was a testament to Kerr's optimism and handling of personnel. It was a notable achievement, but no miracle followed in the Western Division semifinals. Still, it is the most successful expansion season in NBA history.

★ ★ ★ ★

Only a few years after Kerr helped the Bulls break the ice with Chicago fans, coach Dick Motta turned them into winners. His charges won between 47 and 57 games for five straight years starting in 1970, and twice they made it as far as the Western Conference finals.

Two savvy trades set the course for the Bulls' five-year run, as the additions of Chet Walker and Bob Love brought an explosive frontcourt to town. Jerry Sloan became the cornerstone of the back-court, and bulky 7-foot, 265-pound center Tom Boerwinkle was a load in the middle.

JERRY SLOAN

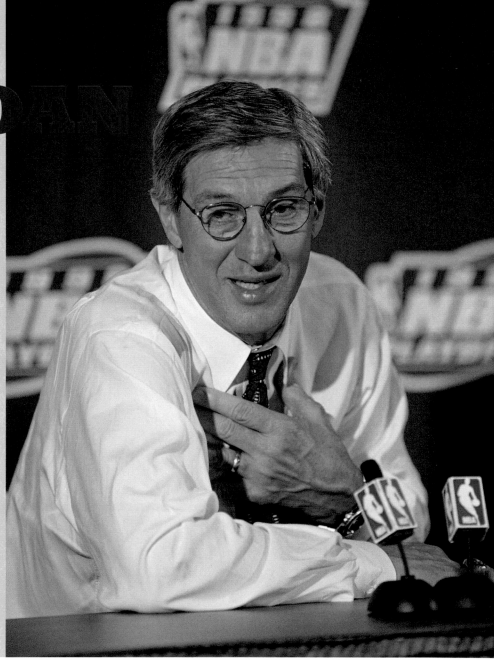

As a player, 6-foot-5 guard Jerry Sloan paid attention to all the little things and did them right. It was in his DNA; he was a scrappy player known for taking charges on defense, diving for loose balls and getting more rebounds (7.4 per game) than a backcourt man should. In his 11-year NBA playing career, of which 10 were spent with the Bulls, he averaged 14 points per game and was a two-time All-Star.

For three years, beginning with the 1979–80 season, Sloan coached the Bulls. His teams weren't great, and he suffered three straight losing records, but the major part of his bench reputation was obtained through his 23-year tenure in Utah. As coach of the Jazz, Sloan methodically molded the team in his vision, and twice they were crowned kings of the west. And although he didn't end up winning a championship in Utah, his long-term success earned him a spot in the Basketball Hall of Fame.

Walker might well have been one of the most underrated great players in NBA history, simply because he was never asked to be top banana, but always shared the stage with other acts.

An exceptionally smooth player, Walker was nicknamed "Chet the Jet." He was 6-foot-6 and a deadly midrange jump shooter with the ability to slither to the hoop between taller defenders. Walker was talented as well as durable. He made seven NBA All-Star Teams and played in more than 1,000 games during a 13-year career.

Even more than his steady scoring, Walker took pride in never suffering a serious long-term injury that knocked him out of more than a handful of games in a season.

"I feel real good about it because it shows that I worked hard and earned my pay," Walker said.

Although the recognition was a long time coming, Walker was selected for the Naismith Memorial Basketball Hall of Fame in 2012.

Love was a 6-foot-8 forward with silky hands who scored at least 19 points per game for Chicago over his seven seasons with the club. A three-time All-Star, Love's No. 10 jersey has been retired by

Norm Van Lier drives past Kareem Abdul-Jabbar in 1973–74, one of three All-Star seasons for Van Lier.

the Bulls. His career almost never happened, though. Love endured a nearly crippling stuttering problem. Basketball was salvation for the big forward. After he retired, however, Love's speech impediment kept him from landing a job that paid enough to keep him above the poverty line. Eventually, while working as a dishwasher for $4.45 an hour, his kindly employer paid for him to undergo speech therapy.

Always a Bulls favorite, Love eventually became the community relations director for the team, giving his first public speech to a room full of children in 1987. Love stepped up to the podium and dialed in, just like on the court. "It was game time," he said.

With Love, Walker, Sloan, Boerwinkle and point guard Bob Weiss acting as key cogs in the system, the 1971–72 season saw the Bulls post a 57-25 record. The franchise rounded out the roster with solid contributors in fiery guard Norm Van Lier and forward-center Clifford Ray.

Ray was solid on the glass, pulling down more than 10 rebounds per game, and was an important backup in the frontcourt, especially after Boerwinkle injured his knee at the end of the regular season. But it was Van Lier, also known as "Stormin' Norman," who really thrust himself into the picture. He averaged 12.1 points and 7.1 assists per game, and his ferocious defensive play made him a fan favorite. It seemed there was a private competition between him and Sloan to see who could give more of their bodies in an attempt to stifle the opposition.

With all due respect to Ray, it is possible that Boerwinkle's injury cost the Bulls a first appearance in the championship series, or even an NBA title. The team had scoring punch, superb passing and a hard-nosed defensive attitude. Chicago had the ingredients to win, and for fans of the era it is hard not to think about what could have been with a healthy Boerwinkle.

Instead the Bulls lost in the seventh game of the Western Conference finals to the Los Angeles Lakers.

"We had a terrific team, but we never could quite get over the hump," Love said.

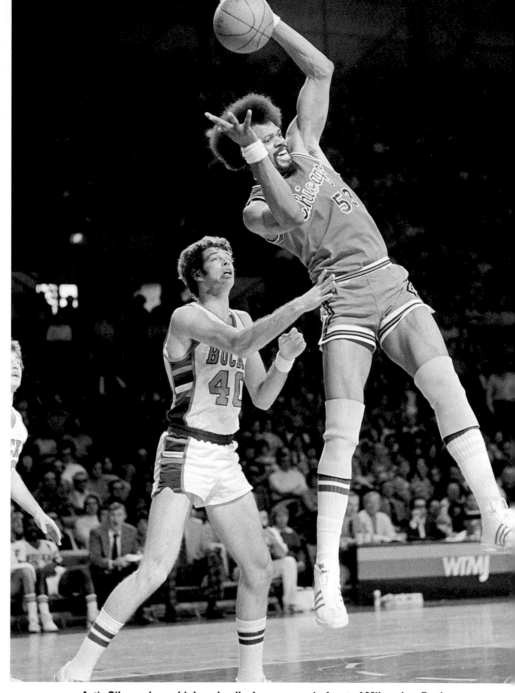

★ ★ ★ ★

The Bulls actually won their only Midwest Division title on Motta's watch with their 47-win campaign of 1974–75, but once again they got hung up in the conference finals, losing to Golden State in seven games.

A year later things fell apart. Chicago finished 24-58, and that was the end for Motta. New coach Ed Badger was handed the keys, and the 1976–77 season looked like it could easily sputter to a halt. But the Bulls got a lucky break. Badger's time came as the merger between the NBA and the American Basketball Association took effect. The NBA absorbed selected teams, but the remaining players were put into a dispersal draft.

The Bulls landed 7-foot-2 center Artis Gilmore, who was probably 7-foot-8 with his Afro haircut. The future Hall of Famer eased right into the Bulls' lineup, and the terrible team of the year before bounced back, recording a 44-38 mark—good enough to make the playoffs. Gilmore contributed 18.2 points per game.

It was a nice coaching job by Badger, but when the Bulls regressed to a 40-42 mark the next year, he was gone. Two coaches later, Sloan, who had retired as a player, finally led the Bulls back to the playoffs in 1981. They didn't stay there very long.

Through the rest of the Sloan regime, through Phil Johnson, Rod Thorn and Paul Westhead, and into the second year of the Kevin Loughery reign, the Bulls were nonfactors. Van Lier, Gilmore and the smoothly talented Reggie Theus labored notably with insufficient reinforcements.

In the 1984–85 season, Loughery's second and last at the helm, the Bulls finished 38-44 and made the playoffs. Much more notably, they introduced

Artis Gilmore leaps high and pulls down a pass in front of Milwaukee Bucks center John Gianelli in 1978.

a new face to the Chicago Stadium spectators. A 6-foot-6 guard of transcendent skill who was drafted out of North Carolina graced the old stadium's floor. Michael Jordan was a sensation. He was chosen the NBA's Rookie of the Year for averaging 28.2 points, 6.5 rebounds and 5.9 assists per game. And the best was certainly still to come. Soon enough Jordan would define a golden era for the Bulls.

Michael Arrives

Perhaps the most scrutinized draft selection in NBA history is the second overall pick in the 1984 draft. It was for this draft that Michael Jordan, after completing his junior year at North Carolina, declared himself ready to play in the NBA.

Michael Jordan, tongue wagging, goes hard to the rim over Cleveland's Craig Ehlo in 1988–89.

During his three seasons with the Tar Heels, Jordan had averaged 17.7 points per game. He vanquished Georgetown with the winning jump shot in the 1982 NCAA championship game, and he was a two-time first-team All-American (1983 and 1984). Jordan was hardly a mystery to talent seekers, but no one predicted he would become the phenomenon that he did. His trajectory had him pegged as an NBA starter, and it wouldn't have been off course to suggest he'd become an NBA All-Star. But the best player who ever lived? Nobody saw that coming.

The Houston Rockets drafted Hakeem Olajuwon with the No. 1 overall pick in 1984. Since big men with grace and ability are always at a premium, there wasn't much need to explain the Rockets' pick.

Michael Jordan puts up the winning shot for the University of North Carolina at the 1982 NCAA finals against Georgetown University.

Besides, although born in Nigeria, Olajuwon was local. The 7-foot center played his college ball at the University of Houston.

Olajuwon went on to become a 12-time NBA All-Star. He finished his career averaging 21.8 points per game, led the Rockets to two NBA titles and was elected to the Basketball Hall of Fame. So Houston did well by their first-round pick.

The Portland Trail Blazers, who had the second overall pick, also decided they needed to go big. Olajuwon was the best prospect at center, but Sam Bowie was no slouch either. At 7-foot-1, Bowie was a superstar in high school and a second-team All-American in 1981 for the University of Kentucky. He struggled with injury, though, and while he was a decent prospect, hindsight illustrates he wasn't in the top four at the 1984 draft—given the Trail Blazers could have also selected future Hall of Famers Charles

Barkley or John Stockton. But the Blazers needed a big man to bolster their lineup and complement Clyde Drexler, the guard they selected the previous year. Jordan was never really on their radar. But, he probably should have been.

As a pro Bowie averaged 10.9 points per game, but he mostly spent his time battling through numerous foot and leg injuries. Today, Bowie's claim to fame is that he was selected one spot ahead of the best player of all time, as the Bull's happily picked Jordan third overall.

★ ★ ★ ★

Jordan's statement to the NBA that he would be a force to be reckoned with came in the third game of the 1984–85 season. His 37 points against the Milwaukee Bucks equaled his total output from his first two NBA starts.

However, despite Jordan's 28.2 points per game in his rookie season, the team was not a

JERRY KRAUSE

A one-time Major League Baseball scout, Jerry Krause showed that his eye for finding talent was just as sharp on the hard court as it was on the diamond. His was the managerial mind that assembled the Bulls roster that won six NBA crowns. Although Krause was frequently overshadowed by Michael Jordan and coach Phil Jackson, and his contributions even sometimes belittled, there is no denying the impact he had on those 1990s Bulls clubs.

Krause's skill drafting players, coupled with his ability to make trades and fill in with new faces at the right time, enabled Chicago to remain on top. He was the man who brought in Scottie Pippen, Horace Grant and Dennis Rodman—and even had the guts to make the unpopular decision to deal away Charles Oakley. Twice Krause was named NBA Executive of the Year.

one-draft-choice fix. The Bulls' biggest offensive threats outside of their All-Star rookie were the oft-troubled guard Quintin Dailey and 6-foot-9 forward Orlando Woolridge. Woolridge was the only other Bulls player to post more than 20 points per game, so it was hard not to argue that Jordan should have the ball in his hands as often as possible.

The fans seemed to agree. During the Bulls' dismal 27-55 campaign in 1983–84, the franchise drew 256,430 fans to home games, ranking them 21st out of 23 teams in the NBA in attendance. With Jordan in the fold the next year, the Bulls nearly doubled their overall attendance, attracting 487,297 fans to home games to rank ninth in the league.

Word spread fast that Jordan was a one-of-a-kind talent.

"If you look up the definition of greatness in the dictionary," Los Angeles Lakers great Elgin Baylor once said, "it will say Michael Jordan."

Praise like that from a Hall of Famer who some say was the precursor to Jordan was a ringing endorsement.

Jordan was a guy who could perform magic with a basketball. He could seemingly score at will, he was willing to dunk from anywhere near the key, and he made gutsy and inventive no-look passes to teammates who were often as surprised as his opponents. All of it provided first-rate entertainment, and even if he couldn't beat other teams single-handedly, he certainly tried.

Jordan did things with a basketball that left those competing against him on the court gasping. On the occasion of Jordan's hitting a famous game-winning 1989 playoff shot against the Cleveland Cavaliers, Cleveland center Brad Daugherty said, "I don't know how he stayed in the air that long."

This was early-era Jordan. Chicago and the rest of the NBA were getting used to his swagger, and its physical manifestations—sticking his tongue out in anticipation—really rubbed some

Bill Cartwright challenges former New York teammate Patrick Ewing during the first round of the 1990–91 playoffs. The Bulls won the game 126–85, handing the Knicks their worst playoff loss ever.

people the wrong way. Comparisons to Wilt Chamberlain's dominance abounded, but mostly, what people started to notice was that the boy who grew up in Wilmington, North Carolina, had an incredible will to win.

"There is no 'i' in team," Jordan said, "but there is in win."

Less apparent, at first, was Jordan's capacity to internalize any perceived insult or slight and use it to later stoke his inner fire. He turned perceived weaknesses into strengths in order to make people eat their words. Jordan had zero tolerance for doubters. Part of that was having the arrogance to be great. Part of it was his need to seize anything he could to feed upon as motivation.

"Obstacles don't have to stop you," Jordan once said. "If you run into a wall, don't turn around and give up. Figure out how to climb it, go through it, or work around it."

Attitude may be half the battle in some people's minds, but even General Custer couldn't do much about the situation when he was outnumbered and surrounded. And to a large extent during Jordan's early years in the NBA, that was his situation. Other teams had much more talent and depth than the Bulls. Jordan could lead Chicago to victories in games it otherwise would not have been in, but he could not overcome every obstacle thrust in front of him by each foe.

His second season was a washout. He broke his foot and played in just 18 regular-season games. Recovered by March, Jordan rejoined the Bulls for the playoffs, and in a game against the Boston Celtics he turned in one of the greatest playoff performances of all time, scoring an incredible 63 points. But the most amazing part of Jordan's night? The Bulls lost 135-131 in overtime.

Famously, Larry Bird, the Celtics' future Hall of Famer, said after the game, "That was God disguised as Michael Jordan. I couldn't believe anybody could do that against the Boston Celtics."

The math was simple: Jordan was extraordinary and the Bulls were underwhelming, which equaled exciting individual highlights and very little team success. And bigger than Jordan's 63-point playoff game was what came next. In his third season (1986–87), clearly fully recovered from his foot problem, Jordan scored at a 37.1 clip. It was the NBA's highest point-per-game total since Wilt Chamberlain posted four years of astronomical numbers between 1959–60 and 1962–63. No one in the league has posted a total as high since. For Jordan it was the first of seven straight scoring titles, all of them at an average of at least 30 points per game.

The 10th coach to lead the Bulls since Dick Motta's eight-year reign ended in 1976 was Doug Collins, who got the job after Stan Albeck floundered in 1985–86.

Collins, a former Olympian and NBA first-overall pick, was a surprise hire by the Bulls for the 1986–87 season, given that he'd never coached a game in his life and had only been an assistant with Arizona State for two years. But his leadership improved the Bulls by 10 wins that season, and a year later Chicago finished 50-32, their best record in 15 years.

"I was the kind of guy to roll up my sleeves and make something happen," said Collins of the attitude he brought with him to Chicago.

General manager Jerry Krause had made sure to provide Collins with some much-needed reinforcements. By 1986–87, depth center Dave Corzine was the only holdover from the pre-Jordan days. Krause's remake included Charles Oakley, who was added for the 1985 season, as well as Scottie Pippen and Horace Grant. Krause had snatched Pippen in a draft-day trade with Seattle and selected Grant at the same draft. Both were rookies for the 1987–88 season.

Pippen famously became Jordan's right-hand man during the Bulls' championship runs, and Grant, who wore some of the most arresting eye protection in NBA history, became a starter and double-figure scorer over a 17-year career that saw four championships.

Krause made a controversial move when he traded Oakley the night before the 1988 NBA draft. He swapped the muscular power forward, a close Jordan comrade, to the New York Knicks for center Bill Cartwright. Cartwright was a ballerina on his feet compared with Corzine and another newcomer, Will Perdue. But Jordan was not happy about the deal, and the Knicks made Oakley a part of their nucleus for 10 years. Cartwright wasn't as good a scorer or rebounder as Oakley, and he was on the back end of his 16-year NBA career. But he added some veteran savvy to a team that, including him, had only three players 30 or older.

Another Krause newcomer was guard Craig Hodges, whom the GM brought in from the Phoenix Suns. Hodges was never a starter in Chicago, instead filling a specialist role off the bench. His pleasure was the long ball, and three times in his

Chicago Bulls' Scottie Pippen controls the ball against the Atlanta Hawks in 1992, Pippen's third of seven All-Star seasons.

career he made between 45 and 50 percent of his attempts from beyond the arc. Hodges won three All-Star Game three-point shooting contests, and in the 1991 competition he sank 19 straight threes.

Krause's wheeling and dealing earned him the executive of the year award for the 1987–88 season. He had constructed a house built to last. Now Jordan had a team to work with. And Collins guided the new-look Bulls to the 1988–89 conference finals. That series ended in a loss to the eventual NBA champion Detroit Pistons. And almost a month to the day after the series ended, Collins was gone—fired for what owner Jerry Reinsdorf called "philosophical differences."

It was a shock to fans, but little did anyone know that his replacement would become one of the greatest coaches in NBA history—and the man to help the Bulls go the last mile. With Phil Jackson at the helm, and Jordan and Pippen leading the way, the recently downtrodden Bulls became a dynasty that ranks as one of the finest in NBA history.

Three-peat

Phil Jackson never started a single game in his 10-year NBA career. Born in 1945, Jackson grew up in North Dakota and played basketball for the university there before being drafted by the New York Knicks in 1967.

Michael Jordan hugs the NBA championship trophy, as teammate Scottie Pippen looks on, following the Bulls' 99–98 win over the Phoenix Suns to win their third straight NBA title.

In the Big Apple Jackson was a role player who won two titles with the Knicks. He wore his hair long and was a liberal political thinker—a member of the counterculture. It was a label that may have made him anathema to conservative NBA owners as he attempted to begin his coaching career.

So, instead of landing a spot in the league as an assistant and working his way up, Jackson took the long way around. He learned the ropes with a professional team in Puerto Rico and most notably the Albany Patroons of the Continental Basketball Association, which won a league title under his guidance in 1984.

Jackson returned to the NBA when he was hired as an assistant by the Bulls in 1987 for second-year coach Doug Collins—it was Jackson who took over when Collins was fired after the 1988–89 season.

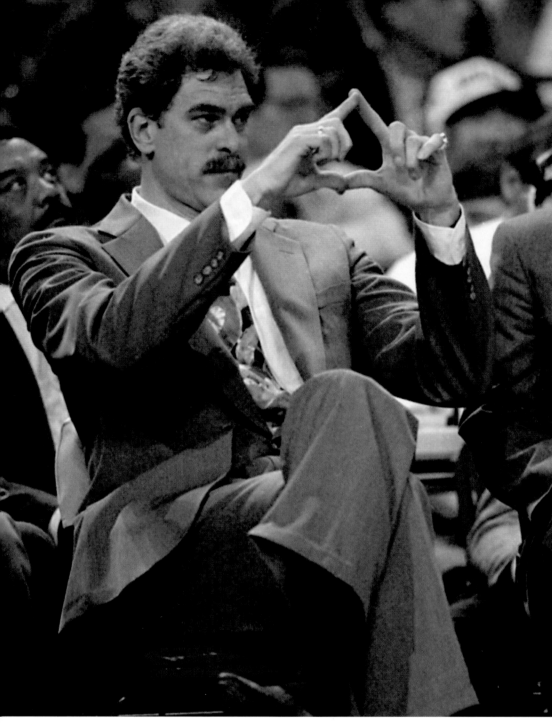

Bulls coach Phil Jackson signals for the triangle offense in 1991.

The offense is a give-and-go style passing attack that is routinely a three-pass offense. It was this formation, also called the triple-post offense, that became Chicago's cornerstone attack under Jackson.

And Jackson did more than adopt the offense. He practically adopted Winter. Jackson picked Winter's brains and relied on his advice throughout the Bulls' glorious era and later even hired him as a consultant with the Los Angeles Lakers when Winter was in his 80s.

Jackson's second order of business was to gain the respect of Michael Jordan. He was the key to the entire enterprise, and he had indicated frustration with past coaches.

At the professional level, the linchpin of success for coaches is the handling of personnel. They must be wise strategists that players will turn to with belief in crunch time as the clock is ticking down. They must believe in the reasoning behind a coach's distribution of playing time, even if they are not always thrilled by it.

As the Bulls' new bench boss, Jackson's first order of business was to install a new offensive philosophy for the team. Borrowing heavily from whiz coach Tex Winter, who had literally written the book on the triangle offense, Jackson introduced the tactic to his squad.

The crux of the offense is a sideline triangle created by the center in the low post, one forward at the wing and one guard at the corner.

Jackson was one coach who took to heart communicating with his players. He had been more backup than star, so he could identify with the bench guys. He had been part of championship teams, so he knew what it took to reach the top and be a winner.

Jackson, known as a deep thinker, was nicknamed "the Zen Master" not only because he sometimes appeared capable of reading minds and motivations but also because he genuinely wanted to know what made his guys tick. As an avid reader, he made a habit of giving gifts of books to individual players whom he felt would benefit from the wisdom contained within.

"I think the most important thing about coaching is that you have to have a sense of confidence about what you're doing," Jackson said. "You have to be a salesman, and you have got to get your players, particularly your leaders, to believe in what you're trying to accomplish on the basketball floor."

✷ ✷ ✷ ✷

For Jordan and the Bulls, the 1990–91 season was the first in which they truly broke away from the pack. Even Jordan was extra special this season, and the Bulls finished with the second-best record in the league (61-21), behind only the Pacific Division's Portland Trail Blazers. The 61 wins was a franchise record.

Even with the season as terrific as it was, it was the task of getting past the Detroit Pistons in the Eastern Conference finals that was a true milestone. The rugged Pistons, two-time defending champs, had bullied the Bulls before and were intent on dispatching them again. It was immensely satisfying for the Bulls to sweep Detroit 3-0.

"This is a team that has humiliated us in the past," Chicago coach Phil Jackson said, "mocked us, beat us physically."

Say goodnight, Pistons.

That playoff triumph sent the Bulls to the NBA Finals to face the Los Angeles Lakers, a team that

Magic Johnson goes head to head with Michael Jordan in the 1991 NBA Finals.

had knocked off the regular-season champs from Portland.

The NBA pumped Chicago versus L.A. as a glamour matchup. The Lakers, led by Magic Johnson, had won five NBA crowns during the 1980s. The showcase showdowns of those wins were against the Boston Celtics and Larry Bird. But now that the Bulls were coming at the Lakers, it was Magic versus Michael—experience versus inexperience. Fans loved the hype.

But the finals proved to be less mano a mano than coronation for the Bulls. Chicago was the hungrier team, the younger team, and Jordan's

Michael Jordan throws down two of his 39 points in Game I of the 1992 NBA Finals.

Paxson, shone on the big stage in Game 5. Pippen (32 points) and Jordan (30 points) did their thing, but the Lakers were blind-sided by Paxson's critical makes, especially after they tied it 93–93 in the fourth quarter. Paxson ran off 10 points in three minutes to help seal the deal in a 108–101 victory. That stretch propelled the 6-foot-2 former Notre Dame star into Bulls lore.

"That's why I've always wanted him on my team and why I want him to stay on my team," Jordan said after Paxson's moment in the sun.

When the game ended and the championship belonged to the Bulls, Jordan cried. He had been to the mountaintop as an individual, but now he had scaled the peak with teammates.

"I never showed this kind of emotion in public before," Jordan said, making his comment sound like an apology, one which no one felt he had to deliver. "We started from scratch, on the bottom, not making the playoffs when I got here. It took seven years, but we won."

It was Phil Jackson, the coach who was poised to begin a record-breaking winning streak of his own, who sounded like the philosopher he's become.

"We were fortunate and we were destined," Jackson said.

Jordan was named the league's MVP for the regular season and the MVP for the playoffs; he was a first-team All-Star selection, a first-team all-defensive team selection and the NBA's leading scorer. He probably had to build a new wing in his house for all the trophies.

By this point in his career, Jordan had stretched the normal boundaries of superstardom. His appearance as the face of the NBA dovetailed with the retirement of Larry Bird and Magic Johnson by the early 1990s. Jordan had wisely signed a shoe contract with Nike, and his rise also coincided with the NBA's effort to begin marketing its product overseas. In 1992 Jordan was one of the dominant personalities on the Dream Team,

star was still ascending. Even though Johnson—a tall and strong ball handler who could work you inside for a shot, or, more likely, make you pay with the perfect pass—had revolutionized the point guard position and was due his top billing, it was clearly Jordan's time. The young star posted per-game averages of 31.2 points, 6.6 rebounds, 11.4 assists, 2.8 steals and 1.4 blocks. Magic could only average one more assist per game than Jordan and a little more than one extra rebound while falling well short everywhere else.

The Lakers won the opener and the Bulls won the rest. The series wasn't exactly a rout because many of the games were close, including one overtime victory. But once the Bulls knotted it they never let the Lakers up again, taking the series in five games.

One of the overshadowed Bulls, guard John

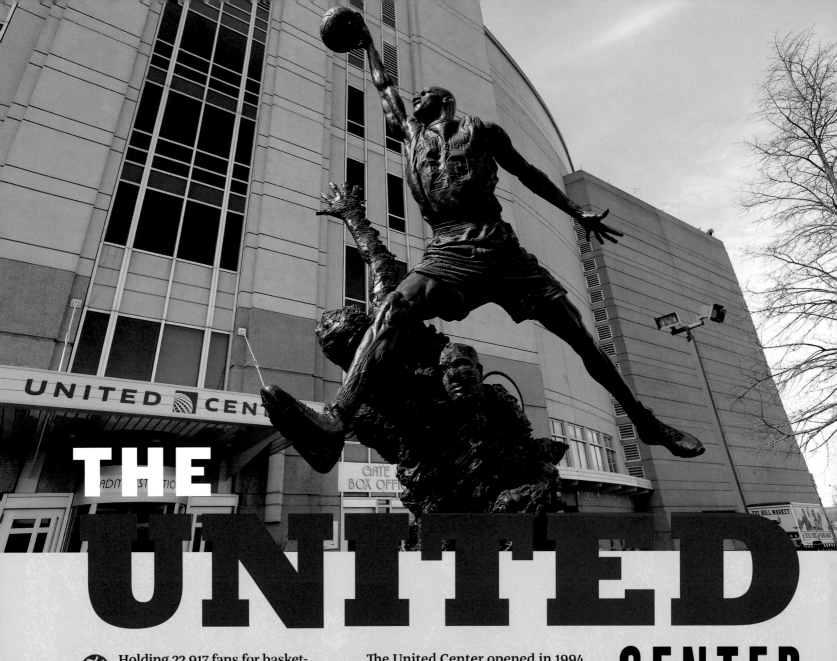

THE UNITED CENTER

Holding 22,917 fans for basketball, the United Center is known as "the house that Michael built." The moniker pays homage to Michael Jordan's popularity as perhaps the greatest player in NBA history. It was almost single-handedly Jordan's talent that made the demand for Bulls tickets skyrocket in the late 1980s and early 1990s, and the popularity of the Bulls and their championship-winning play necessitated a new stadium to replace the storied but long since past its prime Chicago Stadium, which had been hosting hockey since 1929.

The United Center opened in 1994 as a home to both the Bulls and the hockey-playing Blackhawks. Out front of the main gate is a statue of Jordan in his iconic Air Man leap.

Bulls retired numbers or banners hanging from the United Center rafters honor Jordan, Jerry Sloan, Scottie Pippen, Bob Love, coach Phil Jackson, coach and broadcaster Johnny Kerr and general manager Jerry Krause. There is also a special No. 72 banner commemorating the Bulls' 1995–96 season of 72-10, which set an NBA record for wins.

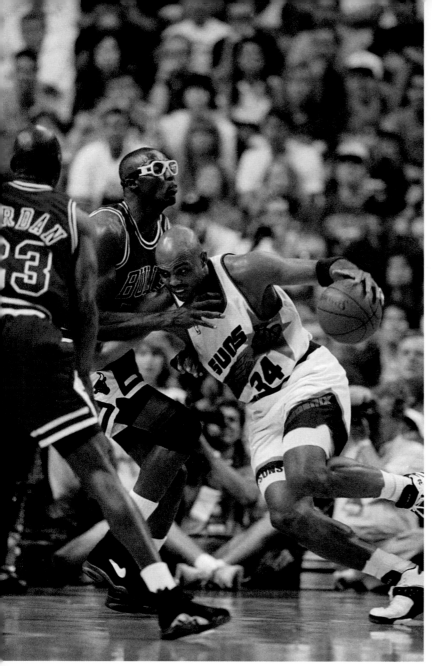

The Phoenix Suns' Charles Barkley drives to the hoop against the Bulls' Horace Grant during Game 6 of the 1993 NBA Finals.

was known for his work ethic. Each off-season he tried to add a new dimension to his game, to raise its level another notch. He was the personification of President Theodore Roosevelt's comment, "Let us rather run the risk of wearing out than rusting out."

The championship had ascended Jordan to godlike status, but he was just getting warmed up after the first NBA title—he and the Bulls liked the taste of champagne and they wanted to sip it every June.

Built for the long haul, the Bulls were even better in 1991–92, going 67-15. Most remarkable was Jordan's own repeat of winning all the same major awards he had been honored with the previous year.

In the playoffs the Bulls battled past Miami, New York and Cleveland and then marched on Portland, topping the Trail Blazers, 4-2, in the finals for a second straight championship. The core of the team was the same, although 6-foot-2 guard B.J. Armstrong played a larger role off the bench. The only team that gave Chicago more than a shrug of competition was the Knicks.

New York had won 51 games during the regular season and featured coach Pat Riley, who liked to run a nasty defense. Future Hall of Famer Patrick Ewing was at center, and other threats like Mark Jackson, Xavier McDaniel and Gerald Wilkins rounded out the squad. They also had power forward Charles Oakley, AKA "Mr. Elbows," who was itching to prove the Bulls made a mistake by trading him in 1988.

New York's defense proved tough as advertised, six times holding the Bulls under 100 points. But in the seventh game Chicago broke free of the shackles and won 110-81.

The finals against Portland contained some indelible moments, notably the Michael Jordan Show in Game 1. Jordan set a playoff record by scoring 35 points in the first half, but the Bulls were in such command that they hardly needed him in the second half. Chicago won 122–89 and Jordan finished with 39 points.

At one point, as Jordan was throwing down

the first all-professional U.S. team to compete in the Olympics. The players were like rock stars in Barcelona, and as this greatest team ever bull-dozed to a gold medal, it set the tone for the future of pro basketball around the world.

No one reaped the benefits as Jordan did. He became more renowned than almost all world leaders, his being arguably the most recognizable human face in the world.

And then things got bigger.

As much as he was admired for his skill, Jordan

one of his six first-half three-pointers, even he looked surprised, and he issued a sheepish shrug. Commentator Marv Albert said, "Did you see that look? Michael indicating he can't believe it."

After their Game 6 victory to win the title, the Bulls retreated to their locker room, but they emerged and returned to the United Center floor and performed a victory dance for their still-giddy fans.

There was no reason to pick against the Bulls for the 1992–93 season, either. Winning three straight NBA titles was not a rarity, and Chicago seemed as ready as ever to defend. The first team to capture three straight crowns was the Minneapolis Lakers between 1952 and 1954. The Boston Celtics blew everyone out of the water during their unbelievable run in the 1950s and 1960s with Bill Russell at center. Boston won eight consecutive titles between 1959 and 1966 and 11 crowns in 13 seasons in all. So, it had been accomplished.

In 1993, it took a little bit more work for the Bulls to join the list of teams with three straight championship trophies. They finished 57-25 during the regular season, and Jordan won his seventh consecutive scoring title, a feat only Wilt Chamberlain had ever accomplished. In the play-offs they topped the Phoenix Suns in six games in the finals.

Those finals stung future Hall of Famer Charles Barkley. It had been the Phoenix forward's best chance to capture a championship ring. At 6-foot-6 and more than 250 pounds of bad attitude, Barkley was at the top of his game, averaging 25.6 points and 12.2 rebounds per game in the regular season while leading the Suns to their best winning percentage in franchise history. His performance landed him the MVP award.

But in the end it was Jordan who would walk away with the finals MVP, even though John Paxson hit the winning shot with 3.9 seconds remaining in the 99–98 Game 6 victory.

After carrying a third championship trophy back to Chicago, it seemed as if the Bulls might be capable of a Boston Celtics–like run. But Jordan

John Paxson is mobbed after nailing a three-pointer with 3.9 seconds left in Game 6 of the 1993 NBA Finals to secure the Bulls' third NBA title.

had different plans, stunningly announcing his retirement from basketball and his intent to begin a professional baseball career.

It was one of the strangest developments in the history of the NBA. It seemed incomprehensible that the game's greatest player would simply walk away while at the peak of his powers. But that is exactly what Jordan did, signing a contract with the Chicago White Sox and being assigned to play minor league baseball in Birmingham, Alabama.

But the Jordan era wasn't over. Far from it.

Chicago BULLS

CHAPTER 26

Repeat Three-peat

No one was sure what to make of Michael Jordan's 1993 retirement from basketball—and they were even more puzzled by his decision to test his mettle at professional baseball.

Michael Jordan of the AA Birmingham Barons prepares for batting practice before a minor league baseball game against the Orlando Cubs on May 9, 1994.

As a right-handed outfielder, Jordan was definitely a curiosity in the White Sox's minor league chain, where he ended up playing the 1994 season with the AA Birmingham Barons of the Southern League. He was 31, ancient for a minor league rookie, and batted only .202.

It became obvious to everyone, including the notoriously stubborn Jordan, that even if at one time he could have become a Major League Baseball player, that ship had sailed.

So he came back to basketball and played the final 17 games of the 1994–95 season. Year two without Jordan had seen the Bulls stumble to a 34-31 record before his comeback. The Bulls' 13-4 run to finish the season made it very apparent that Jordan was the difference. He averaged 24.6 points per game in that limited stretch. But the proof that he was back, or at the very least that he would soon hit top form, came

Some dismiss Dennis Rodman as just a wild and crazy guy—which he is—but he was an important link on three Bulls championship teams. No forward in history has rebounded as well as Rodman. Using his elbows and ferocity to track down loose balls is what the Bulls paid him to do instead of scoring, and Rodman excelled at the task.

Rodman made almost as much noise off the court as he did on it. Sometimes he dressed in drag, sometimes he'd show off his multiple tattoos—before such a thing was commonplace among sports stars—and other times he told tales of wild parties and celebrity friends. More recently Rodman left fans gobsmacked when he visited North Korea to buddy up to dictator Kim Jong-un, whom he has called "a friend for life."

Still, the 6-foot-7 Rodman's importance to the Bulls' second three-peat can't be questioned, even if you can question the habits of the man.

DENNIS RODMAN

in his fifth game. In 39 minutes of basketball Jordan pumped in 55 points against the Knicks in a 113–111 Chicago win.

That pretty much eliminated the skeptics, even if Jordan could not instantly lift the Bulls to another crown in the ensuing playoffs.

Whatever the actual cause of his departure from basketball on that temporary basis, there was no doubt that Jordan was back where he belonged. And because he was back in a Bulls' uniform, it was also clear that the Bulls would be serious title contenders once again.

In its own way, as if anyone needed to be reassured, Jordan's career timeout proved that he was the absolute glue of the Bulls franchise and that despite the capabilities of his teammates, Scottie Pippen included, no Jordan translated to no title.

For Phil Jackson, who had weathered the two years without Jordan as well as any coach could have, there was no way to measure the addition to his 1995–96 team except to say there had been a hole and now it had been filled.

Come the 1995–96 NBA season, Jordan was locked on form—it was as if he had never been away. He even took his old No. 23 down from the rafters after wearing No. 45 for the 17 games he played in 1994–95.

It is difficult to suggest that Jordan was better than ever, but he was at least every bit as good. It was the Bulls, as a team, who were better than ever—in fact, they were the best in history.

Chicago set the still-standing regular-season NBA mark of 72 wins and 10 losses in 1995–96. They led the league in scoring with an average of 105.2 points per game and allowed only 92.9—a differential of 12.3 points, which was far and away the most impressive in the league. Jordan led the NBA in scoring for the eighth time with a mark of 30.4 points per game. When Jordan announced

Toni Kukoc controls the ball during the 1995–96 NBA season. Kukoc was a key cog for the Bulls' repeat three-peat.

Steve Kerr performing at the All-Star Game's three-point competition. Kerr was routinely called upon to deliver clutch threes.

Sensation" a chilly reception. However, as Kukoc continued to prove his usefulness Pippen and Jordan softened, and Kukoc became an important contributor.

Coach Phil Jackson possibly had the hardest job on the whole team, as much of his coaching time was spent massaging egos. It was a talented cast that was full of larger-than-life personalities. Jordan was out to prove he could still do it better than anyone else; Pippen was out to prove he was among the best two or three players in the league, even though he couldn't lead the Bulls to a championship; and Rodman—well he was unexplainable, unpredictable and straight-up weird. But man, those guys could play. Jordan and Rodman set the tone on the defensive end, swallowing up the men they guarded, and Jordan, Pippen and Kukoc set the tone on the offensive side of the ball.

In the playoffs Chicago rolled through the first three rounds, dropping only one game—a 102–99 overtime decision to the New York Knicks in the Eastern Conference semifinals. Chicago then met the Seattle SuperSonics in the finals. This was a team that boasted Gary Payton and Shawn Kemp—as good a one-two punch as there was in the league. But the Bulls paid no mind.

Rodman, a loose cannon on a good day, managed to alienate the entire city on Puget Sound with minimal effort.

"Too many people kill themselves around here," Rodman said. "They got so many damn coffee shops here because of one reason: People are bored and their lives are miserable."

Rodman did not say if he took one lump of sugar or two in his coffee. But he did revel in the boos SuperSonics fans showered on him. And

his comeback with the simple words "I'm back," it seems he meant it.

Scottie Pippen, who gamely led the Bulls in Jordan's absence but couldn't bring them to the Promised Land, returned to option No. 2 on the depth chart. And GM Jerry Krause continued to creatively fine-tune his behemoth. Depth players like James Edwards, Ron Harper, Luc Longley and John Salley were added for their specific talents, and in some cases their willingness to come off the bench.

Dennis Rodman, the rebounding maven who'd helped the Detroit Pistons win two crowns, was probably the acquisition who made the largest impact, becoming an integral piece of one of the league's stingiest defenses.

Relative newcomer Toni Kukoc was the third-leading scorer behind Jordan and Pippen, even though the main duo gave "the Croatian

even though Seattle won two of three games at KeyArena, Rodman still dominated the glass, pulling down a total of 36 rebounds over three games.

With a 3-2 lead in the series and Game 6 in Chicago, the Bulls took control, winning the game by 12 points. Jordan's joy burst forth. He was like a little kid, diving on the game ball to make it his. He then dashed into the locker room and began crying. The game was played on Father's Day, and Jordan was remembering his father, James, who was murdered in 1993, and how much he missed him.

Owner Jerry Reinsdorf said that after the 72-10 campaign the Bulls had to win the title or forever be portrayed as the team that let one get away.

"You get greedier as you go along," Reinsdorf said of capturing the fourth crown. "They're all hard, but this one we had to win or they'd be writing about it for a very long time."

The emotional Jordan reappeared and was as happy about winning this title after the all-around brilliant season as he had been when the Bulls won their first. He showed up at the team's celebration party still in uniform, a bit tear-streaked, drinking champagne and wearing only one of his Nikes.

Of course, since Jordan wasn't planning to try his hand at hockey or football, the expectations were as high as ever following the record-breaking season. The Bulls had to do it all over again or be considered a flop. That's meeting a high standard, but really it was no lower a bar than the Bulls had already set for themselves.

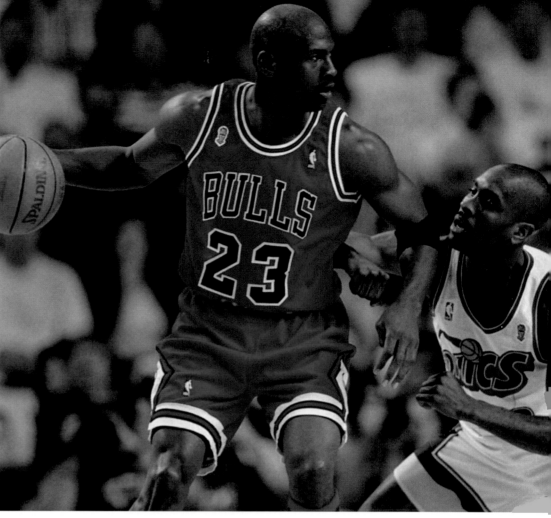

Michael Jordan is hounded by the Seattle SuperSonics' Gary Payton, the 1996 Defensive Player of the Year, in the 1996 NBA Finals. Jordan averaged 27.3 points per game in the finals, his lowest output in any of his six championships with Chicago.

The 1996–97 regular season was pretty much an instant replay of Jordan's first year back, as Chicago finished 69-13—tied with the 1971–72 L.A. Lakers for the second best winning percentage of all time.

Jordan did his thing, averaging 29.6 points per game, good enough for his ninth scoring title. Pippen averaged 20.2 and Kukoc 13.2, and Rodman averaged 16.3 rebounds per game. A group of sharpshooters, including Harper and Steve Kerr, roamed the perimeter, throwing down outside jumpers when needed.

The Eastern Conference playoffs were also nearly identical to the previous season. The Bulls rolled through the preliminary rounds losing only two games, one each in the conference semifinals and conference finals.

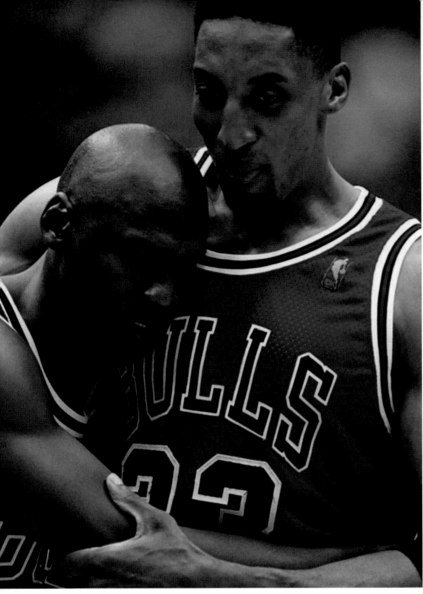

Scottie Pippen supports an exhausted Michael Jordan after the Bulls' 90–88 win in Game 5 of the 1997 finals, referred to as "the Flu Game."

In the finals, the Western Conference champions, Utah, presented a whole new challenge. Karl Malone and John Stockton, future Hall of Famers, had never been this close to a title before. Four games into the finals the teams were knotted at 2-2. Game 5 became the stuff of legend. Jordan was sick with the flu and seemed barely strong enough to stand up, never mind stand up to the muscular Malone.

Jordan woke nauseated and running a temperature.

"I was scared," Jordan said. "I didn't know what was happening to me. I felt partially paralyzed."

Trainers initially indicated he had stomach flu or food poisoning. He stayed in bed all day, and

although he was told it was inadvisable that he play, Jordan climbed to his feet three hours before tip-off in Salt Lake City. He was dehydrated, had lost weight and at times was dizzy.

When Pippen first saw Jordan he didn't believe he would have the strength to even put on his uniform let alone run up and down the court.

"I'd never seen him look like that," Pippen said. "He looked bad—I mean really bad."

Shaky when he took the floor, Jordan seemed sluggish and out of sorts. The Jazz, sensing the kill, ran out to a 16-point lead. Jordan and the Bulls fought back. Woozy throughout and later reporting that he felt like fainting numerous times, Jordan barely rested, playing 44 of the game's 48 minutes.

Jordan scored 15 points in the fourth quarter, 38 in all for the game, and when the buzzer sounded Chicago had a 90-88 victory. An exhausted Jordan fell into Pippen's arms. Jordan's effort became legendary in what was soon referred to as "the Flu Game." Apparently he was not the least bit tired of winning.

"That was the most difficult thing I've ever done," Jordan said. "I almost played myself into passing out just to win a basketball game."

Jordan's health marginally improved by Game 6, and once again he ignored caution. He scored 39 points, the Bulls won 90-86, and the team's fifth title was snapped up, just like that. Heading into the next season, it seemed as if the momentum would never stop.

This time the Bulls won "only" 62 games. Jordan won his 10th scoring title and Rodman his seventh straight rebounding title. How long could the Bulls keep it up? Rodman was 36, Jordan 34, Pippen 32, Harper 34 and Kerr 32.

The playoffs were a little tougher this time around too, and the toughest roadblock on the way to the finals was the Indiana Pacers and Reggie Miller. The Bulls led the series 2-1, but in Game 4 Miller hit one of the shots that defined his career, a three-point buzzer beater to win 96-94 and tie the series. Game 7 was a battle to the end, but the Bulls prevailed 88-83 at the United Center.

That set up a rematch with the Jazz and their stars Malone and Stockton, who having been bested before, were doubly intent on bringing home a championship. But the Bulls—and Jordan—would not let them do it. Game 3 epitomized the Bulls at their best. They slaughtered the Jazz, 96–54, leaving Utah with the lowest one-game point total in playoff history.

But even that doesn't live up to Game 6, which has become one of the most indelible moments in both Bulls' franchise history and Jordan's personal legacy.

Chicago led the series 3-2, and with the clock ticking down and the score tight, Jordan got the ball by virtue of having stripped Karl Malone on a double-team under the Bulls' basket. And with less than 20 seconds left, he headed up court, running the clock and setting himself up for one-on-one coverage from Byron Russell.

Russell closed in and Jordan drove to his right. As Russell sealed him off, Jordan pushed off on Russell, sending him further right as he crossed over to his left for an open-look 17 footer. Up it went. Down it came. Nothing but net. Jordan's outstretched arm hung in the air like an exclamation mark on the bucket that sealed the championship. Utah's last-ditch effort fizzled and the Bulls had their sixth title.

After the game Jackson found his star on the floor and embraced him with a hug. "Oh, my God!" he said. "That was beautiful. What a finish!"

Six world titles—and six finals MVP trophies. Fearful as he aged through his peak early years that he would never win a championship, Jordan had more rings than fingers on one hand.

After 15 seasons, as his 35th birthday neared, Air Jordan felt grounded. He did not wish to start over, either with the Bulls or with another team. In early January of 1999, Jordan retired for a second time. His mentor's contract was running out, and Jordan said he did not want to play under anyone but Jackson.

Pippen, too, wanted out. He asked to be traded and was moved to the Houston Rockets. Rodman became a free agent and was out of the game

Jerry Reinsdorf holds up the **NBA** championship trophy after the Bulls beat the Seattle SuperSonics for their fourth **NBA** championship.

by the end of the 1999–2000 season. Time had caught up to the Bulls and the good times were officially over.

The NBA didn't have to wait long for their next dynasty. Phil Jackson headed to L.A. to lead the Lakers in 1999–2000 and immediately took the purple and gold to their first of three straight titles.

The league's desire to replace Jordan, however, has been a tougher job. Kobe Bryant and LeBron James have been the most heartily endorsed nominees as his successors, but while many insist that every great new prospect could be "the next one," most know there never will be another Michael Jordan.

Chicago BULLS

CHAPTER 27

Fresh Dreams

Since Michael Jordan pushed off Byron Russell to nail the 1998 championship-winning shot, the Chicago Bulls have been in rebuilding mode.

The 1998–99 roster featured only six returning players from the previous year's championship, and the offense revolved around Toni Kukoc, who didn't even average 20 points per game. Between 1998–99 and 2007–08, the Bulls posted better than a .500 winning percentage only three times. And other than an appearance in the 2007 Eastern Conference semifinals, the brightest spot Bulls fans had in the 10 years following the 1998 championship was the drafting of Derrick Rose in 2008.

For Bulls fans the acquisition of Rose represented optimism. The wonder years of Jordan and the six league championships were paid for in frustration. The most glorious of times were succeeded by the worst of times.

Tim Floyd replaced Phil Jackson in 1998–99, and his regime did not last terribly long. A record of 15-67 in 2000–01 was the worst, but the remaining winning percentages were not much different. Floyd was

2011 NBA MVP Derrick Rose is the best player to suit up for Chicago since the heyday of the Jordan-era Bulls; he's seen here in 2014.

exiled in the middle of his fourth season. Bill Berry, Bill Cartwright and Pete Myers coached in the interim, but none could secure a winning record.

It was not until Scott Skiles took command for the 2004–05 season that the Bulls topped .500 again with a 47-35 mark. Once a feisty All-American guard out of Michigan State, Skiles seemed to possess the aggressive, take-it-seriously, play-hard-nosed attitude that Chicago fans liked. Seen as a hard-to-beat overachiever, Skiles carved out an 11-year pro career after developing a reputation in high school and college as a big-game player. He seemed to be the prototype of what many teams looked for in a coach—someone who knows the game and who needed to

have a stake plunged through his heart for him to admit defeat.

The 2004–05 Bulls made the playoffs and fielded a team with some exciting players. At last it seemed as if the makeover was completed. The addition of guards Ben Gordon and Kirk Hinrich, as well as forward Luol Deng, infused Chicago with new life. Prospects Tyson Chandler and Eddy Curry, both 7-footers, helped shore up the low post.

But after taking a gamble on Curry and Chandler, the Bulls made errors in judgment with the duo, dealing both players away and leaving the team perpetually understaffed in the front-court. Skiles, despite leading the club to its first

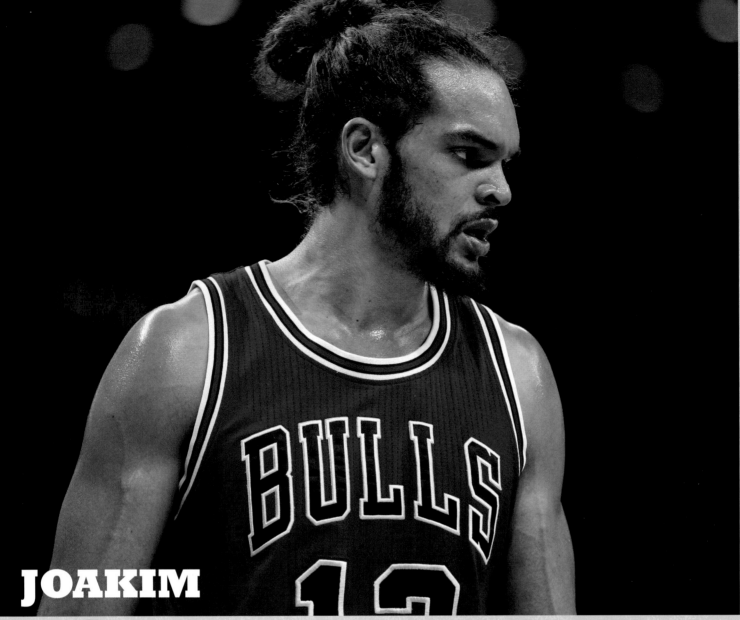

JOAKIM
NOAH

Some fans might not have known what to think when Chicago selected Joakim Noah ninth overall in 2007. He had size (6-foot-11) and pedigree (helping lead the University of Florida to straight NCAA crowns), but Noah seemed to possess iffy scoring skills.

What he really possessed was a deeply serious work ethic that enabled him to excel in the NBA in ways that are commonly described as doing the dirty work. The lanky Noah carries intriguing parental genes: his dad was French international tennis star Yannick Noah and his mother was a Miss Sweden. Noah has dual citizenship, but he plays for the French national team.

Noah made himself into a two-time NBA All-Star by playing extraordinary defense, combined with a hustling rebounding game. Sometimes his biggest contributions as a leader are things that people could not read in the box score. Over the last few years Noah has been selected for three NBA All-Defensive squads, and in 2014 he was the league's Defensive Player of the Year.

Pau Gasol collects one of his 919 total rebounds on the season in 2014–15. In his first year with the Bulls, Gasol posted career highs in total rebounds and defensive rebounds (699).

playoff series win since 1998 in his third year as coach, paid for the mistake before his fourth full season was up in 2007–08.

Although some fans may have thought so, the Bulls were not bad enough in 2007–08 to have much of a shot at selecting Rose in the annual draft. But the basketball gods work in mysterious ways, and Chicago, with a 1.7 percent chance of gaining the first-round pick in the draft lottery, cashed in on their long shot.

Rose was a one-and-done guard for Memphis, a backcourt player who lit up scoring columns when he was in the right mood, or simply elevated his teammates' play when he focused on passing. At 6-foot-3 and 190 pounds he had the muscle to deal with the bigger men in the pros, and his slick ball handling made him an ideal match for Chicago.

Even better, he was a hometown guy: born in Chicago, raised in the Englewood neighborhood and an alumnus of Simeon Career Academy. The only thing that diminished Rose's stature in the Windy City was choosing Memphis over the University of Illinois. Rose had his share of rough times growing up, but he always knew what he wanted to do and be—a pro basketball player.

"The hard part I had to go through in life, period, is living in poverty and not being able to get what I want," Rose said. "When I was younger I just thought about playing in the NBA.

It took no time for Rose to prove he was the real deal, winning the 2009 Rookie of the Year award and then winning the 2011 Most Valuable Player award; at 22 years and six months, Rose was the youngest player to earn an MVP award. From 2010 to 2012 Rose was chosen for three All-Star Teams, and he became the most popular new athlete in town.

His MVP season was guided by yet another new coach, as the Bulls lured Tom Thibodeau from the Boston Celtics, where he was fresh off of building a reputation as a defensive genius. This was a happy match. Along with Rose's MVP award, the 2010–11, Bulls won 62 games and Thibodeau was the Coach of the Year.

Chicago won two playoff rounds, and although the Bulls fell to the LeBron James–led Miami Heat in the Eastern Conference finals, they appeared to be a rising power. Rose had swiftly developed into a point guard extraordinaire. He had an excellent supporting cast and a coach that shaped up as the next coming of Phil Jackson.

Rose was the franchise player. He signed a new five-year contract worth nearly $95 million. There was only one problem. Rose struggled with injuries in 2011–12 and appeared in just 39 regular-season games. Even worse, in Game 1 of the first round of the playoffs against Philadelphia, he tore the anterior cruciate ligament in his left knee. End of Rose's season. End of the Bulls' season. His absence was critical.

The return of Rose for 2012–13 was the most highly anticipated event in the NBA. Only it never happened—his knee never reached full strength. It turned into a Bulls write-off season. It was also a season's worth of rumors. Rose would be back in December. Rose would be back in January. Rose's knee would never heal and he would never play again.

After a long wait, he was declared ready for action for 2013–14. The team and Rose took care not to push too hard in the lead-up to the new season. But once the games began for real, Rose averaged 31 minutes a game, scored at a pace just under 16 points and was making a successful comeback. But he lasted only 10 games. On November 22, he ripped up his right knee, tearing the meniscus. He again underwent surgery and again was out for the rest of the year.

The overall effect was devastating on the Bulls. With a healthy Rose on the roster they were title threats. Without him they were a good team, but they were easy fodder in the playoffs.

In Rose's absence, Joakim Noah stepped up to lead the team. He was named the 2013–14 Defensive Player of the Year and was one of eight players besides Rose (though some of them not full time) who averaged in double figures. In college at Florida, with his long hair in a ponytail, Noah seemed as counterculture as Phil Jackson had been.

In the pros, Noah is an unusual talent. For a big man he can really run the floor, and he uses his lanky 6-foot-11, 230-pound frame to block shots, harass offensive players and pluck balls off the glass. He's also proven himself to be the type of unselfish player that is always valuable to a team. But what makes him extra special is the intensity he brings to the court. His play harkens back to the early Bulls days and Jerry Sloan and Norm Van Lier.

Born in New York, Noah attributes his ferocious style to growing up in the city.

"I always give respect to, and homage to, New York, because I don't feel like I would be the player that I am today if it was not for New York City," Noah said. "It gives you an edge, a certain toughness just growing up in the city."

Rose again had knee issues in 2014–15, missing more time and raising more career question marks. But the Bulls refused to quit. Rising to the occasion along with Noah were All-Star center Pau Gasol and fourth-year guard Jimmy Butler. Gasol's veteran presence and Butler's 20-plus points per game were key factors in the Bulls' ability to survive without Rose. Combined with the surprise stellar play of rookie Nikola Mirotic— who was twice named rookie of the month—the Bulls were anything but pushovers.

And that is good news for Chicago hoops fans. Rose's tender knees aside, Chicago is in as good a spot as they have been since the glory days of Jordan, Pippen and Rodman. It took a long time, but fans hope the revival lasts.

2014–15 star rookie Nikola Mirotic in action against the Philadelphia 76ers in 2015.

Photo Credits

AP Photo

Aaron M. Sprecher 60

Al Messerschmidt Archive 107, 108

Amy Sancetta 57R, 110, 151, 153

Associated Press 33, 38, 44, 45, 46, 49, 74, 76, 77, 78, 79, 82, 85, 87, 89TL, 89TR, 89B, 92, 97, 101, 105, 117, 133L, 137, 138, 139, 166, 169, 172, 173, 207

Beth A. Keiser 226, 227

Bettmann/Corbis 23, 29, 30, 31, 34, 35, 37, 43, 47, 48, 51, 69, 70, 73, 81, 84, 93, 116, 127 TR, 127 MR, 129, 130, 132, 135, 136, 140, 167, 171, 175, 177, 181, 203, 204, 206, 209

Bettmann/Jerry Lodriguss/COR 210

Charles Cherney 179

Charles Knoblock 90

Charles Rex Arbogast 159

Charlie Bennett 106

Cliff Welch 56

Darron Cummings 197

David Durochik 170

David J. Phillip 149, 150

Elise Amendola 191, 192, 231

Evan Vucci 41

Four Seam Images 144

Frank Polich 199

Fred Jewell 104, 141, 183, 218, 221

Greg Thompson 188

Jack Smith 228

Jim Palmer 39

John Lent 100

John Swart 55, 212, 216, 217, 220

John Zich 27

Larry Goren 114, 143

Linda Kaye 152

M. Spencer Green 7

Mark Elias 52L

Mark J. Terrill 205

Matt Slocum 158, 190, 233, 235

Michael Conroy 229

Michael S. Green 211

Mike Groll 147

Mike Wulf 156, 189

Morry Gash 57L

Nam Y. Huh 10

Nell Redmond 232

NFL Photos 63, 95, 103

Paul Beaty 187

Phelan M. Ebenhack 198, 223

Pro Football Hall of Fame 68, 71, 75

Ralk-Finn Hestoft 213

Robert Kozloff 145

Robert Walsh 98

Rusty Kennedy 184

Scott Boehm 24, 219

Scott Troyanos 215

Tom DiPace 52R, 224, 225

U.S. Navy 86

Vernon Biever 91, 94, 111

Front Cover (Top from R-L): Jim Mone, Robin Alam, Four Seam Images, Tom DiPace, Charles Rex Arbogast; (Bottom) Shutterstock: MaxyM

Library of Congress Archives

LC-USZ62-51860: 12

LC-DIG-bbc-0729f: 17L

LC-DIG-ppmsca-19495: 17R

LC-DIG-ppmsca-15619: 18

LC-DIG-ppmsca-13532: 19L

LC-DIG-ppmsca-13533: 19R

LC-DIG-bbc-0734f: 20

LC-DIG-npcc-15254: 67

LC-DIG-bbc-0886f: 121L

LC-DIG-bbc-0757f: 121R

LC-DIG-ppmsca-18323: 122

LC-DIG-bbc-0056f: 123L

LC-DIG-ggbain-15387: 123R

LC-DIG-ppmsca-13542: 124

LC-DIG-ggbain-25384: 125

LC-DIG-ggbain-50311: 127TL

LC-DIG-ggbain-31141: 127TM

LC-DIG-hec-02792: 127ML

LC-DIG-ggbain-11043: 127M

LC-DIG-ggbain-50307: 127BL

LC-DIG-ggbain-50308: 127BM

LC-DIG-ggbain-14167: 128

Hockey Hall of Fame

HHOF 163, 164, 165

HHOF/Imperial Oil-Turofsky 176

Hockey Hall of Fame/Graphic Artists 178

Hockey Hall of Fame/Portnoy 182

Other

The Brian Piccolo Cancer Research Fund 99

Charles M Conlon (1913), Wikimedia Commons/Public Domain 133R

Index